Italian Baroque Paintings

John T. Spike

Italian Baroque Paintings

from New York Private Collections

The Art Museum, Princeton University *in association with* Princeton University Press

Dates of the exhibition: April 27–September 7, 1980

This publication has been edited and produced
at The Art Museum, Princeton University.
Designed by James Wageman
Typesetting: Graphic Arts Composition
Printing: The Meriden Gravure Company

Jacket/cover illustration: Daniele Crespi, *Conversion of St. Paul,* collection of Robert and Bertina Suida Manning (no. 16)

Page 8: Pier Francesco Mola, *St. John the Baptist Preaching in the Wilderness* (detail), private collection (no. 30)

Page 10: Scarsellino, *The Virgin Bestowing a Scapular upon a Saint* (detail), collection of Mr. and Mrs. Morton B. Harris (no. 44)

Library of Congress Catalogue Card Number 79-55743
ISBN 0-691-03955-0 (clothbound)
ISBN 0-691-00325-4 (paperbound)

Published by The Art Museum, Princeton University,
in association with Princeton University Press,
Princeton, New Jersey 08540
In the United Kingdom, Princeton University Press,
Guildford, Surrey

Contents

Works in the Exhibition

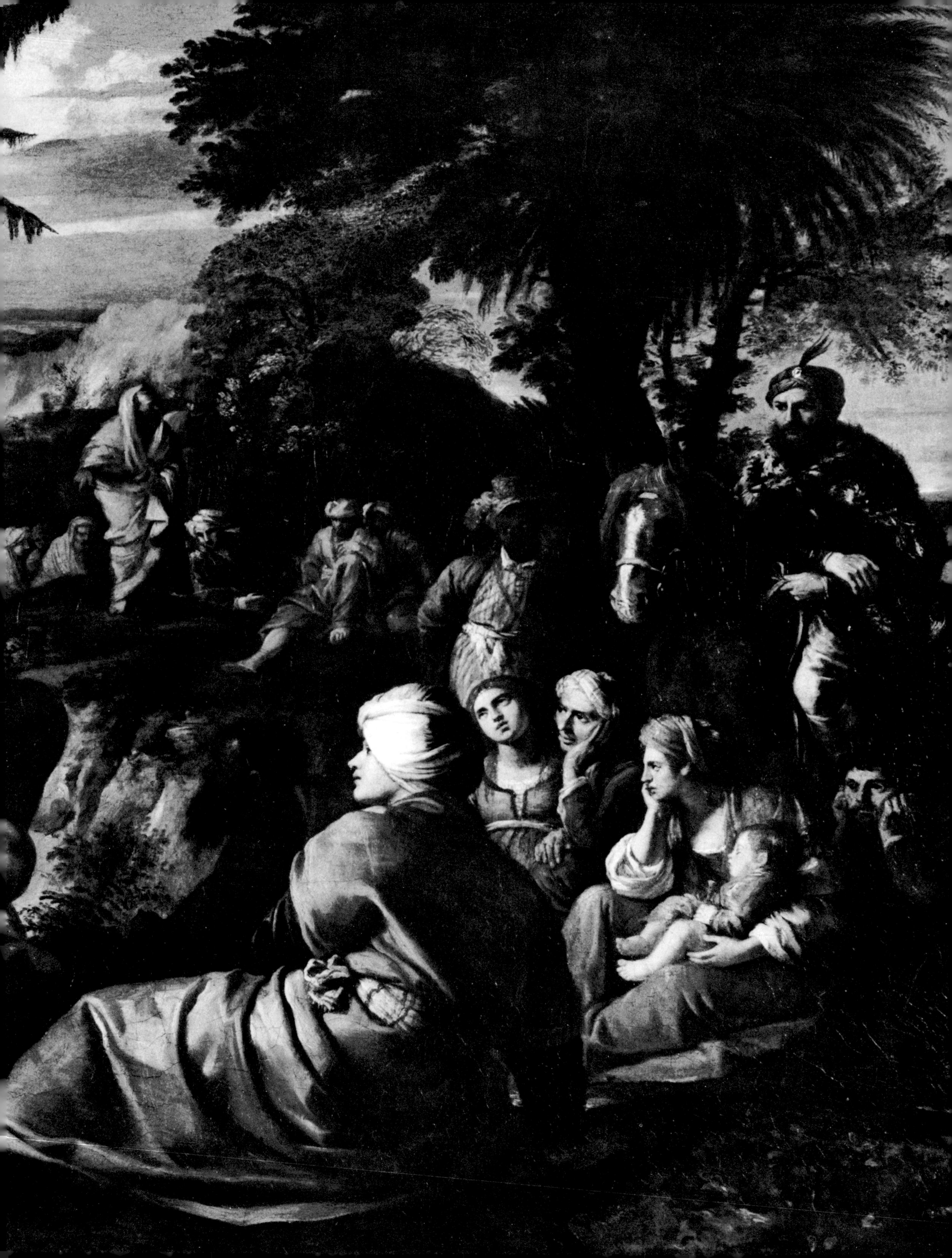

Foreword

This exhibition of Italian Baroque paintings from New York private collections is a happy instance of the advantages Princeton enjoys because of its proximity to New York City. It also says something nice about that special race, too often maligned, the New Yorker. The response of the collectors participating in the exhibition and the generosity with which the loans were forthcoming has been extraordinary. The collectors are exceptional as a group; many are professionals in the fields of art history and conservation. Even those who are not so engaged are remarkable for their sophistication as connoisseurs and for their knowledge not only of their own pictures, but of the history of painting in general. It has been an educational and civilizing experience to have worked with them. A great many lenders to the exhibition have chosen to remain anonymous; happily, I am able to thank by name Richard L. Feigen, Mr. and Mrs. Paul H. Ganz, Mr. and Mrs. Morton B. Harris, Howard and Shirley G. Hibbard, and Robert and Bertina Suida Manning.

John T. Spike, Guest Curator of the exhibition, selected the paintings and wrote the accompanying catalogue. The quality of the pictures in the exhibition speaks eloquently of his taste and the catalogue is scrupulous in its scholarship, impressive in its judgment, and is also very well written. We are greatly indebted to John for the excellent job he has done, especially within the short space of time he was given to produce the manuscript. Our association has been most rewarding.

Virginia Wageman, Director of Publications at the Museum, supervised the production of the catalogue, and James Wageman is responsible for the handsome design. Typesetting is by Graphic Arts Composition in Philadelphia and printing by the Meriden Gravure Company, both of which met an exacting production schedule. Robert Lafond, the Museum's Registrar, arranged to have the paintings photographed and handled the details of transporting the paintings to Princeton with his usual care. Harriet Gault, John Kalajian, and Gunnar Salmonson are to be thanked for their assistance in the installation of the exhibition and JoAnn Carchman for the attendant festivities.

Many of the finest Baroque paintings in the Museum's permanent collection are the gifts of Mr. and Mrs. George L. Craig, Jr., who are among the mainstays of the Museum. On this occasion we have Mrs. Craig to thank for her very thoughtful and generous assistance in support of this catalogue.

Allen Rosenbaum
Director
The Art Museum, Princeton University

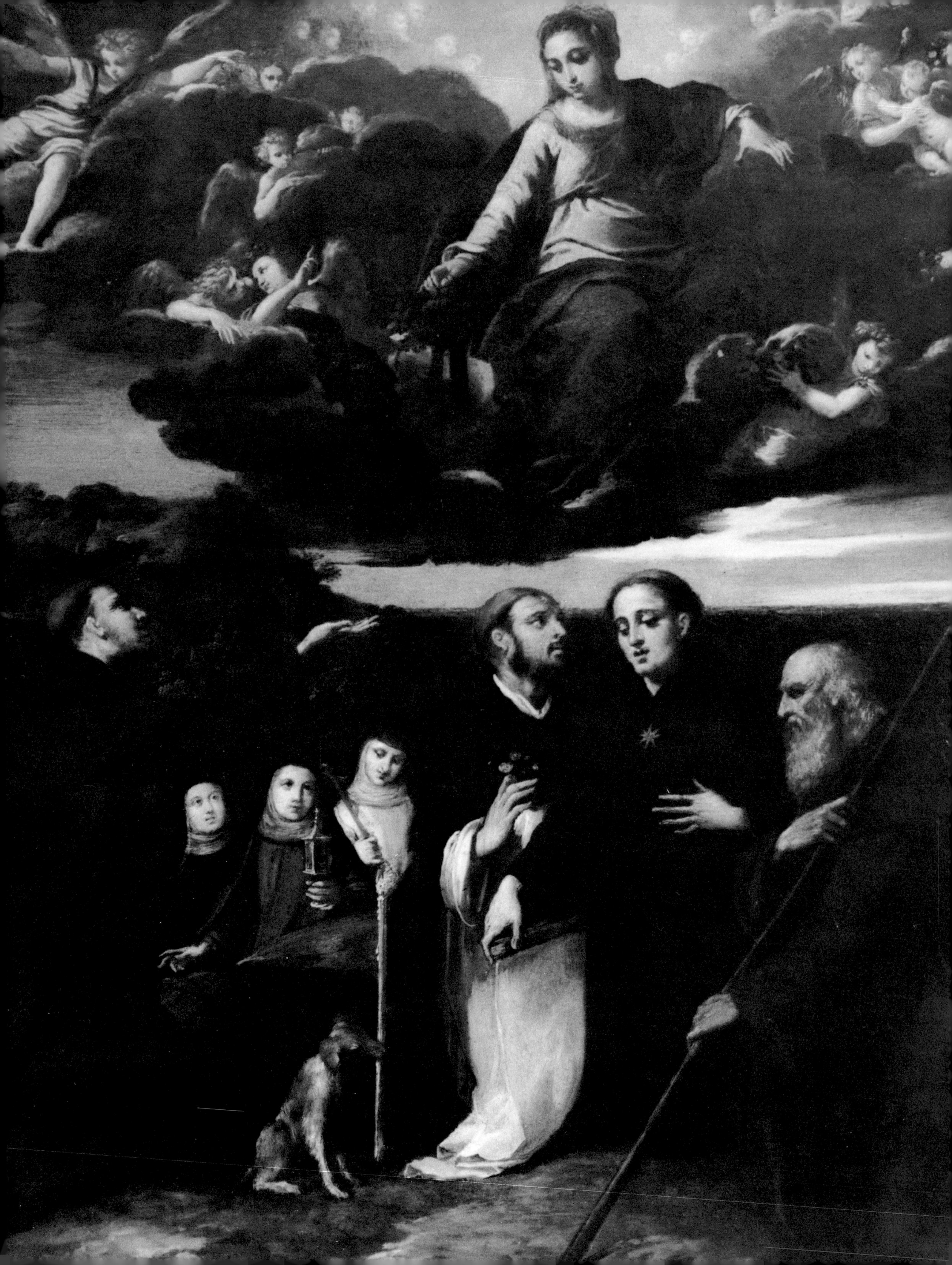

Introduction

In 1944 Hans Tietze, one of the most sensitive connoisseurs of our century, introduced the catalogue of the exhibition *Three Baroque Masters: Strozzi, Crespi, and Piazzetta* (Baltimore Museum of Art) with the following lines:

> Let us not deceive ourselves. There is hardly any period within the art of the past to which we find the approach more difficult than to the Italian Baroque and its counterparts elsewhere. . . . It is not my intention to offer an apology of Baroque art, but my task to explain our opposition to it. [P. 5]

To the relief of one who must introduce an exhibition of Italian Baroque paintings from New York private collections in 1980, the reputations of the Italian contemporaries of Rembrandt and Velazquez have been thoroughly rehabilitated in the intervening decades since Dr. Tietze wrote for an audience he perceived to be hostile. The battle to restore this neglected epoch had of course been joined as early as the end of the last century. The heroes, too many to name, in this reversal of critical attitudes were, as ever, scholars and private collectors (and many persons who were both).

On the American front, the effort was mainly concentrated in the classrooms and apartments of New York City, which is today one of the few cities in the world that could support an exhibition of this kind. In its intention to pay homage to the quality and diversity of New York private collections of seventeenth-century Italian paintings, the present exhibition is much the spiritual heir of the series of exhibitions arranged in the 1960s at the Finch College Museum of Art by Robert L. Manning. Indeed no fewer than eight "alumni" of those shows are again exhibited on this occasion (nos. 1, 9, 10, 13, 24, 36, 38, and 44).

The Finch College shows, now almost legendary in the memories of the cognoscenti, were devoted in turn to the Bolognese (and Emilian), Neapolitan, Genoese, and Venetian schools of this period. The foremost American collectors of Italian Baroque paintings, then as now, were situated in New York. Walter P. Chrysler, Jr. (whose collection now graces the Chrysler Museum in Norfolk, Virginia), Mr. and Mrs. Paul H. Ganz, and Robert and Bertina Suida Manning all collected in this field with enthusiasm and discernment long before most American museums awoke to recognize the curious lack of transition between their overflowing galleries of Italian Renaissance and eighteenth-century (Venetian) pictures. These three collectors were major lenders to the

Art in Italy 1600–1700 exhibition in Detroit, which in 1965 effectively announced the vindication of Italian Baroque studies. Four paintings shown at Detroit are included in the present exhibition (nos. 1, 13, 36, and 39), and the Suida Manning and the Ganz collections are again valued participants.

The scholarly investigations that have once more raised up the Italian Baroque for our admiration have, paradoxically, also lifted the lid of a Pandora's box of unresolved questions. It has become evident that an astonishing diversity of artistic expression and means are crowded together under the historical umbrella of "the Baroque." Indeed this exhibition, although limited to forty-seven paintings, demonstrates a good many of the pictorial and expressive possibilities open to Baroque artists. For instance, while sacred themes predominate, the interpretations of the stories range from the exacting piety of Dolci, Strozzi, and Fracanzano, to name only three notables, to the lighter intimacy of Badalocchio and Guercino, the lyricism of Castiglione, the dramatic urgency of Lanfranco and Preti, and even the sensuosity of Pignoni and Chiari. Subjects from classical history and philosophy may be found treated with antiquarian reverence, as by Testa and Rosa, or plumbed for their erotic content, as in the mythologies of Bellucci and Ricci. The serious intent of Solimena's splendid *Continence of Scipio* traces one of the middle paths. The thorny problem to identify the common pulse(s) of Baroque art has been addressed at length by many distinguished scholars, among them Sir Ellis Waterhouse, Rudolf Wittkower, Andrea Griseri, and most recently, John Rupert Martin. And we are only inching toward the solution of this issue, if such exists.

In the meantime, the cranky apparatus of art-historical terminology, which in the simplest of circumstances tends to separate the flow of artistic thought into a series of pools, has been overwhelmed by the currents within the Baroque, which course across one another and turn back upon themselves as often as they lead on to succeeding developments. What metaphor will describe a period that embraced archaistic strains as well as a proto-Romanticism that anticipated concerns we now think of as typically nineteenth century? Accordingly, art-historical labels have been dispensed with in this catalogue as much as possible. Some definitions are in order, however.

A prime source of confusion stems from the two usages, broad as opposed to specific, that are demanded of "Baroque." As used in the title of this exhibition and thus far in this introduction, "Baroque" refers collectively to the whole panoply of artistic developments that arose at the end of the sixteenth century in reaction against the formal and psychological artificialities of the previous Mannerist period, and which gave way almost imperceptibly during the first half of the eighteenth century to Rococo style (with neoclassicism not far off). The observation of three successive phases in the development of Baroque style—Early, High, and Late Baroque—has become standard and can be useful so long as we account for the separate responses of the regional schools of Italian painting and do not attempt to fix the chronological limits by fiat. My understanding of the distinctions among these phases follows Wittkower's in the main. For the purposes of selection for this exhibition, the Baroque was not considered as synonymous with the seventeenth century; paintings from the transitional period at the turn of the century prior to the Early Baroque have been included: by Annibale Carracci, Scarsellino, Saraceni, Baglione, Manfredi, Bassetti, and Badalocchio. At the distant end of the spectrum, the paintings datable to ca. 1710 by Giacomo del Po in Naples and Sebastiano Ricci in Venice illustrate in their decorative emphases the shadowy boundary between the Late Baroque and Rococo styles: the figure styles retain a directness and sensuosity of physical presence which remain links to Baroque practice.

In its specific sense, "Baroque" describes only one among the sundry artistic currents within this epoch. The Baroque direction is usually conceived as opposed to the precepts of classical style revived by Annibale Carracci in Rome, but the exemplars of the Baroque strain, e.g., Bernini, Cortona, and Baciccio, found much to admire in Annibale's vital, energetic art. The word "Baroque" was coined—its precise etymology is disputed—as a pejorative characterization of these masters' style as eccentric, extravagant, even bizarre. If by way of explanation we must reduce complicated phenomena to truisms, the Baroque artists may be said to have been captivated by the ceaseless flux of nature and human existence, while classicizing artists sought to express timeless quintessences of order and beauty. Between these ideal poles, the painters of the Baroque Age arrayed themselves, never remaining at rest and never quite losing sight of the alternate possiblities.

Our exhibition proposes itself not as an encapsulation of the Italian Baroque, with omissions tidily glossed over, but as a celebration of the period as it is represented in New York private collections. The contribution to scholarship in the presentation of many little-known treasures we hope will not be inconsiderable.

The intrinsic merit of each painting in its relationship to the achievement of its artist was the first and foremost criterion of selection. The desire to illustrate the Baroque in as full dimension as possible without lowering standards of quality was an active, but secondary factor: there was no concern to avoid duplication since our purpose is to reflect the character of New York collections, rather than the Baroque overall.

Some notes on these collections may be of interest to more than future chroniclers of the culture. Cabinet pictures or other paintings of small format (nos. 1, 2, 3, 6, 9, 10, 18, 19, 21, 22, 26, 27, 41, and 44), including many bozzetti or pictures with sketchlike handling, comprise a significant portion of our exhibition. A compelling inducement for the collecting of smaller paintings is of course the space limitations endemic to city dwelling. By the same token, towering altarpieces and the like are conspicuously absent.

New York collectors harbor a decided preference for figure paintings, with, interestingly, the absolute exception of portraiture. Landscapes are rare, and it is characteristic that the landscapes by Guercino, Castiglione, Mola, and Dughet (with figures by Lauri) in this exhibition all depict figural action of greater import than mere staffage. Architectural paintings are hardly to be found: the sole example exhibited here, a *Ruins with a Hermit* by Codazzi, is in many respects an exceptional work for the artist. Still-life paintings too have yet to find a champion in New York, and none were selected for this show, although some isolated works of this genre were worthy. Of the schools of Italian painting, only Rome is represented across the whole span of this century, as befits the crossroads of Europe. The Genoese and Neapolitan (Late Baroque) may be noted as other schools present in some depth.

A number of paintings may be pointed out for their particular interest to current scholarship (and not as any indication of relative quality to works not singled out). This show brings to light many pictures that have never been published or have never been shown in this century. Some major discoveries for our knowledge of certain artists or trends have been made. Saraceni's *Martyrdom of St. Cecilia* is here proposed as the artist's earliest-known Caravaggesque painting, and therefore one of the first emulations of Caravaggio by anyone. A charming *Musical Party in a Garden* has been added to the oeuvre of G. B. Passeri to make a total of only two paintings assigned to Passeri, whose name has endured more as a biographer of artists than as a painter in his own right. Previously known to scholars only through mediocre reproductive engravings, G. B. Castiglione's *Journey of Jacob,* formerly at Stafford House, London, is exhibited for the first time in this century; its new-found signature and date of 1633 establish this painting as the artist's first dated work by more than a decade and a crucial document of his early development in Rome. A powerful *Decollation of S. Gennaro* by Preti, last shown in the landmark exhibition at the Palazzo Pitti in 1922, is discussed in its entry as persuasive grounds for the re-evaluation of the master's late style on Malta, which remains in the shadow of his acclaimed sojourn in Naples, 1656–60. Other painters who are represented in this exhibition by works of especial importance to our understanding of their achievements, for the most part recognized as such in the scholarly literature, are Badalocchio, Baglione, Bassetti, Camassei, Daniele Crespi, Codazzi, Fetti, Forabosco, Fracanzano, Giacomo del Po, Rosa, Scarsellino, and Testa.

Needless to say, this exhibition has been built on the foundation of good faith and personal kindness of all our lenders. When private collectors respond to a show such as this, they commit themselves for the public benefit to a host of sacrifices, not least of which is the time passed in visits and telephone conversations with the cataloguer. For their endless patience and good will I am deeply grateful.

In the course of preparing this exhibition and catalogue I have relied time and again on the assistance of scholars in America and abroad. Among those whose helpfulness I wish to acknowledge are Robert L. Manning, who generously shared with me on innumerable occasions his unparalleled knowledge of the private holdings of Baroque paintings in New York; Sir Ellis Waterhouse, to whom I posed in correspondence all sorts of complicated problems of scholarship—and always received the answer; Dr. Erich Schleier, who sent me his invaluable researches on Lanfranco and Badalocchio prior to their publication; Marco Grassi, for much consultation; Professor Pamela Askew; Elizabeth H. Beatson; Dr. Marie-Nicole Boisclair; Edgar Peters Bowron; Arnauld Brejon de Lavergnée; Hugh Brigstocke; Professor Jonathan Brown; Professor Malcolm Campbell; Dr. Raffaello Causa; Frederick den Broeder; Everett Fahy; Dr. Oreste Ferrari; Mrs. André Hirschler; Terence Hodgkinson; Dr. Jürgen M. Lehmann; Professor Fred Licht, for his confidence in naming me to this assignment; Dr. Manuela B. Mena Marques; Professor John Rupert Martin; Jennifer Montagu; D. Stephen Pepper; Dr. Wolfgang Prohaska; William W. Robinson; Dr. Eduard Safarik; Professor Richard E. Spear; Dr. Nicola Spinosa;

Nicholas Turner. To all these persons, as to all those omitted through inadvertence, my heartfelt thanks.

The professional staff of The Art Museum, Princeton University, deserves every credit for the expert arrangement of this exhibition: Robert Lafond, Jennifer Guberman, Lynda Emery, and especially Virginia Wageman, who edited this catalogue and held us to a tight publication schedule. I cannot thank sufficiently Allen Rosenbaum, Acting Director of the Museum, for his sure direction of this project, his unfailing encouragement, and his keen sensitivity to the art of the Italian Baroque, upon which I relied often.

Two graduate students in the Department of Art and Archaeology of Princeton University found time to aid me: Gregory Clark obtained the photographs for the reference illustrations; Ann Priester's researches into the subject matter of about twenty of these paintings were invaluable additions to their entries.

On a day-to-day basis Mary Schmidt and Ray Ford and the staff of Marquand Library, Princeton University—Grace Claycombe, Elli Walter, and Liza Rolland—went out of their way to assist my researches. My other researches were undertaken at the excellent facilities of the Frick Art Reference Library in New York.

To my wife, Michele K. Spike, I cannot express in these few lines the measure of my indebtedness. To her, and for her, I am eternally grateful.

Catalogue of the Exhibition

Giovanni Battista Gaulli, called Baciccio

Genoa 1639–1709 Rome

No works survive from Baciccio's Genoese youth, when it has been suggested he was a pupil of one of Luciano Borzone's sons. The early sources report that he departed for Rome after his entire family perished from plague: this happened either in 1653 (Pascoli) or in 1657 (Soprani and Ratti).

At first adrift in the Eternal City, Baciccio soon came to the attention of Gian Lorenzo Bernini, who took his career in hand. In 1662 Baciccio was received into the Accademia di San Luca (he was Principe from 1673 to 1675). To this period dates his first public commission, an altarpiece in S. Rocco, Rome, which reveals a painterly naturalism influenced by Van Dyck and reminiscent of the manner of Borzone. However, his careful study of Annibale Carracci is evident in a *Pietà* (Incisa della Rocchetta collection, Rome) painted in 1667 for Cardinal Odoardo Farnese. The young artist had tightened his draftsmanship markedly; one might say in view of Bernini's likely guidance that his intention had become to bring out the "sculptural" presence of the figures. His native genius for color remained constant.

It was Bernini who obtained for Baciccio his first prestigious undertaking in fresco, the pendentives in the cupola of Sant'Agnese in Piazza Navona (1666–72). As part of his painstaking preparations Baciccio visited Parma and Modena in 1669 in order to study Correggio. These lessons were formative on his mature style.

The middle period of Baciccio's career, 1672–85, was primarily occupied with his greatest achievement, the nine frescoes in the cupola and vaults of Il Gesù, the mother church of the Jesuits in Rome. This extraordinary opportunity for the thirty-three-year-old painter was due to Bernini's intervention, who, moreover, guaranteed Baciccio's success. Bernini undoubtedly was consulted for the magnificent design of the nave fresco, the *Triumph of the Name of Jesus* (1677–79), which is a landmark of Baroque illusionism.

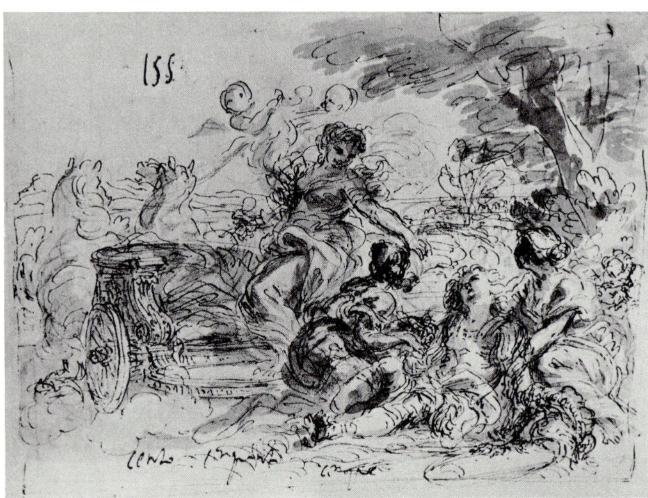

Fig. 1 Baciccio: study for *Rinaldo and Armida,* red chalk, ink, and gray wash on paper. Albertina, Vienna (NI 29012)

Baciccio suffered from the faltering papal patronage of the end of the century. Between 1685 and 1705 he executed no major frescoes and only two altarpieces. Of course, private commissions and portraiture supported him handsomely. His altarpiece for S. Maria in Campitelli (ca. 1698) represents a capitulation to Maratti's brand of classicism: the result is close to G. B. Chiari.

1 *Rinaldo and Armida*

Oil on canvas. 40.95 × 48.9 cm. Ca. 1680–85.

References: Enggass, 1964, pp. 28–29, 133–34, fig. 41; Manning, *Genoese Painters,* 1964, no. 72, repr.; Dowley, 1965, p. 300; Detroit Institute of Arts, 1965, no. 50, repr.; Oberlin, Allen Memorial Art Museum, 1966, no. 11, repr.; Koschatzky, Oberhuber, and Knab, 1971, see no. 88; Pigler, 1974, II, p. 468.

Robert and Bertina Suida Manning, New York

The romantic episodes from Torquato Tasso's *Gerusalemme liberata* (1581) were greatly favored by seventeenth- and eighteenth-century artists, although this is Baciccio's only painting known to be drawn from Tasso. After casting a sleeping spell on Rinaldo, the beautiful sorceress Armida arrived with her retinue on the banks of the Orantes to dispatch the Christian hero. Instead she fell in love with Rinaldo and bid her nymphs to bind him with chains of flowers and to carry him away to her palace.

This bozzetto represents Baciccio's art at its most charming. Robert Enggass has written eloquently on the "gay rhythms and bright colors" in this little canvas and dates it ca. 1680–85, i.e., toward the close of the artist's middle period.[1] Indeed similar landscape settings and angular drapery folds are found in other paintings datable to these years.

On the other hand, the delicate proportions of the figures and their removal from the picture plane as well as the delightfully whimsical spirit so anticipate the Rococo that a slightly later date would be possible. One imagines that a full-scale version of this *Rinaldo and Armida* would compare very well with Baciccio's *St. John Preaching in the Wilderness* (Musée, Dijon), dated by Enggass ca. 1685–95.[2]

The colorful preparatory drawing for this bozzetto is preserved in the Albertina (fig. 1), where it was attributed to Pietro da Cortona until Enggass identified its true author.

NOTES

1 Enggass, 1964, p. 133. 2 Ibid., fig. 125.

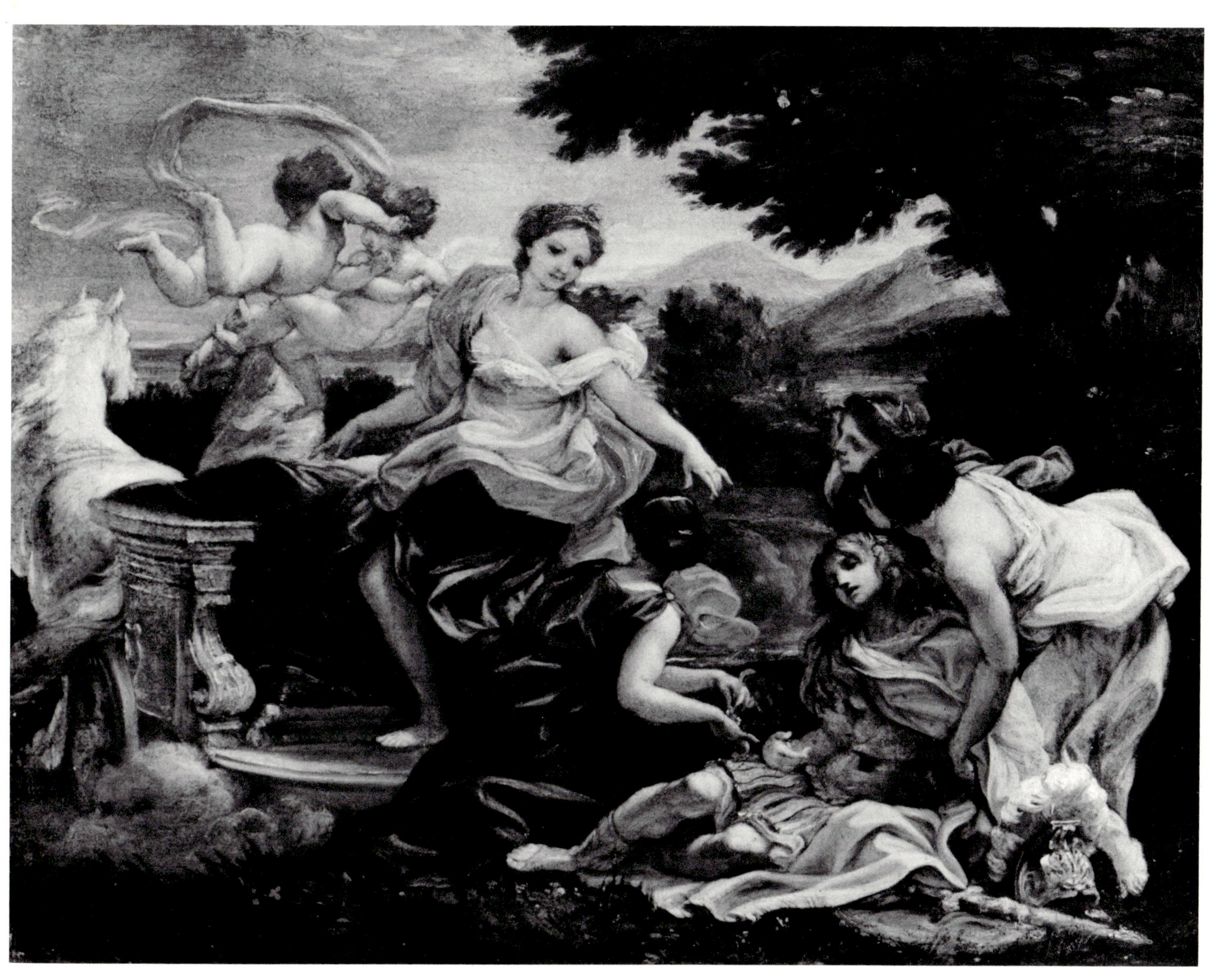

Sisto Badalocchio

Parma 1585–after 1620 Parma

Sisto Badalocchio remains, undeservedly, a little-known figure, overshadowed by his more famous Parmese friend, Giovanni Lanfranco. Badalocchio was a valued member of the Roman studio of Annibale Carracci; his talent as a draftsman was especially esteemed. With Lanfranco, Badalocchio studied under Agostino Carracci in Parma (1600–1602) and then was sent by Duke Ranuccio Farnese to assist Annibale in the Palazzo Farnese in Rome. Lanfranco and Badalocchio published in 1607 a volume of etchings after Raphael's Logge, which they dedicated affectionately to Annibale. Badalocchio's participation is documented or observed by scholars in such important Carracci school undertakings as the lateral walls of the Farnese Gallery (ca. 1604), the Aldobrandini lunettes (after 1603) and the Palazzo Mattei frescoes (under Albani, 1606/7). He was evidently still working in Annibale's studio at the master's death in 1609. Badalocchio then returned to Parma, as did Lanfranco. In 1613 Badalocchio was employed in Reggio Emilia. He returned to Rome about 1615 to work with Lanfranco in the Palazzo Costaguti. The year 1617 found him in Parma being married. This is the last secure date known to us, although Erich Schleier has now postulated a visit to Rome perhaps in 1620/21 on the basis of some prints published in 1621 apparently after his designs.

2 *Madonna and Child*

Oil on copper. 22.8 × 17.2 cm. Ca. 1610.

Provenance: Private collection, England; Thomas Agnew & Sons, London.

Reference: London, Thomas Agnew & Sons, 1978, no. 35, repr.

Private collection, New York

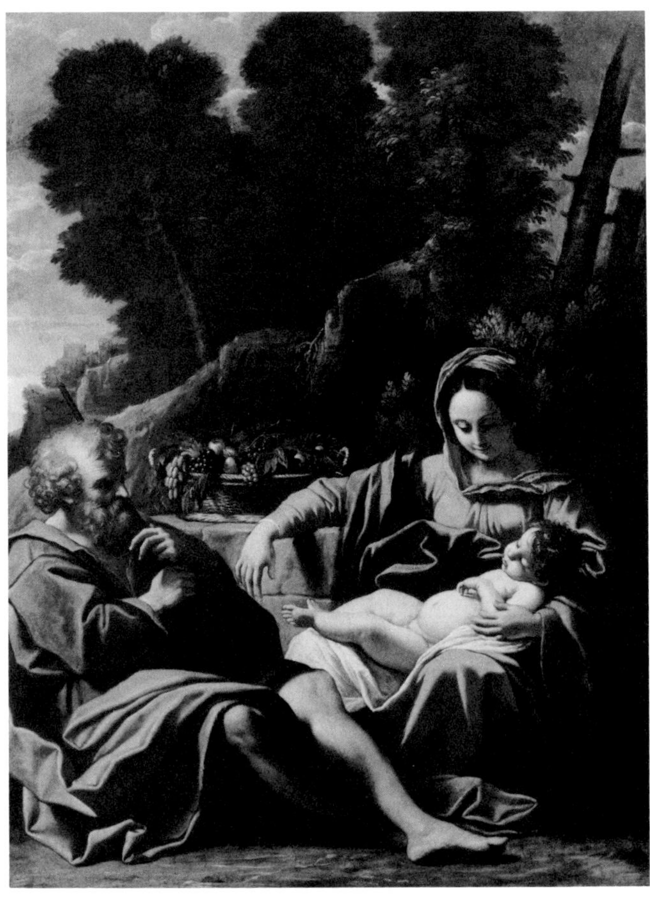

Fig. 2 Badalocchio: *Holy Family,* oil on panel. Wadsworth Atheneum, Hartford, Ella Gallup Sumner and Mary Catlin Sumner Collection (1956.160)

According to Mrs. Jameson in *The Legends of the Madonna*, the Madonna when reading a book is the Mater Sapientiae, and the book is the Book of Wisdom.[1]

When Sisto Badalocchio returned to Parma in 1609 he would have found the Modenese Bartolomeo Schedoni ensconced as painter to Duke Ranuccio I Farnese. Schedoni specialized in diminutive scenes of the Holy Family treated with Correggesque tenderness and fluency. In this painting on copper Sisto's charming characterization of the Infant may be recognized as Schedoni's influence. The conception as a whole, however, is based on Badalocchio's first-hand experience of all that Annibale Carracci had wrought in Rome. His Madonna is ennobled and imposing in her presence, but not wanting for the warmth of human spirit.

Although Badalocchio's chronology remains to be solved, the freshness of his Annibalesque impressions in this painting indicates a date not long after 1609. One of Badalocchio's masterpieces, his *Holy Family* in the Wadsworth Atheneum (fig. 2), compares closely in style and has been dated to this epoch by Denis Mahon.[2] Both pictures evoke the contemporary work of Francesco Albani in their conciliation of intimate expression and grandeur of form.[3]

NOTES

1 Jameson, 1903, p. 157.
2 Mahon, 1958, p. 4, repr.
3 Compare, for example, Albani's *Holy Family* on copper in the collection of the Earl of Yarborough; see Bologna, Palazzo dell' Archiginnasio, 1962, no. 36, repr.

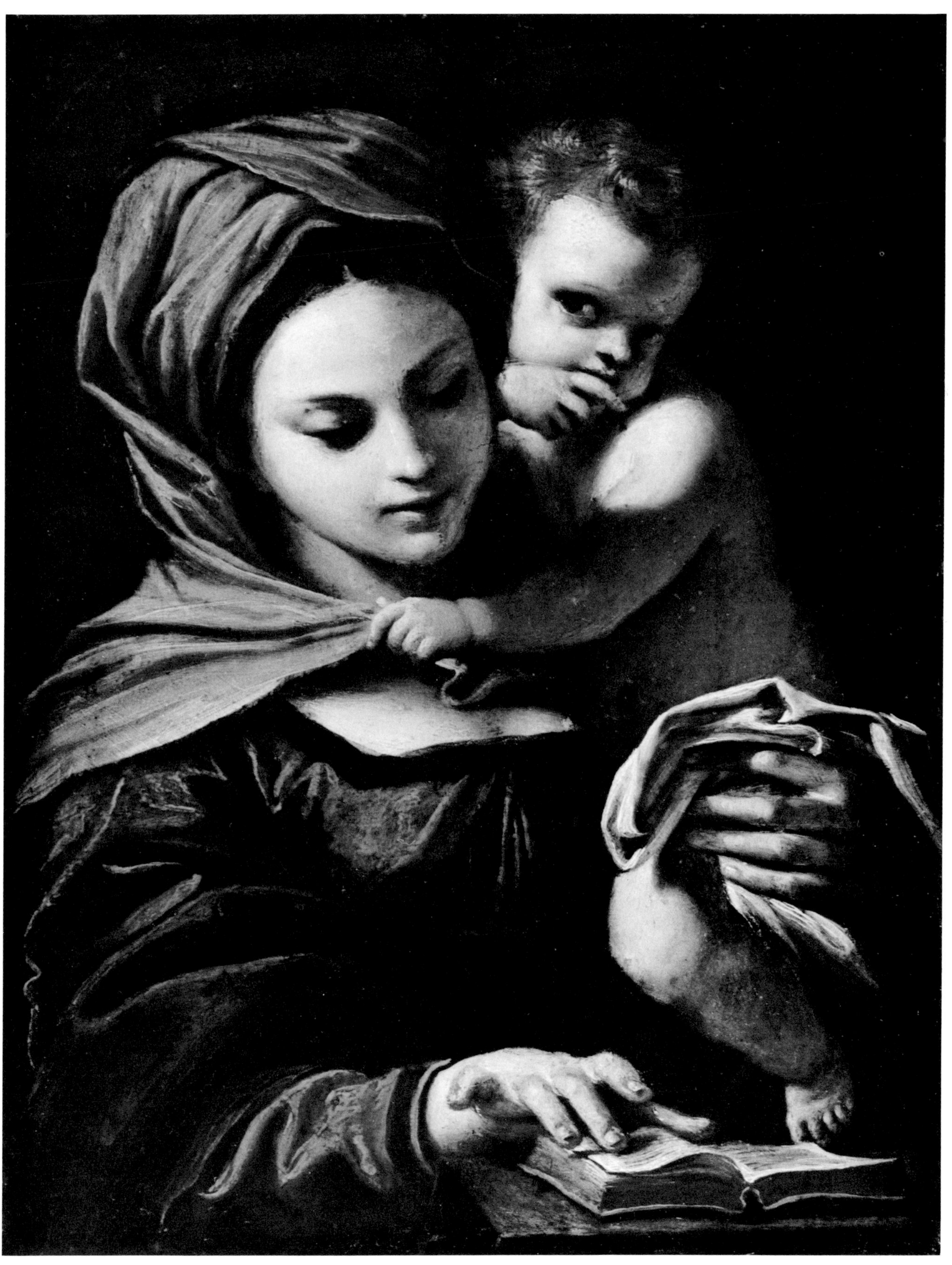

3 *St. Mary Magdalen*

Oil on canvas. 29.2 × 39.35 cm. Ca. 1620.

Provenance: Possibly Maddalena Manini, widow of Bartolomeo Smitti, Parma (1698);[1] sale, Sotheby Parke-Bernet, New York, 22–23 January 1976, lot 184.

Reference: Schleier, forthcoming.

Mr. and Mrs. Morton B. Harris, New York

Badalocchio's portrayal of St. Mary Magdalen in meditation has a delightfully idyllic air.[2] Her pose follows a famous Correggio *St. Mary Magdalen Reading,* which was much copied in the seventeenth century.[3] Erich Schleier has recently pointed out that at this same time, ca. 1620/21, Giovanni Lanfranco painted a reclining *St. Mary Magdalen* with many elements in common with Badalocchio's.[4]

Our present understanding of Badalocchio's development suggests that he felt the influence of Schedoni most keenly after his return to Parma from his Roman sojourn of about 1615 (and after Schedoni's death in 1615). This *Magdalen* could almost be mistaken for a Schedoni in that the bright local colors, the softly modeled volumes and the pervasive sense of atmosphere are so typical of that artist. In comparison to Badalocchio's *Madonna and Child,* no. 2 in this exhibition, we find that within the space of a decade, perhaps, Badalocchio shed his skin of Roman monumentality to show his native Parmese intimacy and sense of humor. It is notable that the landscape glimpsed to the right is comparable to the contemporary landscapes of the young Guercino, one of which is included in this exhibition (no. 26).

NOTES

1 The 1698 inventory of Maddalena Manini (Campori, 1870, no. XXX, p. 408) describes a similar painting of this subject by Badalocchio: "Un quadro di Santa Maria Maddalena coricata, piccolo originale di Sisto, con cornice intagliata bianca."

2 For the subject, see no. 28.

3 Formerly at Dresden, lost during the Second World War; see Gould, 1976, pp. 279–80, pl. 97c.

4 Schleier, forthcoming. I am greatly indebted to Dr. Schleier for sending me a typescript of his article in advance of publication.

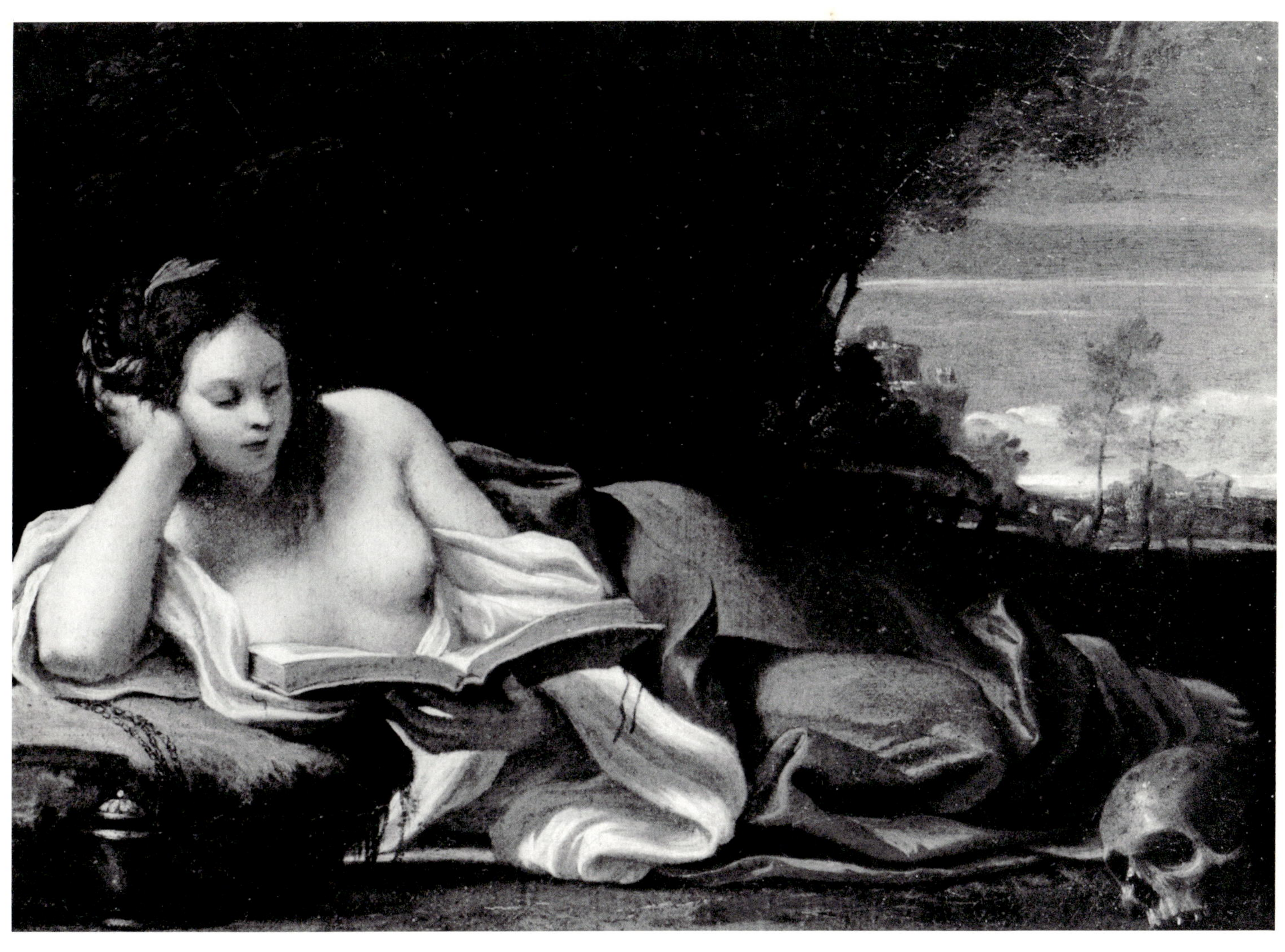

Giovanni Baglione

Rome ca. 1573–1644 Rome

Painter and biographer of artists, Baglione is more remembered for his efforts in the latter office. In retrospect his was an uneven, derivative talent; yet during his lifetime, he won every honor imaginable. Trained in the Florentine circle in Rome and imitative of Giuseppe Cesari and Federico Barocci, the young Baglione participated regularly in the endless decorations commissioned by Pope Clement VIII at the close of the sixteenth century. As part of the observation of the Jubilee year of 1600 Baglione was assigned a major fresco, the *Donation of Constantine,* in S. Giovanni in Laterano.

Between 1600 and 1603 he executed no less than four altarpieces for Cardinal Sfondrato in S. Cecilia in Trastevere. He painted the *Resurrection* (now lost) for Il Gesù in 1603. At this same moment Baglione was experimenting with great sensitivity with the innovative manner of Caravaggio, who evidently resented his attention and, doubtless, his greater success. Baglione brought a suit of libel against Caravaggio's rowdy circle in 1603 (the transcript is fascinating) and closed his Caravaggesque activity.

Baglione passed the whole of his career in Rome (with sojourns in Naples and Loreto), working for many prestigious patrons. In 1620 and 1622 he visited Mantua in the service of Duke Ferdinando Gonzaga, for whom his chief work was a series of *Apollo and the Muses* (Musée, Arras). These were given away in 1624 to Marie de' Medici.

In his later years Baglione devoted himself to his invaluable writings: *Le nove chiese di Roma* in 1639, followed by lives of the early-seventeenth-century artists in Rome, *Le vite de' pittori, scultori, architetti ed intagliatori,* published in 1642.

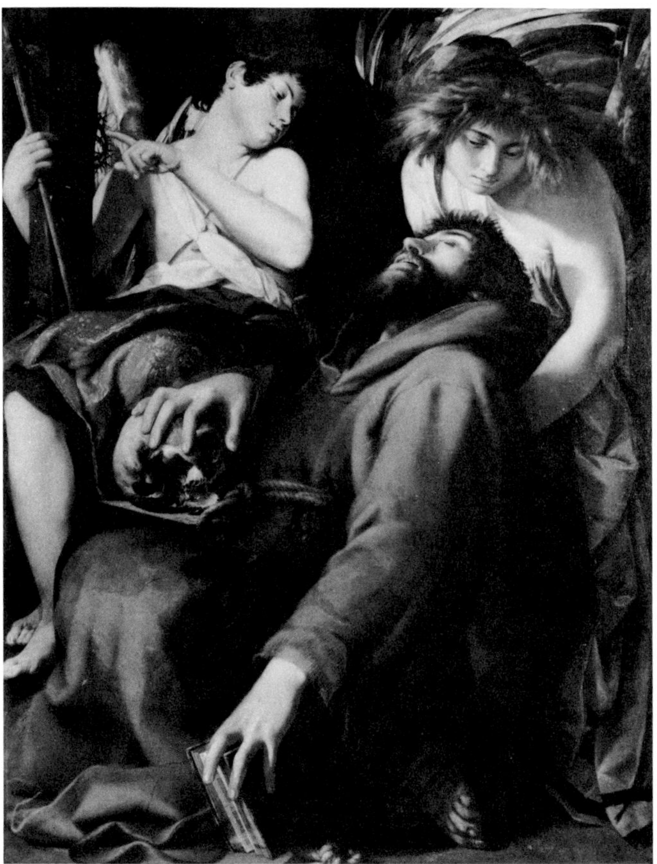

Fig. 3 Baglione: *Ecstasy of St. Francis,* oil on canvas, 1601. Davidson collection, Santa Barbara

4 *St. Sebastian Healed by an Angel*

Oil on canvas. 95.9 × 75.55 cm. Ca. 1603.

Provenance: Cardinal Sannesio, Rome;[1] Anna Maria Sannesio (d. 1724), Rome; V. Camuccini, Rome; Duke of Northumberland;[2] Thomas Agnew & Sons, London (1962); Mr. and Mrs. Paul H. Ganz, New York.

References: "Vecchi maestri," 1962, p. 42, repr.; Longhi, 1963, p. 30, fig. 35; Pigler, 1974, I, p. 468; Spezzaferro, 1975, p. 58 n. 26; Nicolson, 1979, p. 20.

Mr. and Mrs. Morton B. Harris, New York

According to the Golden Legend of Jacopo de Voragine, St. Sebastian was an officer of the imperial guard in Rome under Diocletian. When his Christianity was discovered, he was bound to a stake, pierced by arrows, and left for dead. St. Irene found Sebastian still alive, however, and tended to his recovery. He was finally clubbed to death.

The martyrdom of St. Sebastian was a popular theme in Baroque art, not least because his intervention was invoked against the plagues. Panofsky pointed out that in Renaissance representations of St. Sebastian, the martyr suffers nobly like a Roman hero; in the seventeenth century the saint's healing, his relief from suffering, was emphasized.[3] The significance of Baglione's highly unusual substitution of an angel for St. Irene is not clear. It is noteworthy that Peter Paul Rubens in Italy at this very time painted a *St. Sebastian Healed by Angels* (Palazzo Corsini, Rome).[4]

Baglione, who soon grew to detest Caravaggio, painted the earliest Caravaggesque painting known to us, his *Ecstasy of St. Francis* dated 1601 (fig. 3). This *St. Sebastian Healed by an Angel* reveals Baglione's further

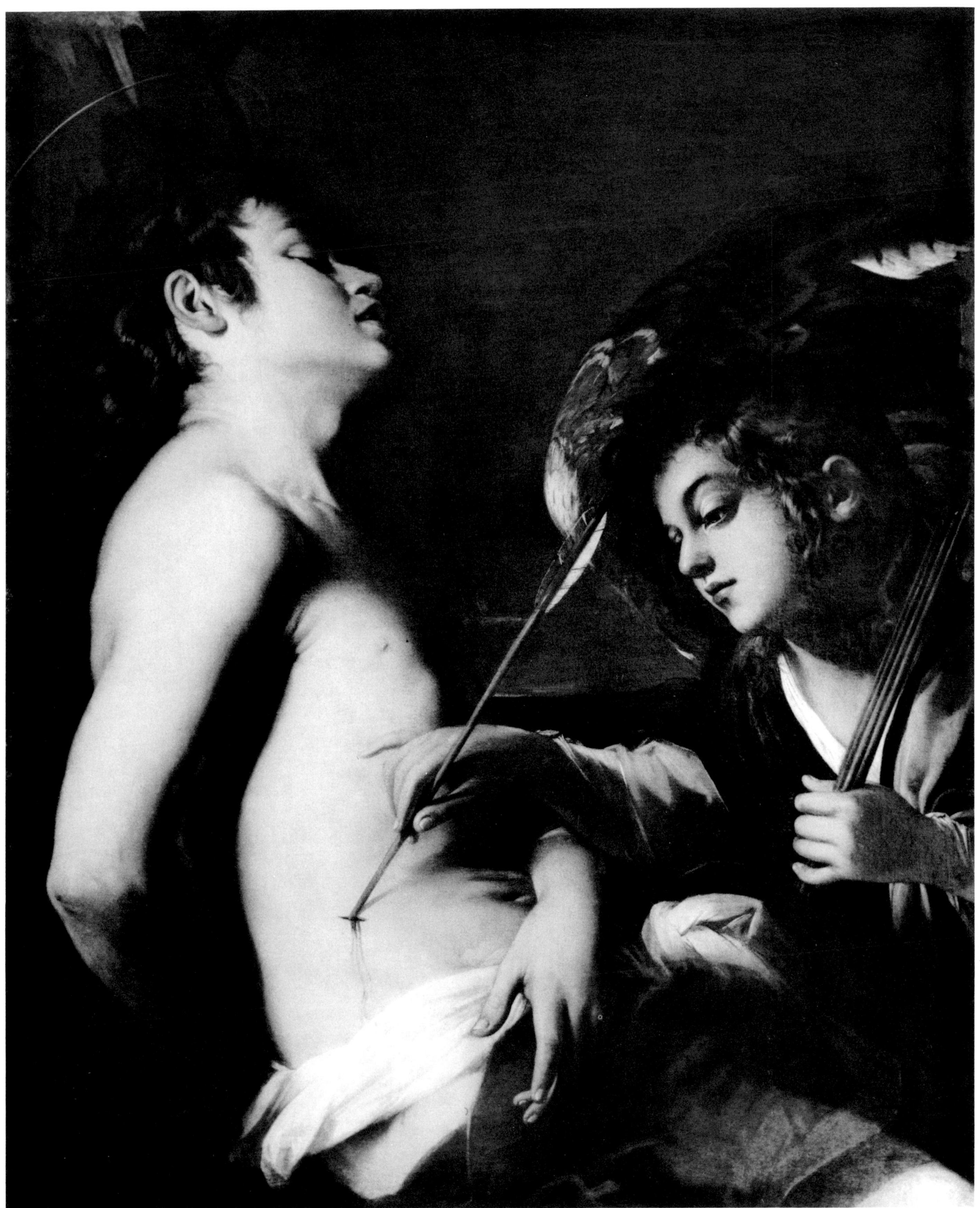

efforts to assimilate the naturalistic basis of Caravaggio's style. Indeed, this picture represents his closest approach to that master. St. Sebastian in particular, while similar in type to the angel at left in the *Ecstasy of St. Francis,* is presented to the viewer with a startling directness that traverses the gap between stylized art and seventeenth-century illusionism. The tending angel still displays idealized features observed from Cavaliere d'Arpino.

If we assume that Baglione's understanding of Caravaggism improved with time, then this painting must be dated to the end of this phase, 1603 at the latest. It would be subsequent to his *Divine and Sacred Love* (Gemäldegalerie, Berlin-Dahlem), which in great part precipitated the events leading to the libel suit of 1603. A contemporaneous work by the artist, the *Madonna with St. Catherine* in S. Cecilia in Trastevere (1603), abounds with d'Arpinesque figures comparable to this healing angel.

NOTES

1 Spezzaferro, 1975, p. 518 n. 26, proposes to identify the present picture with a "quadro in tela di palmi quattro e sette rapp.te San Sebastiano con l'angelo che gli leva la frezza con cornice dorata opera del Baglione" which, with a pendant "quadro in tela rapp.te San Giacomo di p.mi quattro e sette con cornice nera rabescata d'oro mano del Baglioni," is listed in the inventory at death of Anna Maria Sannesio, the last direct heir of the cardinal.

2 The Camuccini and Northumberland references were provided by Thomas Agnew & Sons, London, in 1962 to the then owner.

3 See Hartt, 1964, p. 10.

4 I wish to thank John Rupert Martin for this observation.

Lazzaro Baldi

Pistoia ca. 1624–1703 Rome

Among the pupils of Pietro da Cortona who achieved fame in their own day but soon fell into obscurity was the Pistoiese Lazzaro Baldi. Baldi's career can be traced from mid-century, when he and a fellow *Cortonescho*, Ciro Ferri, painted frescoes in S. Marco, Rome. In 1656/57 Baldi received a considerable share of the fresco decorations in the Gallery of Pope Alexander VII in the Quirinal Palace. Cortona was the superintendent of this grandiose collaborative scheme, which he apportioned in the main to young artists of promise, among them Baldi, Ferri, and Maratti. Unlike Ferri, who based a career on a nearly perfect imitation of Cortona, Baldi gradually modified his *Cortonismo* with classicizing tendencies *à la* Maratti. The graceful, lightened forms of Baldi's late paintings anticipate the mature manner of G. B. Chiari.

Between 1680 and 1682 Baldi endowed and decorated in SS. Luca e Martina (the church of the Accademia di S. Luca) a chapel dedicated to St. Lazzarus. He published a short biography of his name-saint in 1681. Pascoli records that upon Baldi's death his body was transferred in a solemn nocturnal procession to his chapel and there interred.

5 *Ecstasy of St. Benedict*

Oil on canvas. 94 × 69.2 cm. Ca. 1685.

Provenance: Private collection, Berlin (1924).

References: Voss, 1924, p. 554, repr. p. 276; Bosi, 1961, pp. 44 and 57; Griseri, 1962, p. 39; Waterhouse, 1976, p. 53.

Private collection, New York

Baldi has portrayed with admirable urgency and drama the last moments in the life of St. Benedict. Supported by his monastic disciples, the saint raises his hands in prayer and deceases at the steps of the altar. His earlier vision of the soul of his sister, St. Scholastica, is shown at the top of the canvas.

Hermann Voss identified this painting as the bozzetto for Baldi's altarpiece (5.20 × 2.90 m.) in the left transept of S. Maria in Campo Marzio, the church of a Benedictine monastery secluded in the center of Rome.[1] Following Voss, later writers on Baldi have regarded his *Ecstasy of St. Benedict* along with his two lateral paintings of *St. Benedict Writing His Rule* and *The Virgin and Child with St. Gertrude and Other Benedictine Saints* as among the artist's finest works.[2] Voss proposed to date them about 1700; however, Sir Ellis Waterhouse first pointed out that Filippo Titi's *aggiunte* to his Roman guidebook of 1686 state clearly that Baldi completed all three paintings just before the time of publication.[3]

Some variations between oilsketch and altarpiece may

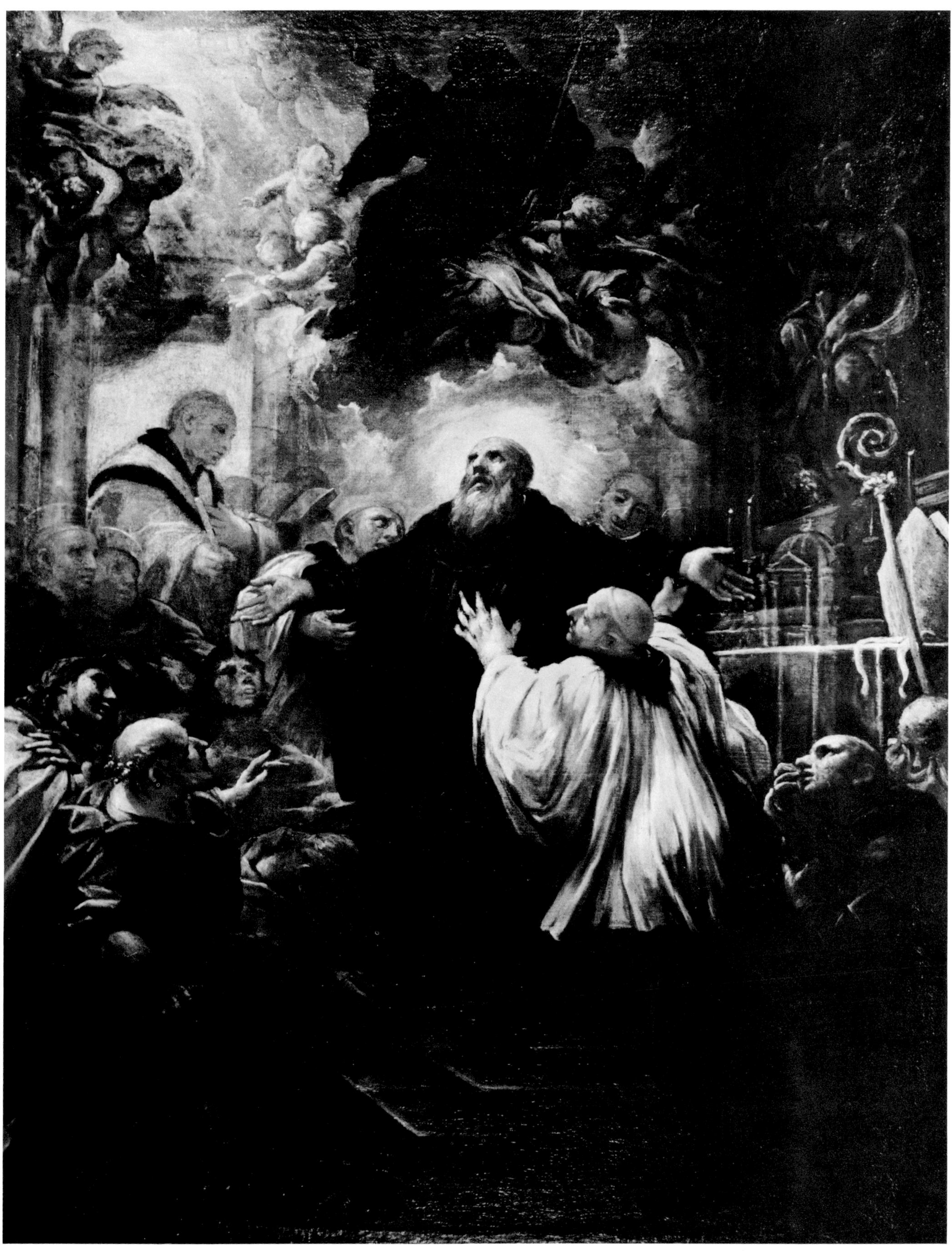

be noted. In particular, the final version of the composition is less crowded; several onlookers at left have been replaced by an open doorway. This modification was visible when Voss knew the bozzetto, but was subsequently removed during cleaning. Baldi's finished drawing, squared for transfer (presumably onto the present bozzetto), was published by A. Griseri.[4] The drawing accords in all respects to the oilsketch, except, interestingly, the composition does not extend to the right beyond the saint's proper left hand. Baldi may have composed the altar and the weeping monks below it directly on this canvas. The painting over the altar apparently represents St. John the Baptist; if any significance may be attached to this association, it was nonetheless not retained for Baldi's final version, where no altarpiece can be seen.

NOTES

1 Voss, 1924, p. 557.
2 Bosi, 1961, p. 44.
3 Waterhouse, 1937, p. 47; Titi, 1686, p. 434.
4 Griseri, 1962, fig. 45.

Marcantonio Bassetti

Verona 1586–1630 Verona

Bassetti was a pupil of Felice Brusasorzi (d. 1605), a Veronese Mannerist, but his keen awareness of the naturalistic elements in the contemporary paintings of Leandro Bassano, Domenico Tintoretto, and Palma Giovane confirms Ridolfi's notice of an important sojourn in Venice. Bassetti, newly arrived in Rome, wrote to Palma in 1616 of the "tante e infinite obbligazioni" owed to the older master.

Carlo Saraceni recognized Bassetti's talents and seems to have provided him with employment in the Sala Regia in the Quirinal Palace (1616/17) and recommended him for some (now lost) paintings in the church of S. Maria dell'Anima, Rome. Saraceni's conciliation of his Venetian heritage with Caravaggism impressed Bassetti deeply, as did the paintings of Saraceni's old friend Orazio Borgianni (1578–1616).

To Bassetti's first Roman years can be dated his *Paradise* (Museo di Capodimonte, Naples), which he based on a painting of the theme by Saraceni (Metropolitan Museum, New York), which itself derived from Francesco Bassano's *Adoration of the Trinity* in Il Gesù, Rome. A *Deposition* in the Borghese Gallery, Rome, was influenced by Saraceni and also Borgianni. By 1619 Bassetti had assimilated his lessons with his native instinct for dramatic expression and was capable of such monumental conceptions as his Varelli Chapel altarpiece sent to Verona and his *Martyrdom of S. Vito* commissioned for Munich. At this time he evidently felt prepared to return to Verona, where his presence is documented after 1625.

Bassetti's mature style in his productive Veronese period continues to abound with references to Saraceni and the Bassani, but the solemn expression and ponderous form are fully his own. In his mature style Bassetti's concern for compositional balance became overtly classical. He placed altarpieces and frescoes in several churches, especially S. Tomio (1627/28), before he died of the plague in 1630.

6 *Christ Bound for the Flagellation*

Oil on slate. 40 × 26 cm. Ca. 1616.

Provenance: J. Weitzner, London.

References: Longhi, 1959, p. 36, fig. 15; Ottani, 1964, p. 166 n. 22.

Private collection, New York

A turbaned jailer binds Christ prior to his flagellation and mocking. The depths of the prison and the sorrowfulness of the moment are represented by the opaque

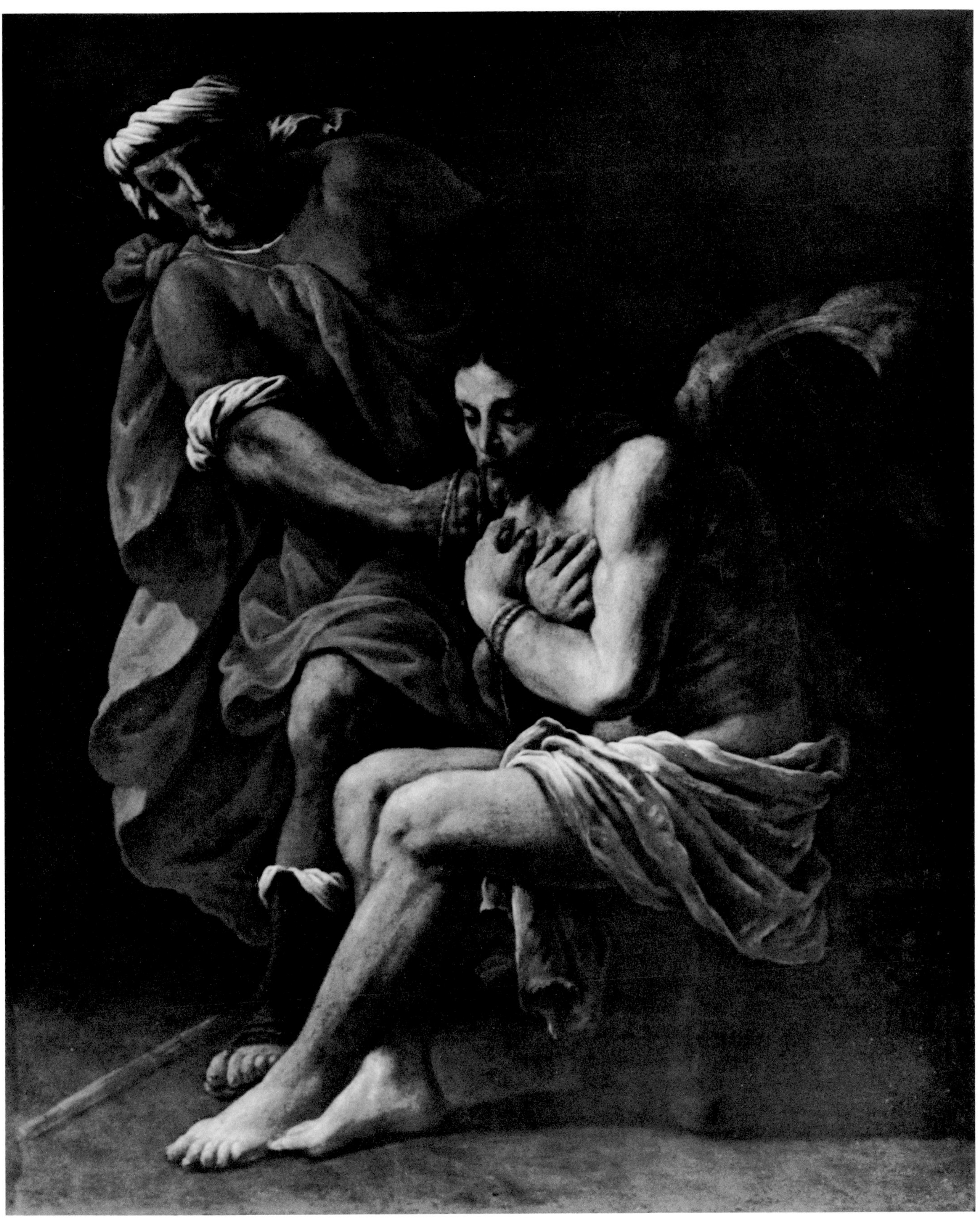

blackness of the slate upon which Bassetti painted this story.

This powerfully compact composition was first published in 1959 by Roberto Longhi. In the opinion of that scholar, shared here, the work can be dated to the beginning of Bassetti's Roman period, ca. 1616.[1] The ponderous figures, as if comprised of the stone they are painted on, anticipate the more expansive monumentality of Bassetti's *Deposition* (Borghese Gallery, Rome). In the Borghese picture a luminism and sense for open air derived from Saraceni modify the grave influence of Borgianni, which dominates in this *Christ Bound*. Bassetti observed from Borgianni's version of Caravaggism more than the details of colored turban and heavy-lidded features; he also appreciated the Venetian-influenced accomodation of the figures to their tenebrist setting.[2] The light does not rake across their forms as in Caravaggio's pictures, rather each figure emerges from the shadow by virtue of seemingly an internal illumination.

NOTES

1 Longhi, 1959, p. 36. Ottani, 1964, p. 166 n. 22, subsequently proposed a somewhat later date, close to the *Risen Christ Appearing to His Mother* (Museo di Castelvecchio, Verona).

2 An example of the type of composition by Borgianni that would have influenced Bassetti is the *Christ among the Doctors* (Almagià collection, Rome) illustrated in Spear, 1975, no. 6.

Antonio Bellucci

Pieve di Soligo (Treviso) 1654–1726 Pieve di Soligo

According to Orlandi, Antonio Bellucci was a pupil in Venice of Domenico Disnigo, a Dalmatian artist. He may also have studied under one or more of the Venetian masters who most influenced his early development, namely Pietro Liberi, Antonio Zanchi, and Andrea Celesti. From these diverse sources Bellucci emerged a tenebrist painter with a propensity for decoration. He was in fact the eldest of the itinerant Venetians—Ricci and Pellegrini most notably—who brought Late Baroque decoration to countless ceilings throughout the continent and England. Bellucci's luminous frescoes in the Chapel of the Blessed Franco in the Venetian church of the Carmines are dated 1674. During the first two decades of his career he worked mainly in Venice, Vicenza, and Verona. About 1692 Bellucci became known to patrons in Vienna; from 1696 to 1702 he was painter to the Viennese court of Joseph I, and was extensively employed by Giovanni Adamo, the prince of Liechtenstein. A new coloristic delicacy and buoyancy of spirit appears in his canvases of this period.

After a brief return to Venice, Bellucci departed in 1705 for Düsseldorf to paint for the Elector Palatine until the latter's death in 1716. Bellucci then went directly to England for six years before retiring with his honors, riches, and gout to his native city in 1722. Although his large-scale decorations often lacked the unfailing inspiration of Giordano or Ricci, Bellucci's more carefully conceived works were an influential transition into the Venetian Rococo.

7 *Diana and Endymion*

Oil on canvas. 101 × 132 cm. Ca. 1700–1710.

Provenance: Baron Lazzaroni, sale, Nice, 16–21 June 1952, lot 17 (as Luca Giordano, *Le Rêve d'Adonis*).

Reference: E. Young, 1974, pp. 301–3, 305 n. 19, figs. 4, 5, and 6.

Private collection, New York

On the slope of Mt. Latmus the handsome youth Endymion lay in perfect slumber. His beauty touched even the cold heart of Luna, who caressed him every night without his awakening. In the pictorial tradition of this theme, the figure of Luna came to be replaced by Diana, who also represents the moon. The role is an uncharacteristic one for the chaste huntress.

Bellucci's authorship and the exceptional charm of this painting among his oeuvre can be established at once by

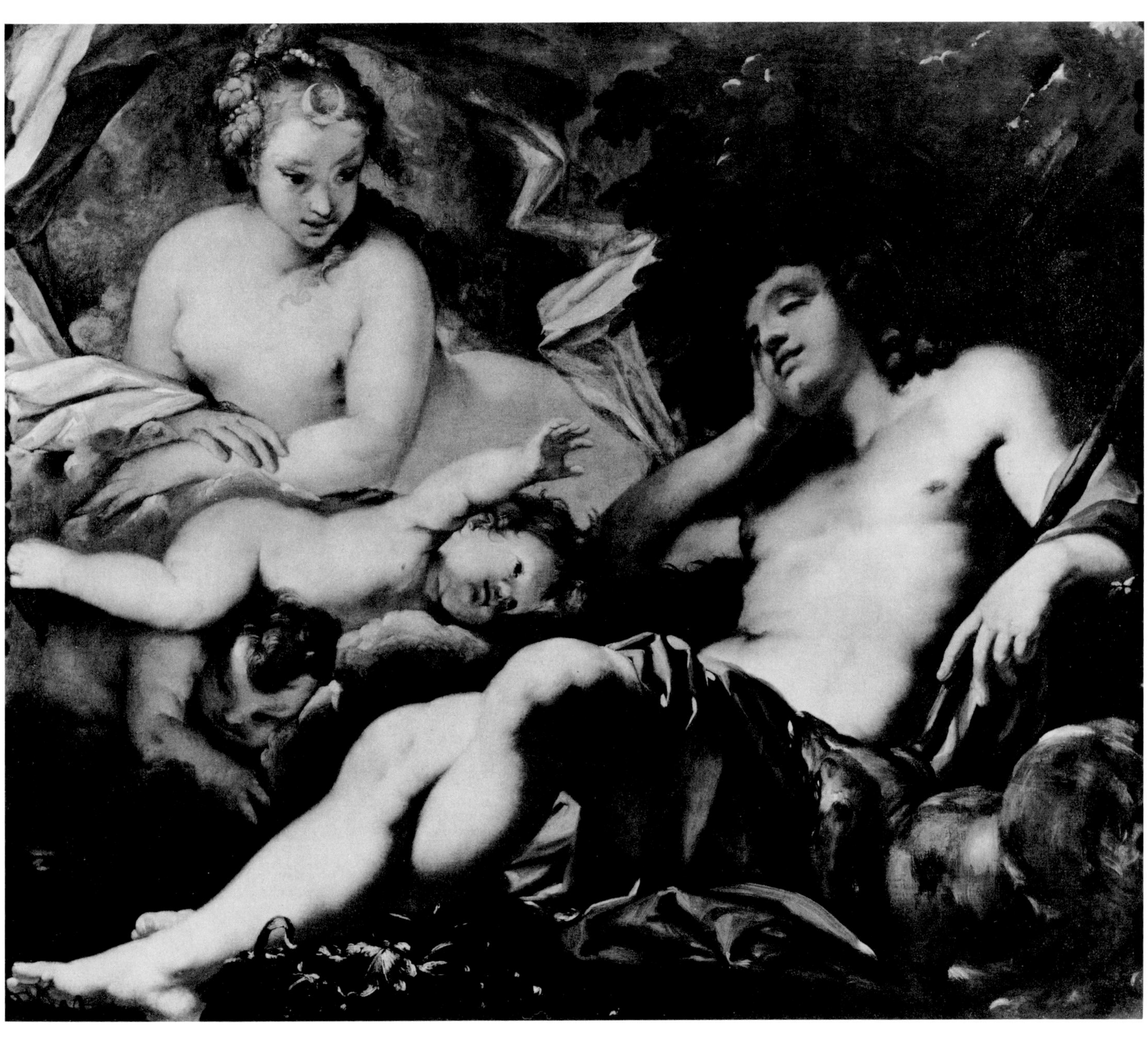

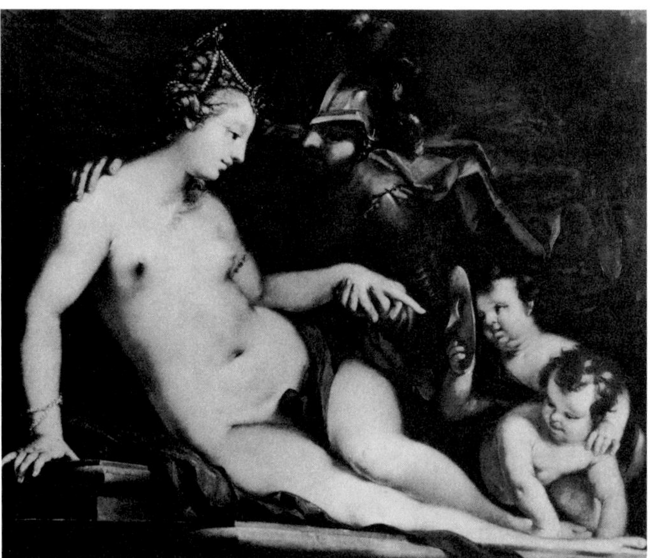

Fig. 4 Bellucci: *Venus and Mars,* oil on canvas. Professor Franco Steffanoni collection, Bergamo

comparison with one of his signed canvases of an analogous subject (fig. 4). The artist usually favored rather heavy facial features; the winsome eyes and pushed-in nose of the kittenish Diana make for one of his happiest conceptions of female beauty.

Eric Young has rightly dated this painting prior to Bellucci's English period.[1] Although the figural arrangement shows the incipience of decorative pattern-effect, Endymion's outstretched legs comprise a diagonal axis that draws the viewer's eye into spatial depth. The brilliant colorism, as of Endymion's cinnabar mantle, indicates a date near the turn of the eighteenth century.

NOTE

1 E. Young, 1974, p. 303, who notes that in 1973 Francesco Valcanover proposed in conversation a date in the English period (1716–22).

Andrea Camassei

Bevagna 1602–1649 Rome

It was the good fortune of Andrea Camassei to enjoy the protection of the Barberini family during the papacy of Urban VIII. Impressive commissions came to him at an early age, and although the limits of his gifts became evident in time, the Barberini never abandoned their support.

By 1626 Camassei was resident in Rome. He maintained close relations with his native Bevagna and during this period painted several works for local churches (possibly in 1627). His master was Domenichino, but the primary source for his style became Andrea Sacchi, his contemporary. Camassei worked alongside Sacchi and Cortona at the Villa Sacchetti, Castelfranco, in 1629. In that same year and the next, Camassei received commissions for altarpieces in S. Andrea della Valle (now lost) and Sant'Egidio in Trastevere.

The 1630s were devoted in the main to Barberini commissions, often of great prestige. The artist received in 1630 a first payment for an overdoor fresco in St. Peter's of *St. Peter Baptizing SS. Processus and Martinianus in Prison* (final payment was in 1635). Before 1632 he had frescoed ceilings of two rooms in the Palazzo Barberini. Along with Sacchi, Cortona, and Reni, Camassei contributed an altarpiece to the new Capuchin church of S. Maria della Concezione, whose decoration (1631–35) was one of the most important collaborative enterprises of the decade. Among other churches in Rome to receive his paintings were the Propaganda Fide (by 1635), the Pantheon (1638, in deposit), S. Maria in Via (1642), and the Lateran Baptistry (1644–48).

The fall of the Barberini after the death of Urban VIII in 1644 was a blow to Camassei, but between 1645 and 1648 he was already employed in the Palazzo Pamphili in Piazza Navona, which frescoes are his last documented works.

8 *St. Peter Baptizing SS. Processus and Martinianus*

Oil on canvas. 76.2 × 50.8 cm. 1630–35.

Provenance: Possibly Don Taddeo Barberini, Rome (before 1648); Don Maffeo Barberini, Rome (inv. 1672, 1686);[1] sale, Christie's, London, 1962; private collection, London.

References: Cortese, 1968, p. 286, fig. 5; Sutherland Harris, 1970, p. 53, fig. 11.

Private collection, New York

According to the Apocryphal Acts of Linus, SS. Processus and Martinianus were Roman soldiers stationed at the prison in which St. Peter was held. Peter converted his captors, and as he baptized them with the sign of the

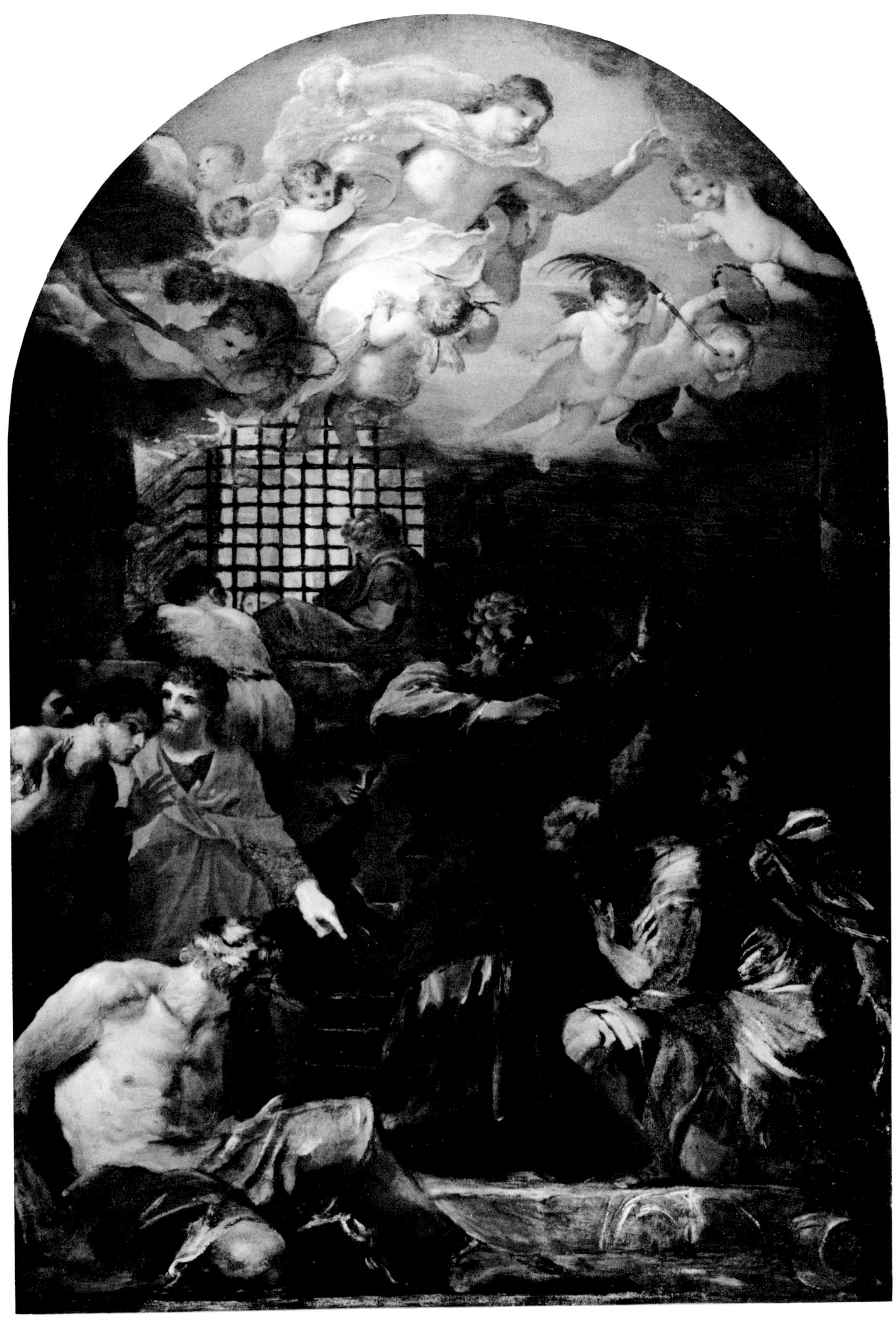

cross, a spring of water miraculously poured from the rock.

Camassei painted this story in a fresco over a door in St. Peter's in the Vatican between 1630 and 1635.[2] The fresco was replaced late in the eighteenth century by Canova's tomb monument for Clement XIII. To judge from this lively bozzetto, the commission—the most important of his career to that date—spurred the young artist to heights that he rarely ascended again.

Two other bozzetti[3] and a drawing[4] preparatory to Camassei's fresco have been preserved. The bozzetti in the Pinacoteca Vaticana[5] and the Petit-Horry collection (Levallois, Seine)[6] have elements in common that are not found in the present canvases, which Ann Sutherland Harris has demonstrated to be the closest to the fresco as executed. The earlier bozzetti are alike in that the principal figures fill the foreground and obstruct any compelling view into depth. This is one of Camassei's typical faults. However, the solution reached finally allows for considerable movement amongst the figures. The prominent window in the rear wall admits light and air into the scene in more than one sense.

Perhaps some consultation with Andrea Sacchi lies behind this new openness of design. The ample, expansive figures and the freshly varied palette are extremely intelligent adaptations of Sacchi's style, noticeably more so than in the other two bozzetti.

NOTES

1 This Barberini provenance is based on three successive inventory references to a Camassei bozzetto; see Lavin, 1975: V.inv. 48–49.89; VII.Alpha.72+.382; VII.inv.86.232. Lavin, however, identifies these entries with the sketch acquired by Sir Ellis Waterhouse at the sale of the Barberini paintings (L'Antonina, Rome, 16–23 January 1935, lot 262) and given by him to the Pinacoteca Vaticana in 1937. Sutherland Harris, 1970, p. 53, suggests that the Vatican sketch is identical to no. 111 in an 1844 Barberini inventory, described as "Eredita Colonna" (see *Catalogo dei Quadri . . . nel Palazzo . . . Colonna*, Rome, 1783, no. 579). The 1844 Barberini inventory lists a second sketch by Camassei (no. 249), which was presumably the picture already in the collection in 1648. It may be identical with the present bozzetto or with a version in the Petit-Horry collection.

2 See Sutherland Harris, 1970, p. 50, on whose thorough outline of Camassei's career this entry is based, save for style notes.

3 Waterhouse, 1976, p. 61, notes that Camassei was one of the first artists to employ bozzetti.

4 Kunstmuseum, Düsseldorf (FP 644); see Sutherland Harris, 1970, fig. 9.

5 Cortese, 1968, fig. 4.

6 Sutherland Harris, 1970, fig. 10.

Giulio Carpioni

Venice 1613–1678 Vicenza

Carpioni stands out as a singular figure in Venetian painting of the seventeenth century for the linear style that he developed as a youth and hardly varied the whole of his life. His use of a pronounced, rather clotted outline to emphasize volume had been anticipated by Paolo Farinati. Not surprisingly, Carpioni's etchings are among the finest of the age. Carpioni studied under Il Padovanino, an influential master who painted seemingly uninformed that the sixteenth century had closed. Carpioni was instructed to turn to the Venetian Renaissance for inspiration, which he did with profit, creating in his mythologies his personal vision of a thickly populated arcadia.

The artist had moved to Vicenza by 1638, where he received steady commissions from the local churches and nobility and apparently felt little compulsion to travel elsewhere. The presence of several fine paintings in the church of S. Leonardo in Verona, and the testimony of Dal Pozzo indicate that he was active in Verona for a few years late in his life.

He remained well informed on the state of art in Venice and his early works reveal his receptivity to the diverse manners of Fetti, Muttoni, Strozzi, and Renieri. The former's specialty in cabinet pictures conceived in series must have impressed Carpioni who took it up. In Vicenza Carpioni competed with Francesco Maffei. Despite the antipodal differences between their styles, Carpioni's works frequently evoke the energetic compositions of Maffei.

9 *Pan and Syrinx*

10 *Artemis and Chione*

Oil on canvas. Each 39.4 × 47 cm. (oval).

Provenance: David M. Koetser, New York.

Reference: Manning, *Venetian Baroque Painters*, 1964, nos. 29 and 30.

Robert and Bertina Suida Manning, New York

Carpioni often painted in an oval format, with the possible intent to evoke antique cameos with his multifigured compositions. This pair of pendants, happily together still, depicts Ovidian subjects of the passions of the gods.

Pan's pursuit of the nymph Syrinx was a favorite theme of Carpioni's, who painted it separately and as a pendant to other mythologies of love. As Syrinx found her escape obstructed by the River Ladon, Pan drew close to seize her. At that moment she was metamorphosed into a reed. The beautiful sound of the wind through the

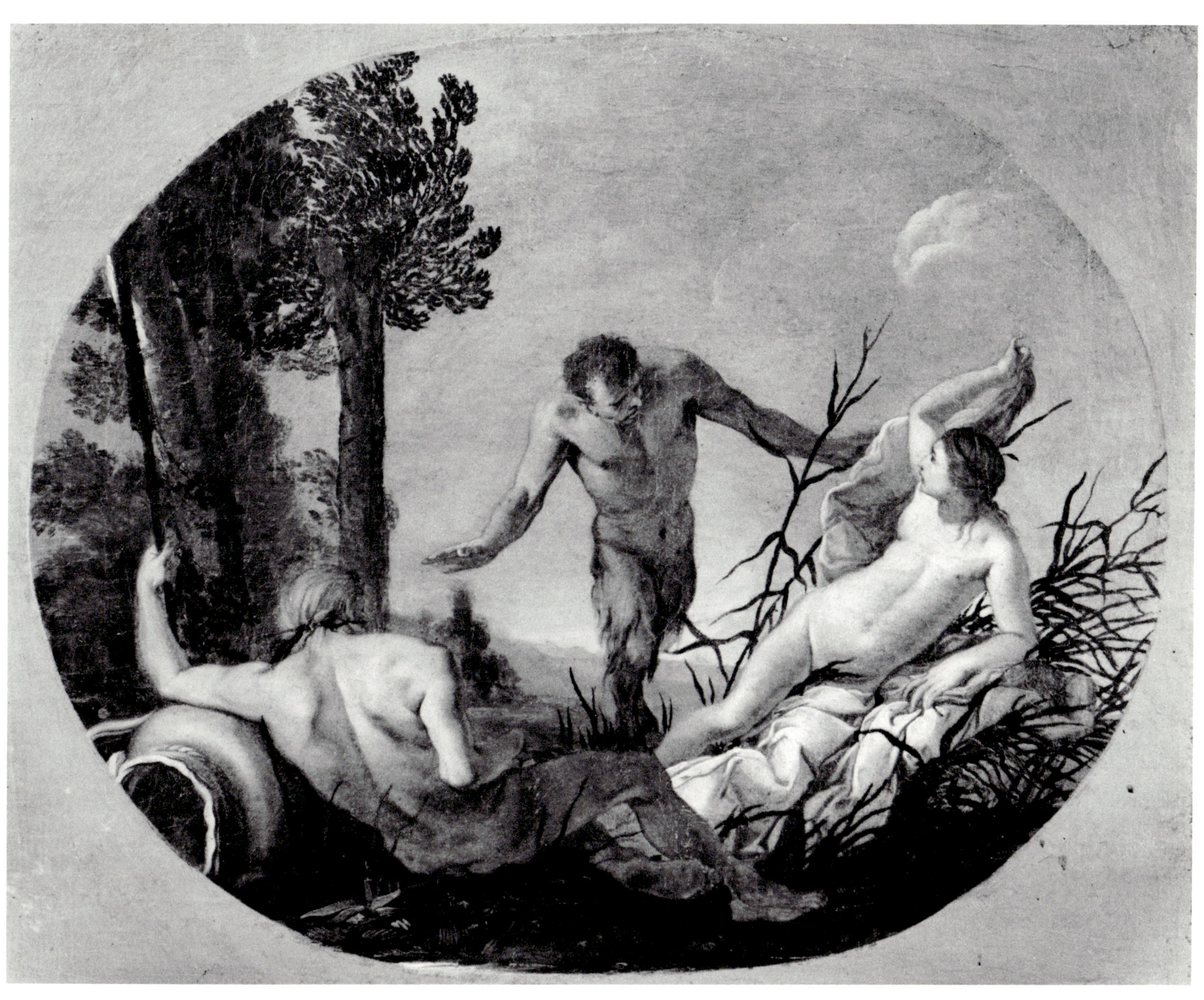

reed moved Pan to make a flute of it which became his attribute (*Metamorphoses* 1.689–713).

The subject of Artemis and Chione, identified by the owner, appears to be unique in the artist's oeuvre. Because she had dared to compare herself in beauty to Artemis, the goddess shot Chione with an arrow. Her unconsolable father, Daedalion, threw himself off Mt. Parnassus, but Apollo mercifully changed him into a hawk in mid-air (*Metamorphoses* 11.301–27).

These pendants are datable to Carpioni's late period. An oval *Pan and Syrinx* in a private collection in Venice and Carpioni's altarpiece of *S. Mauro Healing Invalids* (SS. Nazaro e Celso, Verona) exhibit similarly slender figure types and the economical handling of the master's advanced style.

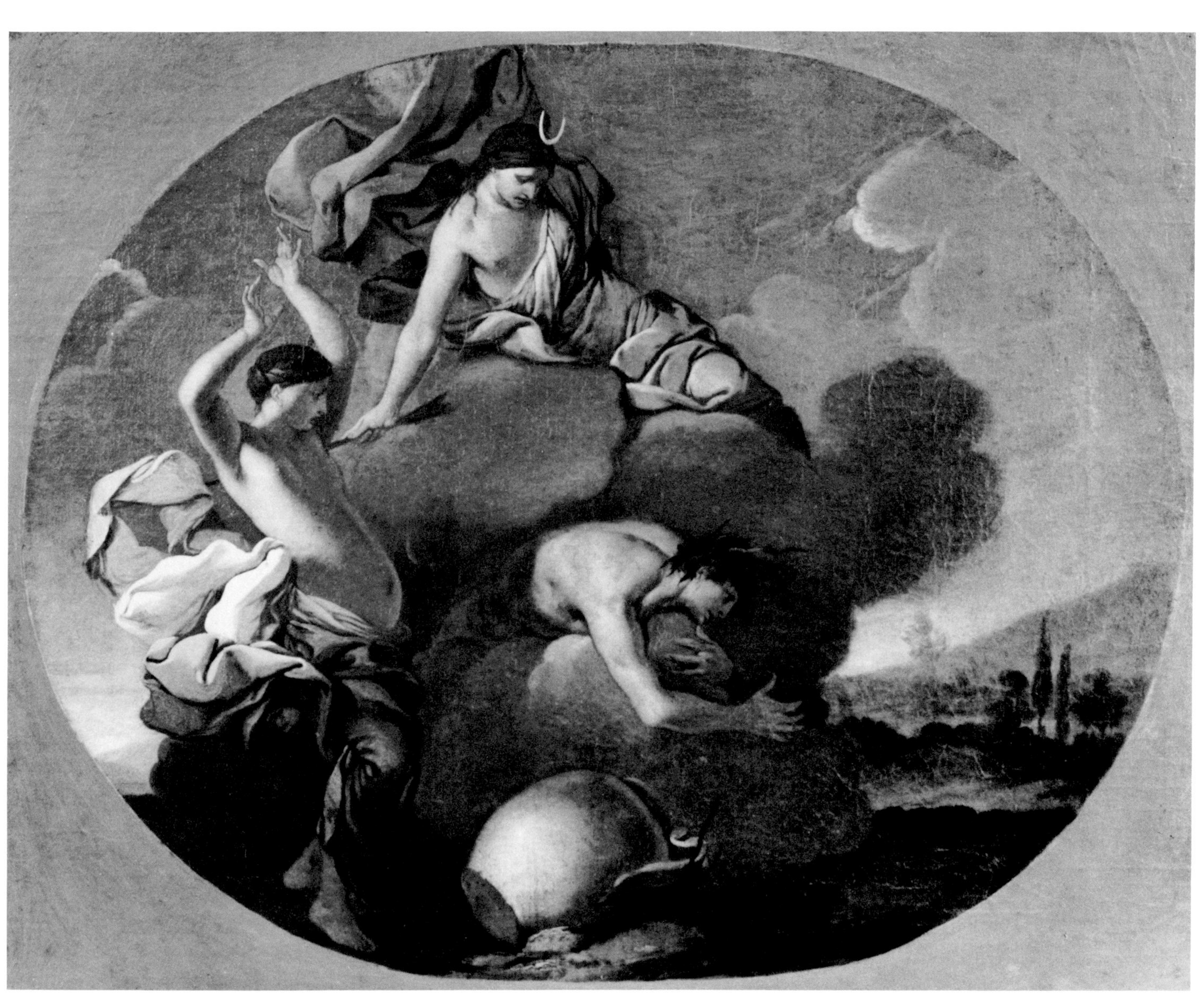

Annibale Carracci

Bologna 1560–1609 Rome

Annibale Carracci learned the fundamentals of painting from his elder cousin, Ludovico, but his earliest works, for example his *Crucifixion* of 1583 (S. Maria della Carità, Bologna) and his genre subjects, the *Butcher Shop* (Christ Church, Oxford) and the *Bean-Eater* (Galleria Colonna, Rome), reveal him most responsive to the naturalistic tendencies in the art of Bartolomeo Passarotti, a local Mannerist, and of the Campi in Cremona. Annibale's elder brother, Agostino, taught him how to engrave and encouraged him in his studies of the Venetian Renaissance. In 1582 the three Carracci opened a humanistic school of painting in Bologna, the Accademia degli Incamminati.

During the 1580s Annibale broadened his formation through visits to Tuscany, Parma, and Venice. With Ludovico and Agostino, Annibale frescoed stories of Jason in the Palazzo Fava, Bologna, 1584. His deep studies of Correggio and Barocci came to the forefront in many works of this period, including his altarpieces of the *Baptism of Christ* (S. Gregorio, Bologna) of 1585 and the *Assumption of the Virgin* (Pinacoteca, Bologna), indebted as well to Venetian models, signed and dated 1592. The Carracci collaborated on equal terms in decorative frescoes in a room of the Palazzo Magnani in Bologna, done between 1588 and 1591.

Annibale was called to Rome in 1595 by Cardinal Odoardo Farnese, who first engaged him to decorate the camerino in the Palazzo Farnese. Agostino joined him to undertake the splendid frescoes on the ceiling of the galleria of the Palazzo Farnese (ca. 1597–1600), which became the most famous decorative enterprise of the century in Italy and the indispensable textbook for nearly every artist in Rome. After his arrival in the Eternal City, Annibale had ordered his vital, sensuous style according to the ennobling and clarifying tenets of Roman classicism.

For the lateral walls of the Galleria Farnese and for many other important commissions—such as the Herrera Chapel, S. Diego degli Spagnuoli (1602–7) and the landscape lunettes with sacred subjects for the chapel in the Palazzo Aldobrandini (after 1603/4; now in the Galleria Doria-Pamphili, Rome)—Annibale employed his Bolognese pupils, Reni (who was mostly independent at this date), Domenichino, and Albani, and Agostino's Parmese pupils, Lanfranco and Badalocchio, to execute his designs. Annibale's years after 1605 were tragically clouded by an illness that seems to have robbed him of his will to work. After a brief visit to Naples in 1609, which did not revive his health, he died in Rome that same year. Through the currency of his own art and the careers of his brilliant students, the Carraccesque tradition became pervasive in Rome and Bologna and was felt in every school of European painting.

11 *Study of an Old Man*

Oil on paper pasted on panel. 44.5 × 26.7 cm. Ca. 1590.

Provenance: P. & D. Colnaghi and Co., London.

References: New York, Wildenstein & Co., 1967, no. 35, repr.; Posner, 1971, II, no. 53, repr.; Pepper, 1972, p. 263; Pepper, "Annibale Carracci ritrattista," 1973, p. 131, fig. 9; Cooney, 1976, no. 53, repr.

Mr. and Mrs. Paul H. Ganz, New York

This *Study of an Old Man* seems not to have been painted by Annibale in preparation for a larger composition or as a portrait in the strict sense of the word. It relates instead to Annibale's studio exercises, almost always made in chalk, in which for his own instruction he would set down his observations from the model as directly as possible. The present sketch in oils on paper is the only work in this technique for which Annibale's authorship is universally accepted. Such sketches belong to Venetian tradition and it does not surprise that Annibale should have experimented with the medium.

The unadorned handling of this almost uncolored study distinguishes it from Annibale's portraits in colored chalks, which have a more posed character and are rightly considered in connection with similar portraiture by the Bassano family. A most apt comparison is furnished by a chalk-drawn *Portrait of a Boy* (collection of H.M. the Queen of the Netherlands), recently attributed to Annibale by Felice Staempfle, which exhibits the same daringly blunt quality of observation.[1]

The dating of this painting is made difficult by its very nature, since it does not readily lend itself for comparison with either Annibale's drawings or his more finished paintings. Donald Posner has proposed to associate this picture with the period of Annibale's frescoes in the Palazzo Magnani, Bologna, ca. 1589/90.[2] On the occasion of its exhibition in 1967 a slightly earlier date of ca. 1587/88 was put forward.[3] D. Stephen Pepper would prefer a more advanced date of about 1593.[4]

NOTES

1 New York, Pierpont Morgan Library, 1979, no. 118, repr.
2 Posner, 1971, II, no. 53.
3 New York, Wildenstein & Co., 1967, no. 35.
4 Pepper, 1972, p. 263.

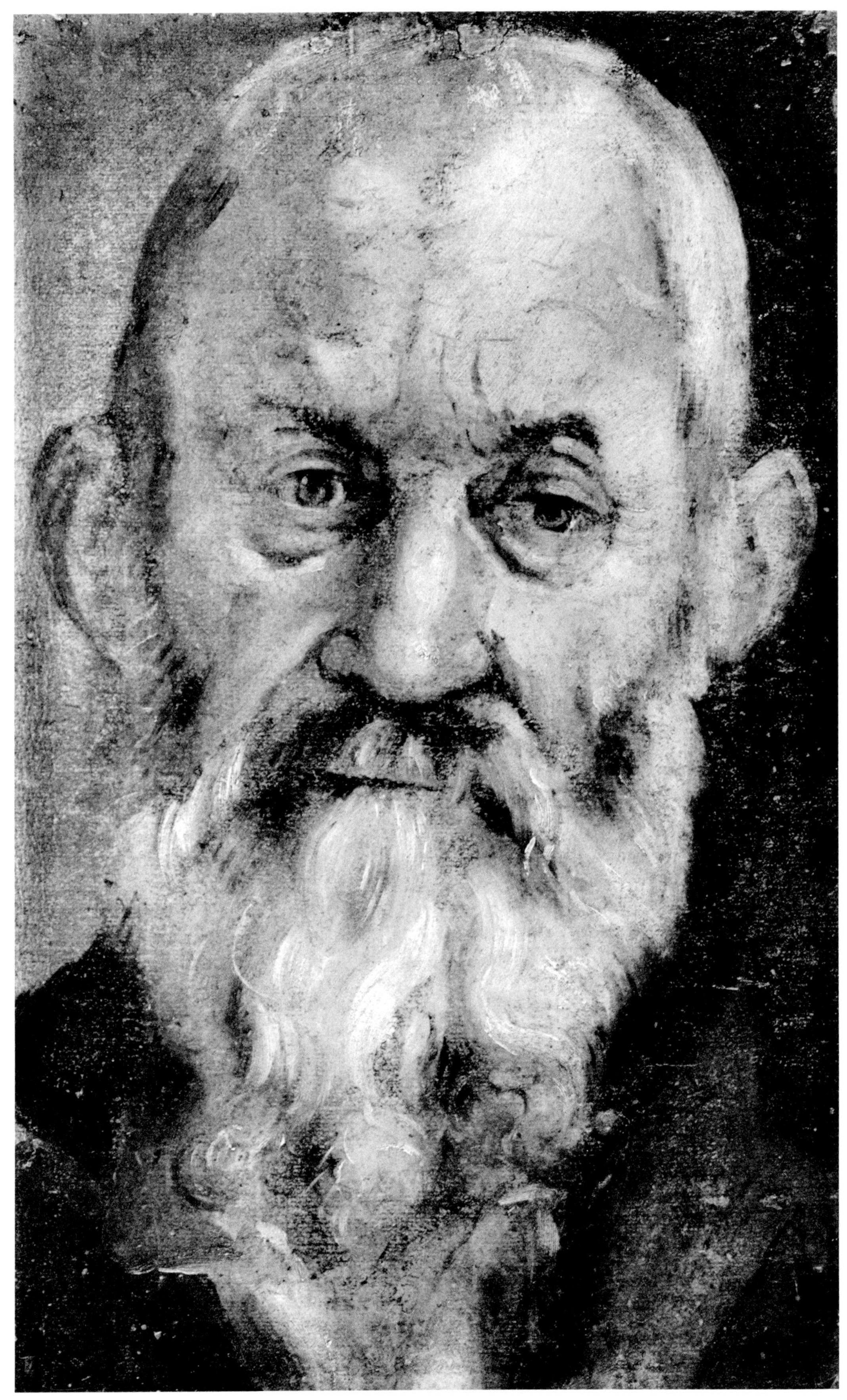

Giovanni Benedetto Castiglione

Genoa 1609–1665 Mantua?

Recent documentary discoveries have illuminated somewhat the peripatetic life of G. B. Castiglione, called Grechetto. The chronology of his copious oeuvre remains unsettled due to the scarcity of dates and the confusion between his paintings and the works of his son, Francesco (1641?–1716?) and of his brother, Salvatore (1622?–after 1676), who was more active as a picture dealer.

Castiglione was a pupil in Genoa of Giovanni Battista Paggi (d. 1627) and G. A. de Ferrari, but he was most receptive to the animal paintings of Sinibaldo Scorza (d. 1631) and Jan Roos. The Genoese activity between 1621 and 1627 of another Fleming, Van Dyck, made a considerable impression on him, most noticeably during the 1640s.

By Easter of 1632 Castiglione had arrived in Rome, and in 1634 he entered the Accademia di San Luca. In the next year he visited Naples, where his influence was immediately felt in the landscapes of Andrea de Leone. Castiglione's earliest dated painting (1633), exhibited here for the first time, reveals that Castiglione was attracted to the neo-Venetian style of Poussin earlier than has been suspected.

Luigi Salerno (1977/78) has pointed out that Poussin must have inspired Castiglione (as he did Testa and Rosa) to classical and stoic subject matter. Castiglione's own proto-Romantic absorption with necromancy and occult ideas of fate and genius were influential for Rosa, especially through the medium of his etchings.

Castiglione probably passed the early 1640s in Rome, although visits to Genoa are documented in 1639 and 1641 (by a portrait etching). During an important Genoese sojourn of 1645–47 Castiglione studied Van Dyck in depth, as may be recognized from his *Nativity* in S. Luca, Genoa, of 1645 (previously his first dated work) and strikingly so from his *Immaculate Conception* (Minneapolis Institute of Arts), painted in Rome in 1650, where he resided from 1647 to 1651.

The abundance of paintings by Castiglione in the Gonzaga collections as well as testimony of early writers have indicated to scholars a Mantuan sojourn during the 1650s. Recent archival investigations in Mantua have found no reference to Castiglione prior to 1659. Letters of that year place Salvatore in Mantua and Giovanni Benedetto in Genoa, the latter clearly informed on Mantuan affairs.

In his last years, Castiglione suffered painfully from gout. In 1660 he traveled to Venice for his health before settling in a "new and commodius" house provided him in Mantua. However, he very quickly returned to Genoa at least through 4 March 1663, when his return to Mantua had evidently been arranged. The date on his memorial in the Duomo of Mantua is 1665.

12 *Journey of Jacob*

Oil on canvas. 95.9 × 133.35 cm. 1633.

Signed and dated lower right: IO: BENEDITTVS/ CASTIGLIONVS/IANVENSIS./1633.

Provenance: The Honorable T. H. Brand (later Lord Dacre); Marquis of Stafford, Cleveland House (by 1808); Duke of Sutherland, Stafford House, sale, Christie's, London, 11 July 1913, lot 49; Saunders.

References: Britton, 1808, no. 80; Ottley, 1818, no. 66 (engraving by I. H. Wright after drawing by W. M. Craig, 1813); J. Young, 1825, I, no. 106, pl. XL; Percy, 1971, p. 51 n. 52; Newcome, 1978, p. 166, fig. 3 (engraving by I. H. Wright after drawing by W. M. Craig, 1813); H. Brigstocke, "Castiglione," *Burlington Magazine*, forthcoming, repr. (cover).

Private collection, New York

Due to its distinguished provenance this *Journey of Jacob* by Castiglione was recorded at an early date and even engraved by 1813. One can imagine, however, that the picture wanted cleaning when it hung in the drawing room at Cleveland House, for no one noticed the proud signature (in serviceable Latin) nor the date, 1633.

Knowing the ex-Stafford painting only from the engraving, Ann Percy[1] and Mary Newcome[2] reasonably judged it a "Castiglionesque" variant version of a *Departure of Jacob* by Andrea de Leone (Kunsthistorisches Museum, Vienna).[3] In her recent study on Castiglione's influence on de Leone, Newcome observed with interest that the ex-Stafford painting combines elements from the de Leone canvas in Vienna and another version attributable to him, which was with Delbanco, London, in 1933.[4]

The problem of the relationship of de Leone's Vienna painting to Castiglione is elucidated by the reappearance of the ex-Stafford *Journey of Jacob*. The latter may have been the actual model for both the de Leone compositions in Vienna and London; in any event it provides us with a clear idea of the style that Castiglione introduced to Naples two years later, in 1635.[5] During that visit Castiglione was already mentioned in a Roman court

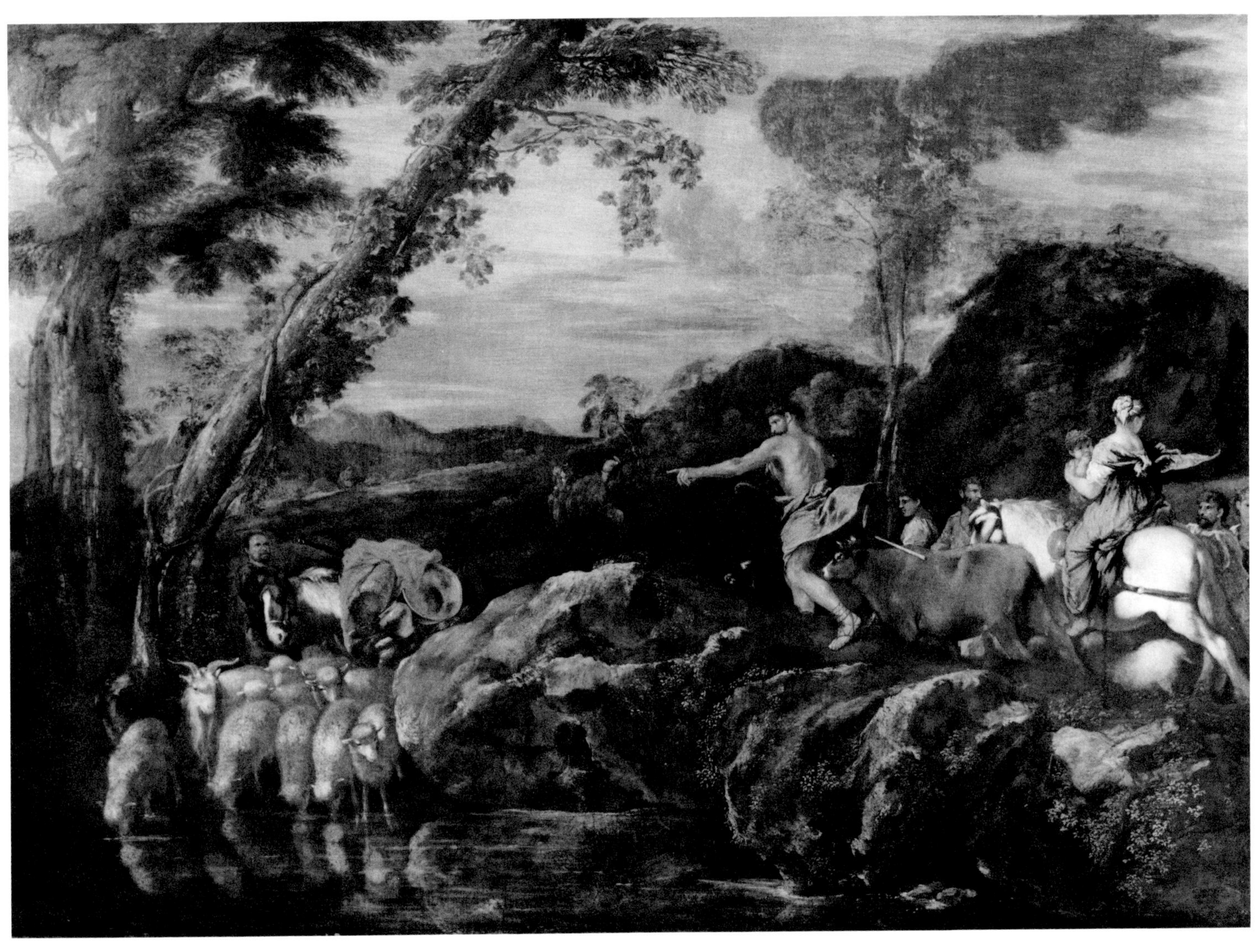

proceeding as a painter who specialized in "voyages of Jacob" (Genesis 31:17–18).[6]

Castiglione's lyrical, even dreamlike landscape belongs to a world distinct from the crisp descriptions of de Leone, who shows himself a faithful pupil of Aniello Falcone.[7] Poussin's neo-Venetian paintings of the late 1620s were Castiglione's direct inspiration. If the young Genoese had seen Poussin's *Arcadian Shepherds* (Duke of Devonshire Collection, Chatsworth) only, he would have found his source not merely for the blue accent of Jacob's mantle, but also for the sweeping flow of atmosphere and the elegiac relationship of man to timeless nature.[8]

NOTES

1 Percy, 1971, p. 51 n. 52.

2 Newcome, 1978, p. 166 and fig. 3.

3 Ibid., fig. 1.

4 Ibid., p. 166 and fig. 2. Percy, 1971, p. 51 n. 52, was the first to call attention to the Delbanco picture as well as to its preparatory drawing (sale, Christie's, London, 22 December 1938, lot 138, as Castiglione). Percy dates these works by de Leone to 1635–45.

5 The problem arises as to whether de Leone could have seen this very painting prior to his Roman sojourn of the later 1640s, unless it had been sent to Naples, or unbeknownst to us, Castiglione visited there in 1633. Castiglione's drawing in the Cooper-Hewitt Museum, New York (1931-66-15), a close variant of this composition, reminds us that Castiglione may well have painted more than one version in oil.

6 It is possible that the theme of one or another of the paintings discussed here might be the Bitter Waters of Marah Made Sweet (Exodus 15:23) since that is the title of a Pietro Monaco etching (1743) after a lost Castiglione composition with drinking sheep and pointing shepherd (repr. in *G. B. Castiglione,* 1975, fig. 44); Newcome, 1978, p. 169 n. 12, also called attention to this print.

7 Of course, the Delbanco *Departure of Jacob,* if in fact by de Leone, does approach Castiglione's style of 1633 quite closely. A crucial piece of evidence is the preparatory drawing (see note 4, above), which seems to have more affinity with de Leone's draftsmanship as established by Newcome (1978, compare especially pl. 34), than Castiglione's.

8 Hugh Brigstocke will discuss in depth this painting by Castiglione and its relationship to Poussin in a forthcoming article in *Burlington Magazine.* In Brigstocke's opinion, the Cooper-Hewitt drawing (see note 5, above) is preparatory to the present painting.

13 *Pastorale*

Oil on canvas. 77.15 × 85.1 cm. 1650s?

Provenance: Private collection, England; David M. Koetser, New York.

References: Birmingham, Ala., Museum of Art, *Italian Art,* exh. cat., 1958, p. 11, no. 5; Manning and Manning, 1962, no. 22, repr.; Manning, *Genoese Painters,* 1964, no. 44, repr.; Detroit Institute of Arts, 1965, no. 170, repr.; Percy, 1971, p. 60 n. 160; Shapley, 1973, p. 91.

Robert and Bertina Suida Manning, New York

[The photograph was made before recent restoration.]

This *Pastorale* may illustrate an episode from Genesis (29:4–6), wherein Jacob stops to inquire of some men of Haran the whereabouts of Laban.[1] It is typical of Castiglione's paintings of biblical journeys that the provisions and livestock are accounted for down to the smallest pot, but no motif clearly identifies the actors. Nonetheless, the charm of these pictures is not based merely on the still-life. As Luigi Salerno has observed: "Castiglione was one of the first to realize the romance of the secret, the emotional potential of the obscure."[2]

The dates of Castiglione's paintings are frequently no less problematic. This widely exhibited *Pastorale* has been taken by one scholar to exemplify Castiglione's earliest works in Genoa (before 1632),[3] while another scholar has proposed an attribution to his son, Francesco, which implies a date after ca. 1660.[4] However, the controlled, precise brushwork, although unusual for Giovanni Benedetto, is never found in the art of Francesco, so far as we know it.[5] Francesco employed the soft forms of his father's broader manner and never aspired to such incisive characterizations as of these two wizened men of Haran.

The impressive monumentality of this *Pastorale* would seem out of place amongst Castiglione's juvenilia, especially in light of his development in the *Journey of Jacob* of 1633 (no. 12), which admittedly pertains more to the artist's intense involvement in his new Roman experience than to his origins. This present painting must date to Castiglione's maturity.

The frequent borrowing of motifs from this *Pastorale* testifies to the high regard in which it was held by Castiglione and his circle, and constitutes circumstantial

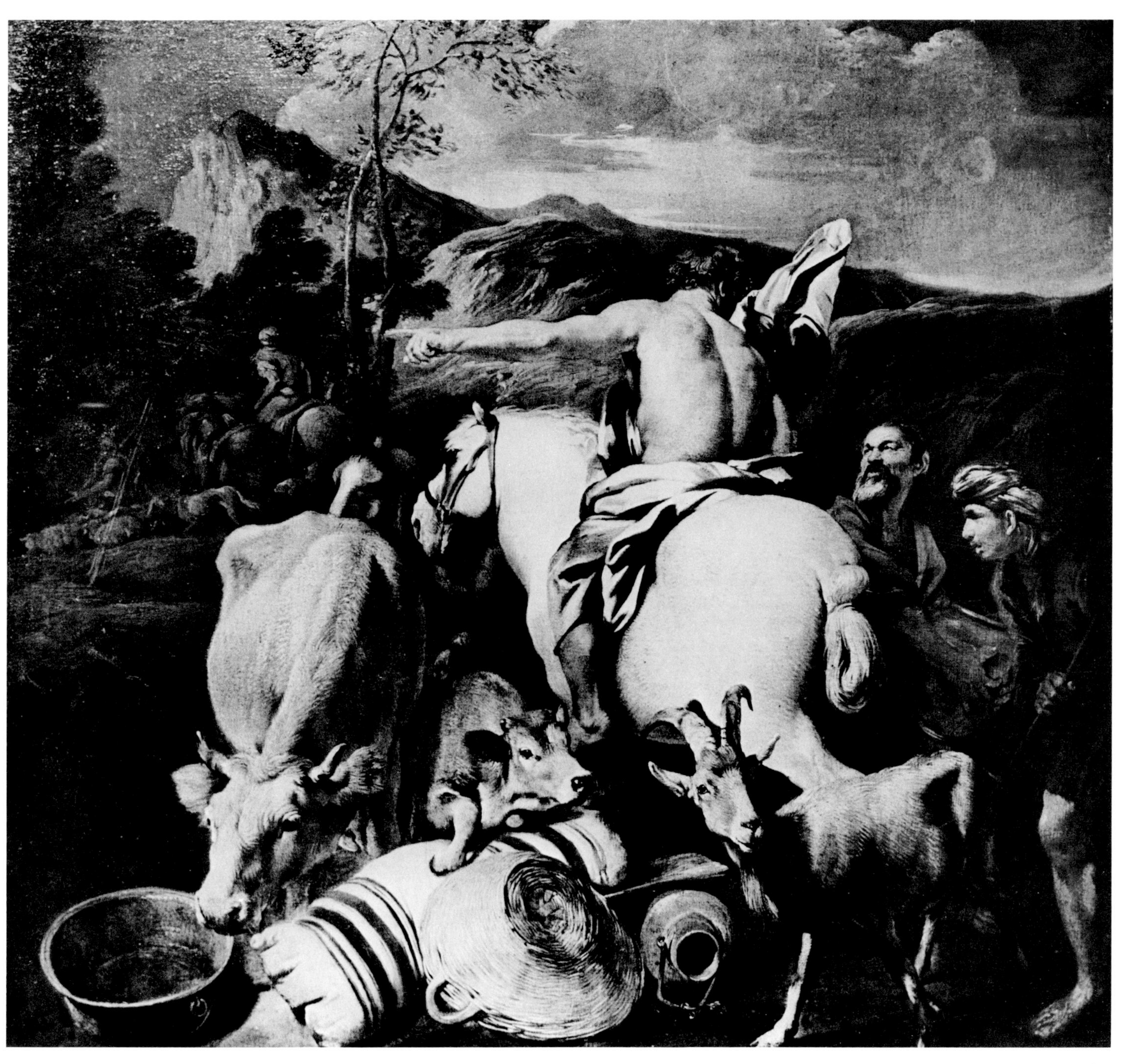

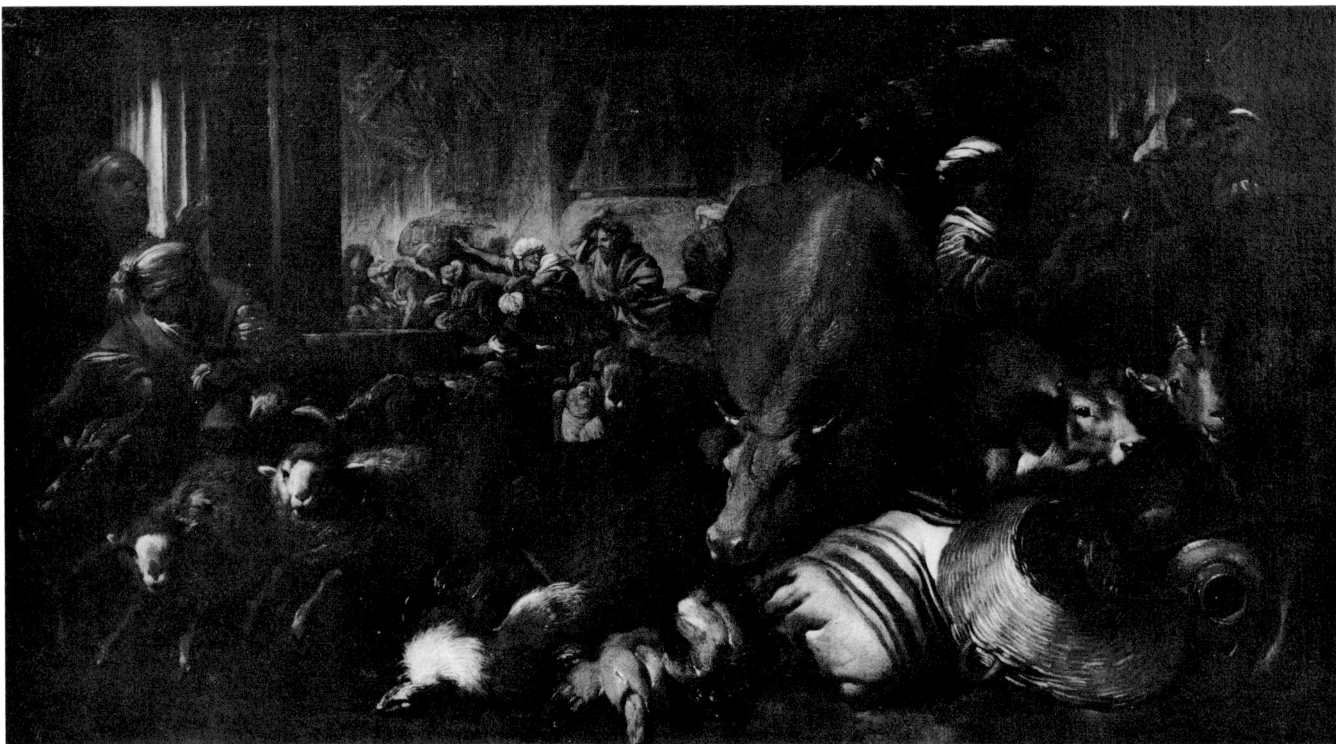

Fig. 5 Castiglione: *Christ Cleansing the Temple,* oil on canvas. Bowdoin College Museum of Art, Brunswick, Maine, gift of the Samuel H. Kress Foundation (1961.100.12)

evidence for a later dating. The whole ensemble of cows, goat, and wicker basket recurs, slightly compressed, in a *Christ Cleansing the Temple* in the Bowdoin College Museum of Art (fig. 5), which has always been attributed to Giovanni Benedetto.[6] The stressed outlines of the animals and the somewhat lost expression of this static group within its furious context indicates that the Bowdoin picture derives from this *Pastorale* and not vice versa; Ann Percy would date the *Christ Cleansing the Temple* in the 1650s.[7]

The central cow who clambers onto the sack of grain may be found once more, as the frightened offering in a *Pagan Sacrifice* (Hermitage, Leningrad), which appears from the photograph to be a late studio work.[8]

NOTES

1 Manning and Manning, 1962, no. 22; see also R. L. Manning in Detroit Institute of Arts, 1965, no. 170.

2 Salerno, 1977/78, II, p. 313 (translated by C. Enggass).

3 Shapley, 1973, p. 91.

4 Percy, 1971, p. 60 n. 160.

5 Two signed paintings by Francesco were formerly in the Balbi di Provera collection in Genoa (Percy, 1971, figs. 36 and 37). A *Sacrifice of Noah* in the El Paso, Texas, Museum of Art exhibits Francesco's typically squat, rather frivolous types (first attributed by Percy, 1971, pp. 46–47, fig. 41).

6 Shapley, 1973, p. 91 (K1775B).

7 Percy, 1971, p. 57 n. 122.

8 *The State Hermitage,* 1957, fig. 175 (attributed to Giovanni Benedetto Castiglione).

Giuseppe Bartolomeo Chiari

Rome 1654–1727 Rome

By 1666 Chiari was already studying with Carlo Maratti, with whom he remained in close association until Maratti's death in 1713. As the favorite pupil of the most renowned painter of the late seicento in Italy, Chiari never wanted for lucrative or honorific commissions. He succeeded his master as the Roman *caposcuola,* and served a productive tenure as Principe of the Accademia di San Luca between 1723 and 1725.

Chiari's distinctive style is a more intimate, rather fresher variation on Maratti's classicizing summation of the Carraccesque tradition in Rome. While Maratti's career was a sustained paeon to *disegno,* Chiari nourished his own art with sidelong glances at the colorism and vitality of Pietro da Cortona and Baciccio. Like the other leading *Maratteschi*—Giuseppe Passeri and Benedetto Luti—Chiari's pleasurable alternative to Maratti's grandiosity marks the transition into the Roman Rococo.

14 *Bathsheba at Her Bath*

Oil on canvas. 135.9 × 97.8 cm. Ca. 1695.

Provenance: Moratilla, Paris.

References: Possibly Kerber, 1968, p. 80; Clark, 1970, p. 190.

Private collection, New York

One evening, while strolling on the roof of his palace, King David espied the beautiful Bathsheba at her bath. In order that he might have Bathsheba for himself, David had her husband Uriah, a Hittite soldier in his service, sent into battle to be killed. David married the widowed Bathsheba, but for these actions he was later punished by the Lord (2 Samuel 11:2–21).

Although previously attributed to Carlo Maratti,[1] this enchanting *Bathsheba at Her Bath* may be reassigned with certainty to G. B. Chiari, whose finest visions often exceeded Maratti's for charm.[2] The figural composition derives in reverse from Maratti's *Bathsheba* in the Liechtenstein Gallery (fig. 6), which dates from 1693–95.[3] Comparison of these paintings points out at once the temperamental distinctions between the artists. Maratti employs the cool, linear elegance of Reni for his conception; Chiari unabashedly strives to convey the sensuosity of the theme through the palpable softness of flesh and gossamer drapery and the heady profusion of color.

A number of Maratti's drawings preparatory to the Liechtenstein picture have been identified;[4] none hitherto for the *Bathsheba* attributed here to Chiari. However, a drawing ascribed to Maratti in the National Gallery of Scotland (fig. 7) is, in fact, an early study for this *Bathsheba* that serves to confirm Chiari's authorship.[5] Bathsheba's arms and hands as sketched were essentially

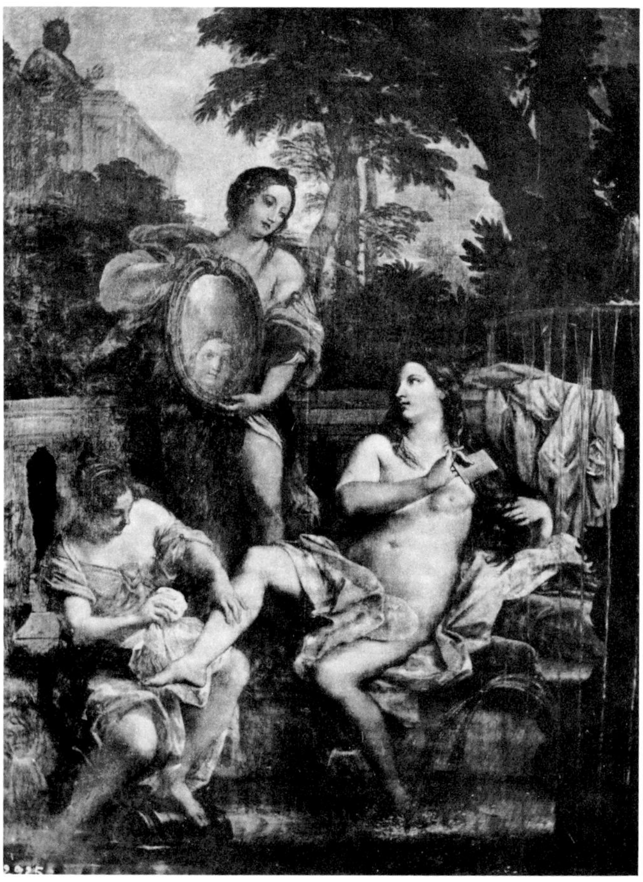

Fig. 6 Carlo Maratti (1625–1713): *Bathsheba,*
oil on canvas, ca. 1693–95.
Liechtensteinische Staatliche Kunstsammlung, Vaduz

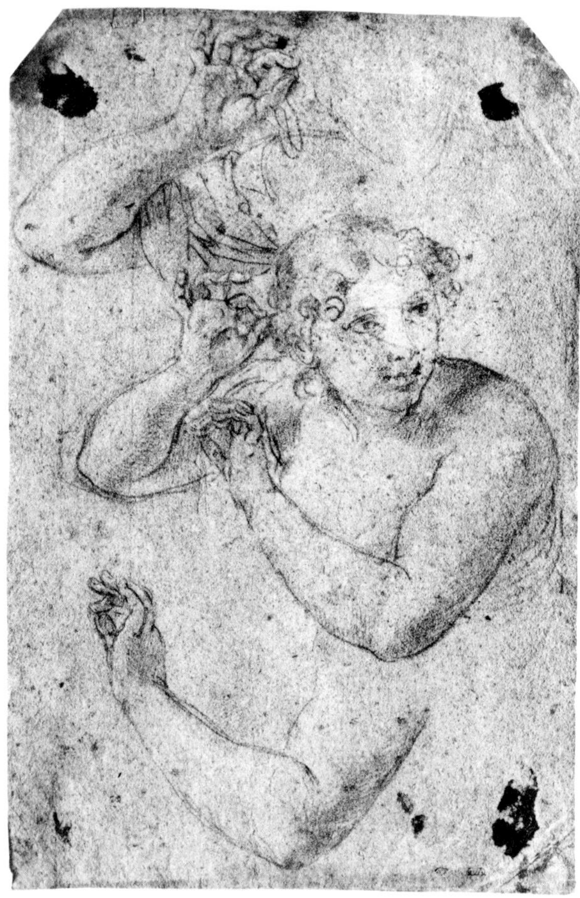

Fig. 7 Chiari: study for *Bathsheba at Her Bath,*
red chalk on blue paper.
National Gallery of Scotland, Edinburgh (D1680)

unchanged in the painting; her somewhat frivolous expression is a standard type for Chiari, which he fortuitously transformed into a noble, more affecting profile.

Chiari's *Bathsheba* may be dated on style grounds to the last decade of the seventeenth century, i.e., contemporaneous with Maratti's. In this period Chiari's works, such as the *St. Anthony Resurrecting the Dead Man,* San Silvestro in Capite, Rome (1696),[6] and the fresco of the *Birth of Pindar* in the Palazzo Barberini,[7] are reminiscent of Romanelli for their animated figures arranged in carefully ordered compositions. The later paintings became progressively freer in handling and softer in description, sometimes untidily so.

NOTES

1 See Clark, 1970, p. 190, where the picture is described as a "Chiari-like variant" by Maratti himself of the *Bathsheba* in the Liechtenstein Gallery.

2 I am most grateful to Dr. Manuela Mena for this attribution to Chiari.

3 Mezzetti, 1955, p. 347.

4 See Nieto Alcaide, 1965, pp. 287–90, pl. II, figs. c–f.

5 The drawing has been entitled *Studies of a Woman Holding an Earring;* see Andrews, 1968, I, p. 70. However, from the painting it is clear that in the drawing Bathsheba is not holding an earring; rather she is tying a ribbon in her hair.

6 Kerber, 1968, fig. 7.

7 Ibid., fig. 6.

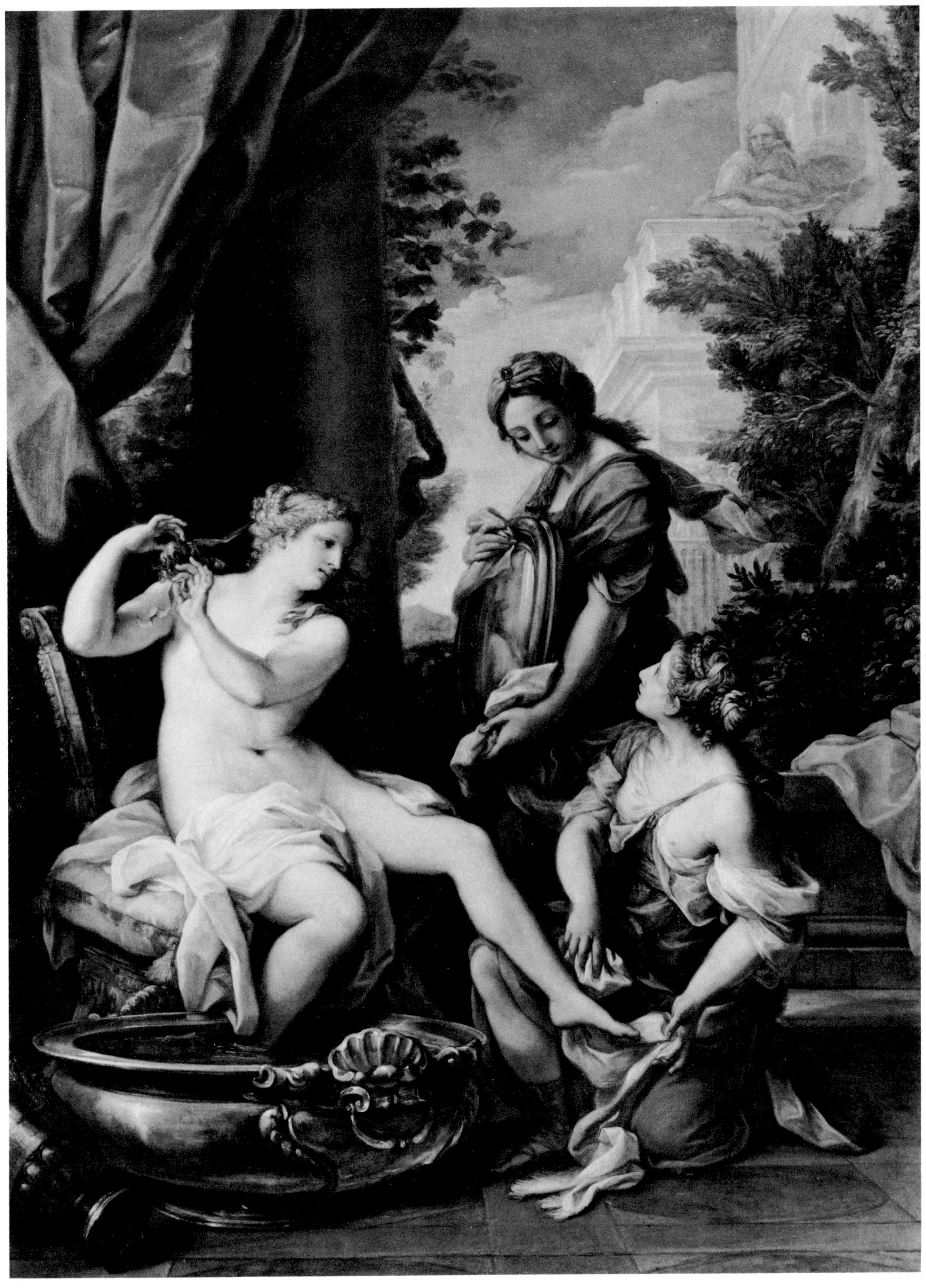

Viviano Codazzi

Bergamo 1603/4–1670 Rome

The origins of Codazzi's style are unclear. He realized the expressive potentialities of architectural paintings as had no one since the Renaissance. With equal sympathy he studied the ruins of antiquity and the dilapidated taverns of his own day, and he painted his observations in imaginary views assembled with an eye for evocative detail.

Codazzi seems to have proceeded directly to Naples with little time for studies in Bergamo or in Rome en route. Upon his marriage in 1636, he declared that he had lived in Naples for fifteen years. In addition to his easel paintings, usually with figures added by Micco Spadaro, Codazzi was employed frequently in Naples to paint architectural backgrounds, columns, stairs, and such in other artists' frescoes. He worked with Lanfranco in SS. Apostoli and Stanzione in the Certosa di S. Martino.

At the Masaniello revolt of 1647, Codazzi left Naples for Rome. He apparently resided uninterruptedly in Rome for the next decade. At least in 1657 he was described in a census as a Bergamesque painter, fifty years of age, living in via Vittoria (al Campo Marzio) with his thirty-three-year-old wife, seven children, and not a rich man (Bertolotti). During the undocumented years, 1659–67, he may have traveled abroad. After that period, he was once more in Rome, where he died.

Codazzi's paintings can often be dated by his collaborator for the figures. The *Bamboccianti* found his dark architecture amenable backdrops for their genre scenes. Cerquozzi's hand is only found in Codazzi's Roman period, Jan Miel's in the period between 1647 and 1653, and G. B. Castiglione's at mid-century.

Codazzi had innumerable followers, most of whom have detracted from his reputation. Ghisolfi and Gagliardi were the most worthy. Canaletto and the other view-painters were the spiritual heirs of Codazzi.

15 *Ruins with a Hermit*

Oil on canvas mounted on panel. 34.3 × 40.6 cm. 1655.

Monogrammed lower right corner: VC 1655.

Provenance: Malcolm Waddingham, London.

Mr. and Mrs. Morton B. Harris, New York

A vaulted chamber of venerable antiquity has become the grotto of a solitary hermit in prayer before a crucifix. The brick walls have collapsed in ages past, but the great arches stand indomitably, their notches supporting the roots of shimmering vines.

This little painting holds especial significance for our appreciation of Codazzi, and not merely because, unusually, he noted his initials and the date upon it. Codazzi was fascinated most of all by the stones that traverse space in a curved span; he rarely painted architecture without the adornment of arches. However, in no other picture by Codazzi do the stones so loom overhead as to draw the viewer into the picture space. The nostalgic aura of ancient ruins was a principal concern of seventeenth-century painters, but in this particular painting Codazzi involves the viewer with such immediacy that the metaphor of age and decay is sensed on a deeply personal level. This is truly the birth of Romanticism as Caspar David Friedrich practiced it.

The simple hermit may well be from Codazzi's own brush. It seems improbable that a figure specialist should have obscured the face in shadow and neglected to paint both feet.

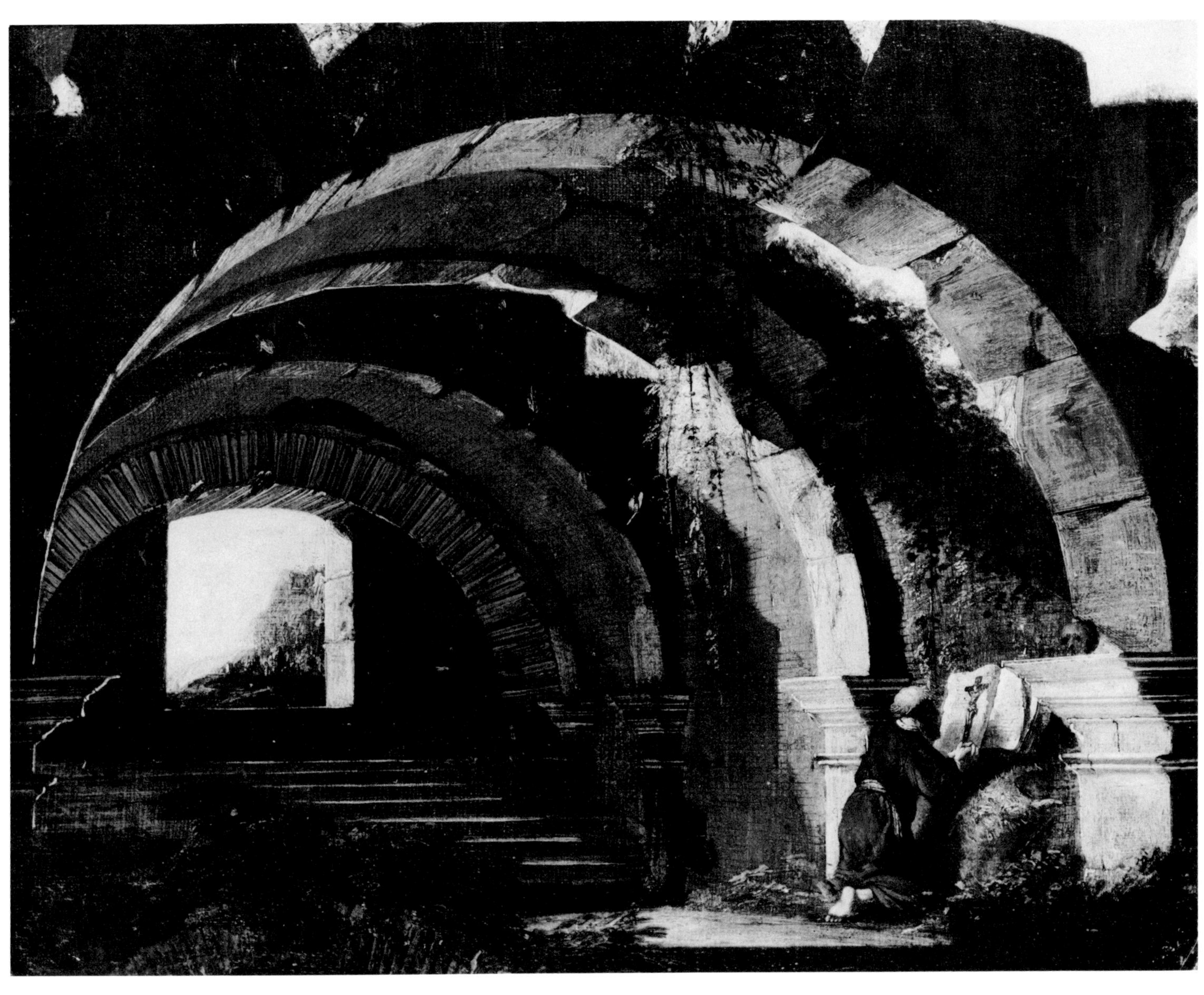

Daniele Crespi

Busto Arizio ca. 1597–1630 Milan

Although his life was cut short by the plague of 1630, the precocious Daniele Crespi had already demonstrated his genius in ample measure. According to tradition he was born in Busto Arizio; by 1610 he had come to Milan. In 1619 we find him working alongside Moncalvo in the cupola of S. Vittore al Corpo. His frescoes and canvases in the chapel of St. Anthony Abbot of that church (also 1619) reveal his study of his compatriots Camillo Procaccini and Il Cerano as well as of the Michelangelesque Mannerism of Tibaldi.

By order of Cardinal Federico Borromeo in 1621, Crespi was accepted into the classes held by Cerano at the Accademia Ambrosiana, but he seems to have been too occupied with commissions to attend. Three paintings of 1623 for the chapel of St. John the Baptist in S. Protaso ad Monachos (removed to S. Giovanni Battista, Busto Arizio) evince a hard-won naturalism and his sensitivity to a profound range of human emotion. In the few remaining years allowed to him, Crespi softened his descriptions of external form as if to devote himself to the life of the spirit. Fresco series in the charterhouses of Garegnano (1629) and Pavia (1630) were his last works.

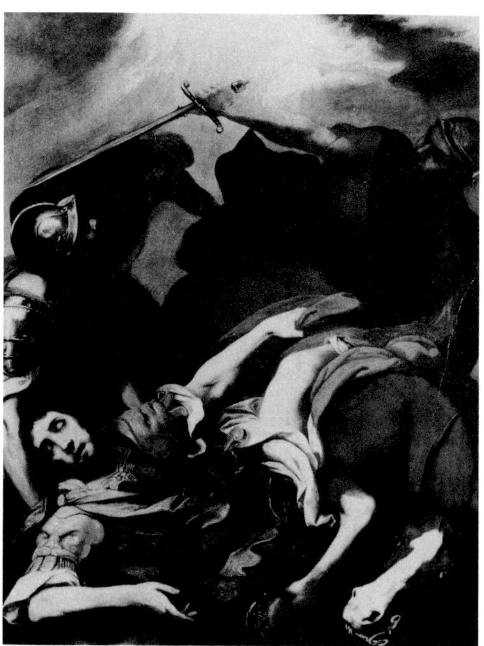

Fig. 8 Crespi: *Conversion of St. Paul,* oil on panel. Galerie Heim, Paris

16 *Conversion of St. Paul*

Oil on panel. 118.75 × 84.5 cm. Ca. 1623.

Provenance: Reininghaus collection, Vienna, sale, 29–30 May 1933.

References: Ruggeri, 90, 1967, p. 56, fig. 11; London, Heim Gallery, 1976, see no. 7; H. Brigstocke, "G. C. Procaccini and Daniele Crespi," *Revue de l'art,* forthcoming.

Robert and Bertina Suida Manning, New York

Saul of Tarsus was a Roman of Jewish descent and a persecutor of the early Christian church. On a journey from Jerusalem to Damascus, "suddenly there shined round about him a light from heaven: And he fell to the earth, and heard a voice saying unto him, Saul, Saul, why persecutest thou me?" (Acts 9:3–4). After his conversion Paul, as he came to be called, was one of the most zealous apostles and influential teachers of the church, traveling throughout the Hellenistic world. He was martyred in Rome under the rule of Nero.

At the moment of his conversion Paul is usually shown blinded by the miraculous light and, often, in the very act of being struck out of his saddle. In Crespi's reading of the story Paul does not share, as it were, in the confusion and turmoil of his companions. His absorption in the stirrings of his soul isolates him from them. Paul thrusts out his arm seemingly not to ward off the light of revelation, rather to receive it and reject the distractions of the crowd about him.

The unnaturally compressed arrangement of men and horse within this picture is a Mannerist trait that Crespi ingeniously employs to heighten the sense of immediacy and excitement. The expansive, weighty figures and their rugged facial types are comparable to those in Crespi's great *Way to Calvary* (Brera, Milan), which has been dated ca. 1623 or slightly earlier.

Crespi interpreted this theme similarly in a *Conversion of St. Paul* (fig. 8), also attributed to the artist by Hugh Brigstocke. An earlier dating is preferred by Brigstocke for that version, a view shared here. The technique and the less forceful presentation of the earlier picture seem closer to the manners of Camillo Procaccini and Cerano.

Various sources from Parmigianino to Ludovico Carracci have been proposed for the composition of the Manning *Conversion of St. Paul,* none compellingly. In actual fact, Crespi found his inspiration in his own city of Milan and from a most prominent model; his painting derives in reverse from Cerano's cartoon in grisaille for the sculpture of this subject, which was in place before 1619 over the portal of S. Paolo alle Monache.[2] It is interesting that Cerano's compositions of the latter 1610s, according to Rosci, typically appear to tumble forward out of the picture format.[3] Indeed, Crespi's picture evokes a sculpture in high relief through its piling up of bulky masses that hardly seem to recede into depth.

NOTES

1 London, Heim Gallery, 1976, see no. 7.

2 Rosci, 1964, fig. 166.

3 Ibid., see pp. 103–6.

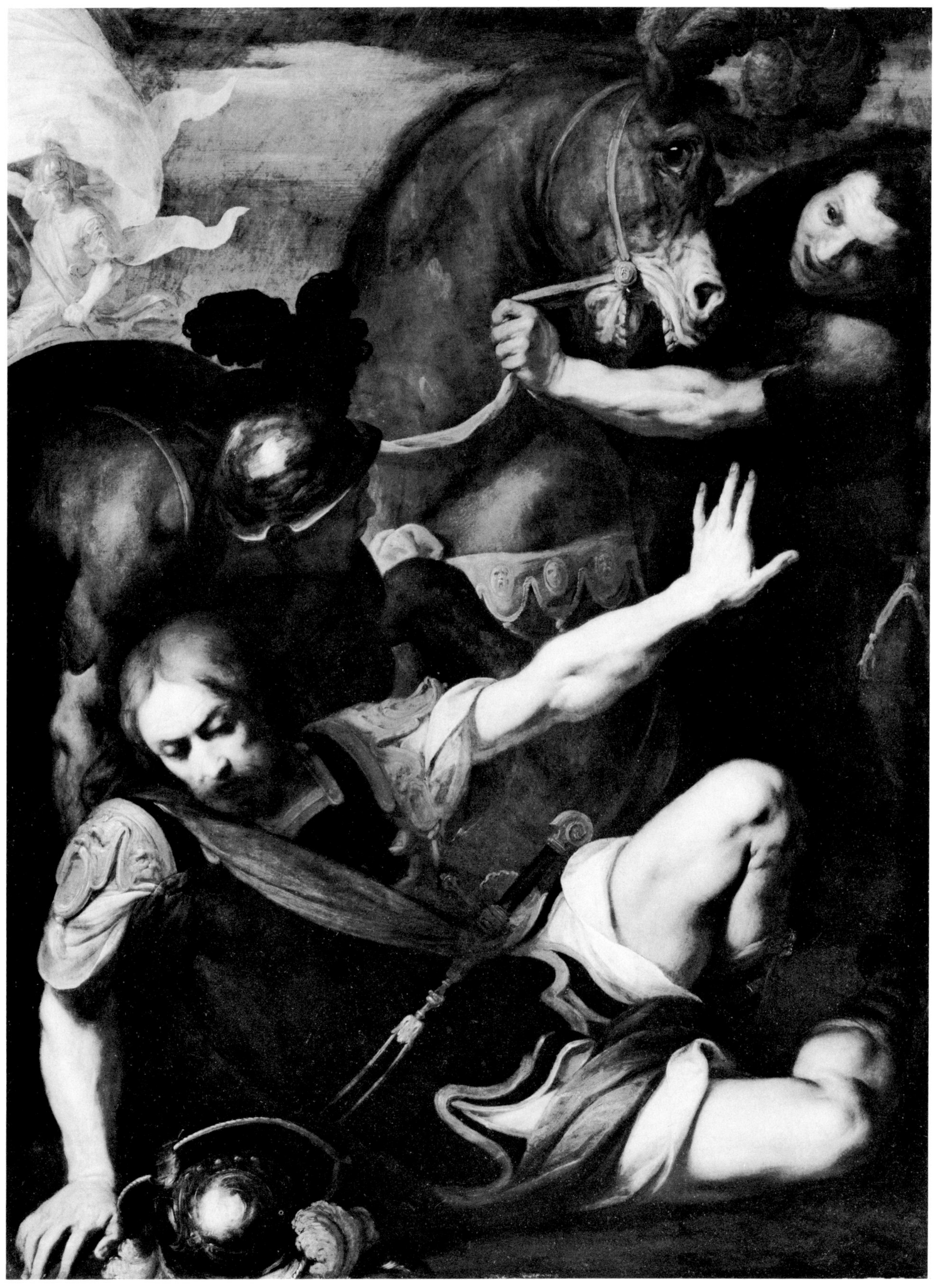

Cesare Dandini

Florence 1596–1656 Florence

Dandini's life is amply described by Baldinucci. At the age of twelve he was apprenticed to Francesco Curradi; thereafter he studied briefly with Cristofano Allori and then with Domenico Passignano, who used his assistance in the cathedral at Pisa. The *Christ Mourned by Angels* of 1625 in SS. Annunziata, Florence, is his earliest dated work. For the same church Dandini painted a major altarpiece in 1631.

Baldinucci remarks on Dandini's avid admiration for Dürer prints, of which he painted copies in the 1620s for Don Leopoldo Medici. He was also much attracted to the stiff elegance of the Florentine Mannerists of the previous century. Through his exposure to the art of Orazio Riminaldi in Pisa, and possibly from a sojourn in Rome, Dandini occasionally exhibited traces of Caravaggesque technique.

Although he placed his share of large altarpieces in churches in Florence, Volterra, and Ancona, Dandini's talent was best suited for paintings on a scale intended for private collectors. His half-length pictures of allegorical or mythological themes were especially sought after. In Dandini's mature style after the 1630s his figures typically referred to the Bronzinesque tradition of aloof detachment and glasine textures. Among Cesare's pupils was his brother, Vincenzo (1607–75).

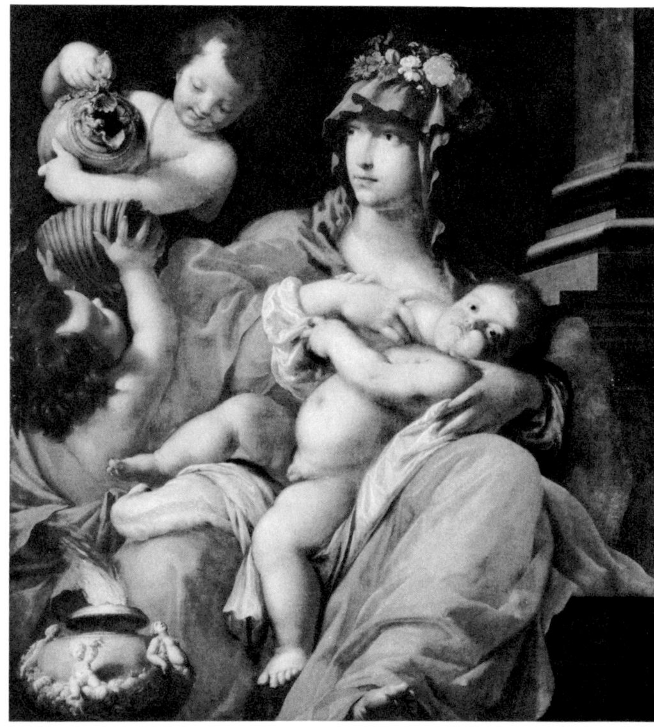

Fig. 9 Dandini: *Charity,* oil on canvas.
Metropolitan Museum of Art, New York,
gift of Mr. and Mrs. Ralph Friedman, 1969 (69.283)

17 *Charity*

Oil on canvas. 115.6 × 101.6 cm. Ca. 1656.

References: Possibly Baldinucci, 1847, IV, p. 559; Gregori, 1965, p. 46; Zeri and Gardner, 1971, p. 212.

Mr. and Mrs. Paul H. Ganz, New York

The *Iconologia* of Cesare Ripa codified the allegorical personification of Charity as a woman who holds three infants, one of whom she nurses.[1] The three infants imply that Charity nourishes the related virtues of Faith and Hope. The act of drinking by one of the putti alludes to one of the Seven Acts of Mercy. The flame symbolizes that Charity is an ardent love for God and neighbor. The inclusion of an angel to trumpet the fame of Charity is unusual.

Dandini painted this theme on numerous occasions. A very similar figure of Charity was used by the artist in a well-known version in the Metropolitan Museum of Art (fig. 9). Otherwise the two pictures diverge dramatically in technique. The Metropolitan *Charity* was painted to an enamel-like perfection of finish, with richly varied values of red and blue. Its *di sotto in sù* perspective suggests that Dandini painted it with a specific hanging in mind. By way of contrast, the unadorned handling of the present *Charity,* which is dominated by a metallic blue tonality, presents a stark, not a lavish expression.

The spare quality of Dandini's means in this *Charity* lends credence to Mina Gregori's suggestion that the Ganz picture was one of two paintings of this subject that Baldinucci reports were left unfinished at Cesare's death and completed by his brother, Vincenzo.[2]

In a smaller Dandini *Charity* in a Milanese private collection, an identical putto drinking from a bowl appears.[3] A drawing by Dandini in the British Museum[4] contains various studies for a *Charity* close to the Ganz composition.

NOTES

1 Ripa, 1611, pp. 71–73.

2 See Gregori, 1965, p. 46.

3 Ibid., no. 10, repr.

4 Inv. no. 1930-4-14-17, red chalk, 22 × 16.8 cm.; see Thiem, 1977, no. 155, repr. A later inscription incorrectly describes the subject as the Holy Family.

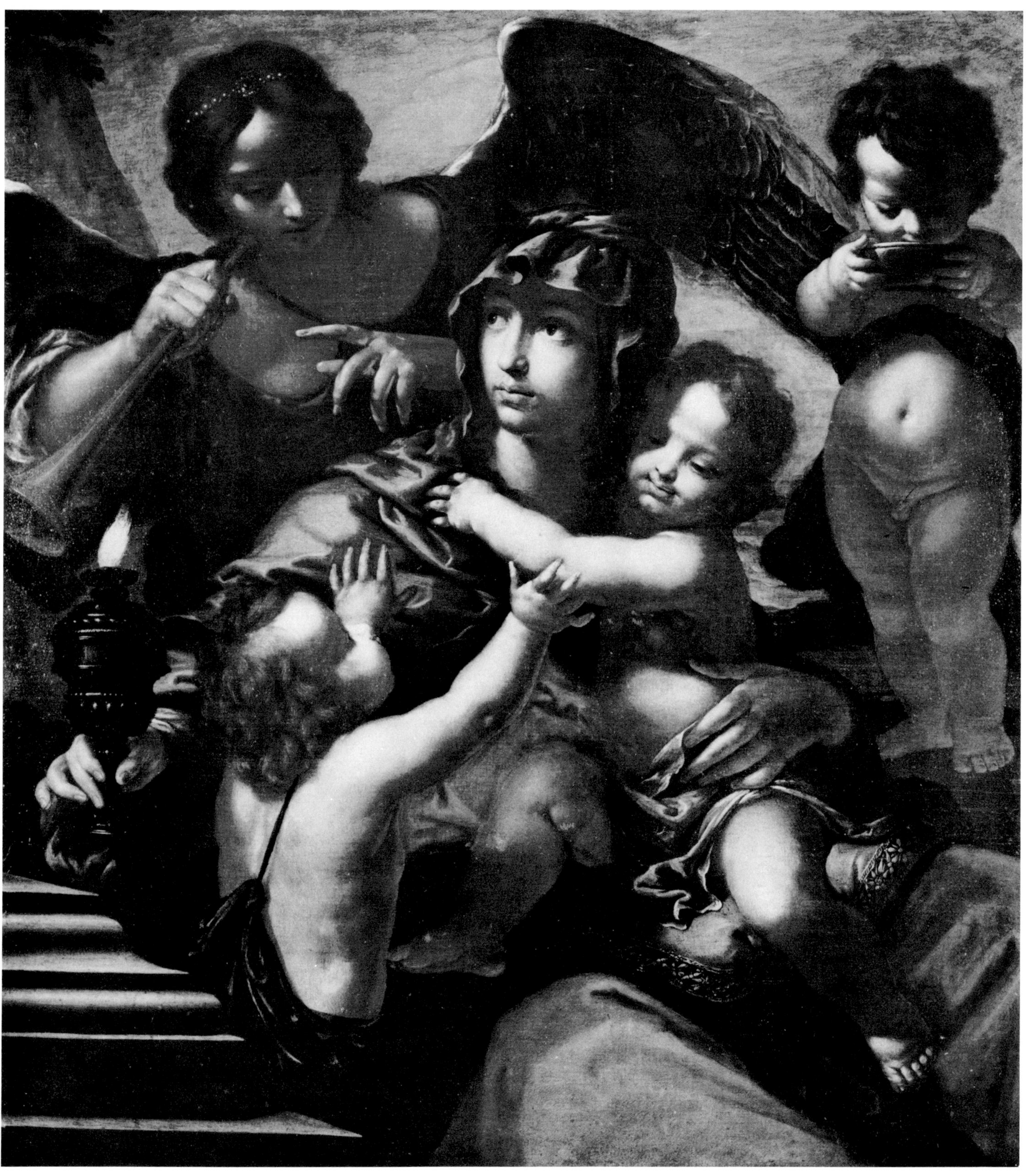

Carlo Dolci

Florence 1616–1686 Florence

Carlo Dolci exemplifies the Florentine Baroque, so much so that when his paintings were despised for their "sentimentality," as they were early in this century, the whole school fell into obscurity with him. It is only recently that Florentine painting of the seventeenth century has regained our appreciation for its highly refined sensibilities and its virtuoso technique.

Dolci, a child prodigy, was trained in Florence and passed the whole of his career in his native city. His fame attracted countless commissions from connoisseurs abroad. His master, Jacopo Vignoli, had looked beyond the confines of Florence to Guercino and to Venetian painting for elements of naturalism and breadth of handling, both of which Dolci typically excluded. However, Charles McCorquodale has traced in Vignoli's impassioned religiosity of the 1620s the source for the rigorously pious interpretations that are distinctive to Dolci. With imperceptible brushwork Dolci painted ever more illusionistic renditions of idealized saints and their every precious tear. His exquisitely detailed pictures are analogous to silk flowers: the closer they approach to nature, the more they mean to surpass it.

18 *St. Jerome in Penitence*

Oil on panel. 29 × 21.5 cm. (oval). 1647.

Inscribed on verso, partly illegible: 1647 a 14 di febrario restano/che questo fare . . . di quanto/gli fussi stato debitore e sin' a detto giorno.

Provenance: Possibly Antonio Lorenzi, Florence (1647); Mrs. E. Hooper, Vancouver.

References: McCorquodale, *Painting in Florence 1600–1700*, 1979, p. 48; McCorquodale, "Some Unpublished Works by Carlo Dolci," 1979, pp. 145–46, fig. 8.

Richard L. Feigen, New York

St. Jerome (ca. 342–420) was the most learned of the Latin Fathers of the church; he is revered above all for his translation of the Bible from Hebrew and Greek into Latin—the version known since the thirteenth century as the vulgate. The saint's emaciated frame, the wilderness setting, and his beloved books refer to this labor and to his many other writings accomplished in Bethlehem in a monastery that he had founded under an ascetic rule.

The inscription in Dolci's own hand on the verso of this small panel indicates that Dolci gave this painting to settle a debt.[1] This curious circumstance lends credence perhaps to McCorquodale's proposed identification of this St. Jerome with "un altro San Girolamo in atto di battersi il petto col sasso,"[2] which Baldinucci tells us Dolci painted for Antonio Lorenzi, his physician.[3]

Dolci rather specialized in small-scale paintings for private collectors, not a usual practice among the major Florentines. As McCorquodale has noted, this *St. Jerome* is the unique dated example of his small, more freely handled works. The softly brushed foliage and the saint's febrile emotion contrast movingly with the firmly defined still-life of books and death's head.

NOTES

1 Professor Nicola Spinosa (in conversation, 1979) was able to decipher this difficult inscription; previously only the date had been read.

2 McCorquodale, "Some Unpublished Works by Carlo Dolci," 1979, p. 145 n. 16.

3 Baldinucci, 1847, v, p. 351.

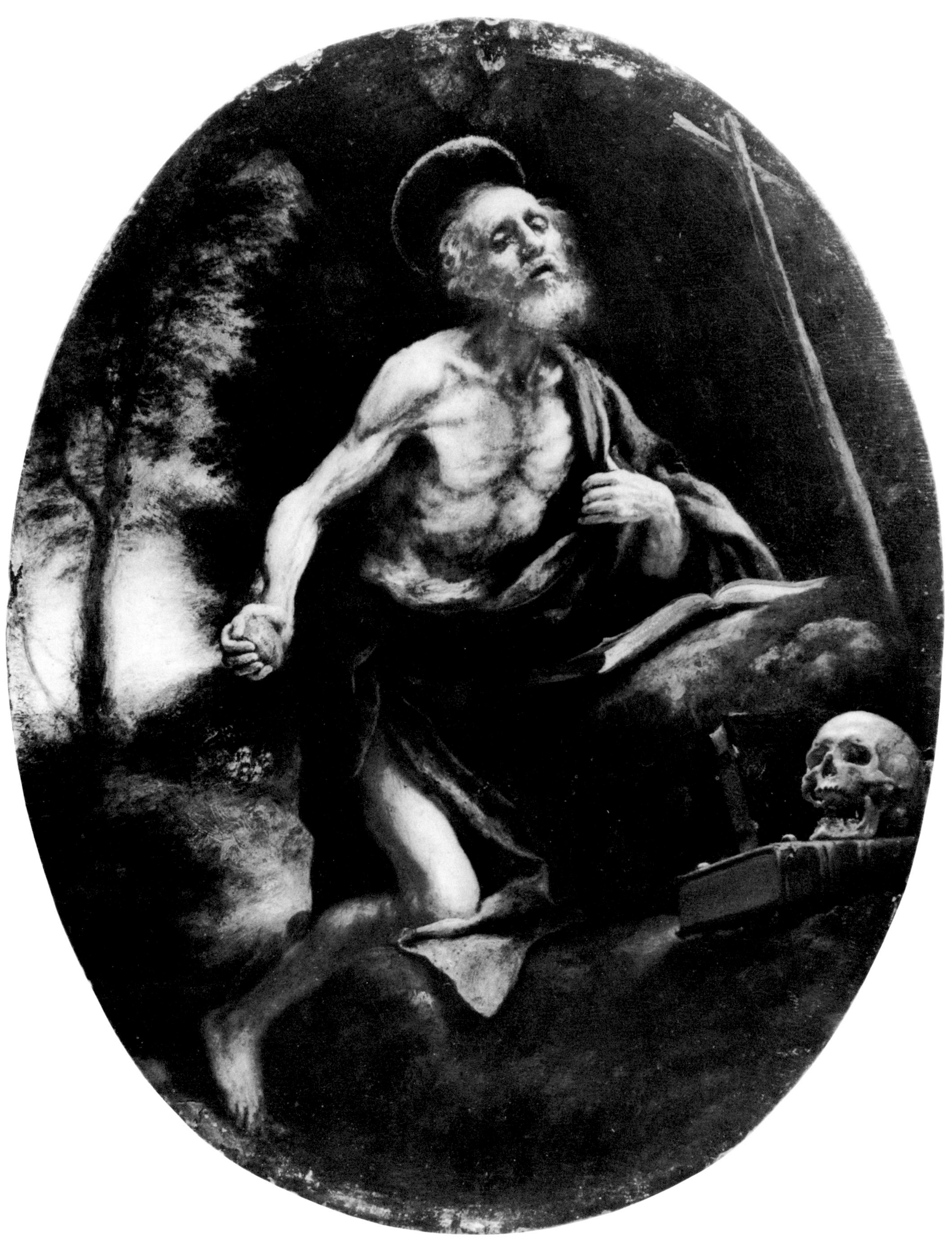

19 *Christ Child with a Wreath of Flowers*

Oil on panel. 23.2 × 17.15 cm.

Inscribed on verso, inside an orb: IHS/VENI CORONOBERIS.

Reference: Heinemann, 1969, p. 97.

Robert and Bertina Suida Manning, New York

This superb painting on copper relates to a large canvas (103 × 71 cm.) (fig. 10) by Dolci now in the Thyssen-Bornemisza collection, which Baldinucci described in glowing terms: "Jesus at the age of about six years [is] seated on the entrance to the garden in the pose that is used during the Sacred Hymns and with a garland of the most beautiful flowers in one hand, as if he were inviting the soul to crown itself with Christian virtues."[1] The Thyssen *Young Jesus* by Dolci is signed and dated 1663. Baldinucci reports that the artist executed a replica of this painting which was presented in 1675 to Empress Claudia Felice; this version has not been traced.[2] A painting of Jesus' head and the upper portion of the wreath only is in the Alte Pinakothek in Munich.[3] The Wadsworth Atheneum, Hartford, acquired a copy of the entire composition in 1937.[4]

As observed in the previous entry, Dolci produced a number of small-scale paintings on panel or copper, several of which exhibit greater interest in atmospheric and softer tactile effects than are found in his large compositions. The Manning *Christ Child* pursues these freer tendencies to an unparalleled degree in the artist's oeuvre. Indeed, in no other known work by Dolci does the technique resemble so clearly that of his master Vignali, who often juxtaposed impastos of color to splendid effect.

McCorquodale has remarked the influence of Vignali in Dolci's small paintings of the 1640s and 1650s.[5] Such a date would of course indicate the precedence of this copper before the Thyssen canvas, which does not seem likely, given the numerous sensitive variations, one might even say clarifications, between the Manning and Thyssen pictures. For example, in the former, the spaces added through the garland and beneath the Child's arms make the contours of the figure more legible, an adaptation no doubt dictated by the reduction in scale. Similarly, the elaborate balustrade was eliminated and the step above allowed to elucidate the space within the painting on copper. The opportunity in this exhibition to compare two small works by Dolci should be most informative for this special aspect of his art.

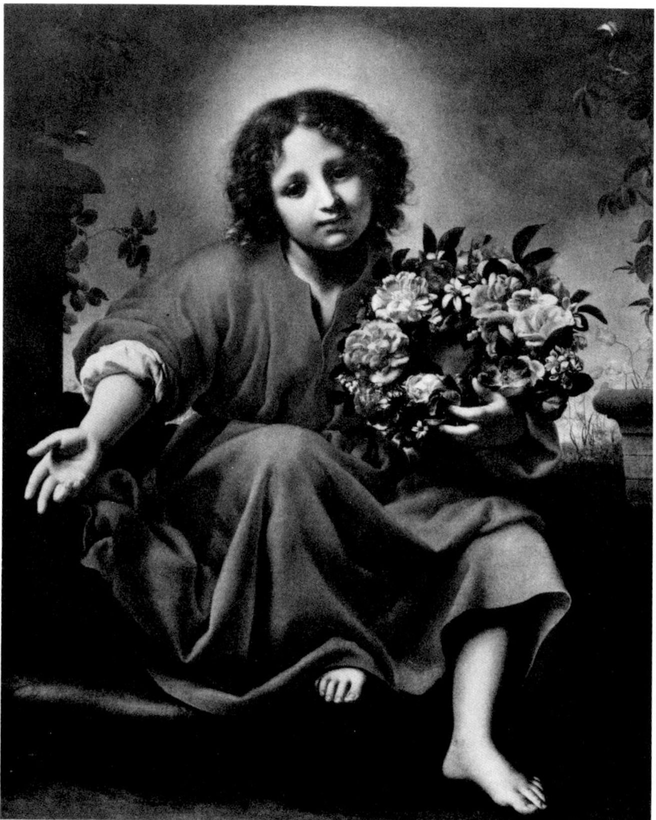

Fig. 10 Dolci: *The Young Jesus with a Wreath of Flowers*, oil on canvas, 1663.
Thyssen-Bornemisza collection, Castagnola

NOTES

1 Baldinucci, 1847, V, pp. 350–51. This translation is adapted from Heinemann, 1969, p. 97.

2 Heinemann, 1969, no. 86.

3 Munich catalogue, 1908, no. 1225, *Der Jesusknabe*. This information is on the mount of the photograph in the Frick Art Reference Library, New York.

4 See *Wadsworth Atheneum Bulletin*, December 1937, p. 3.

5 McCorquodale, *Painting in Florence 1600–1700*, 1979, no. 16; and McCorquodale, "Some Unpublished Works by Carlo Dolci," 1979, pp. 145–46.

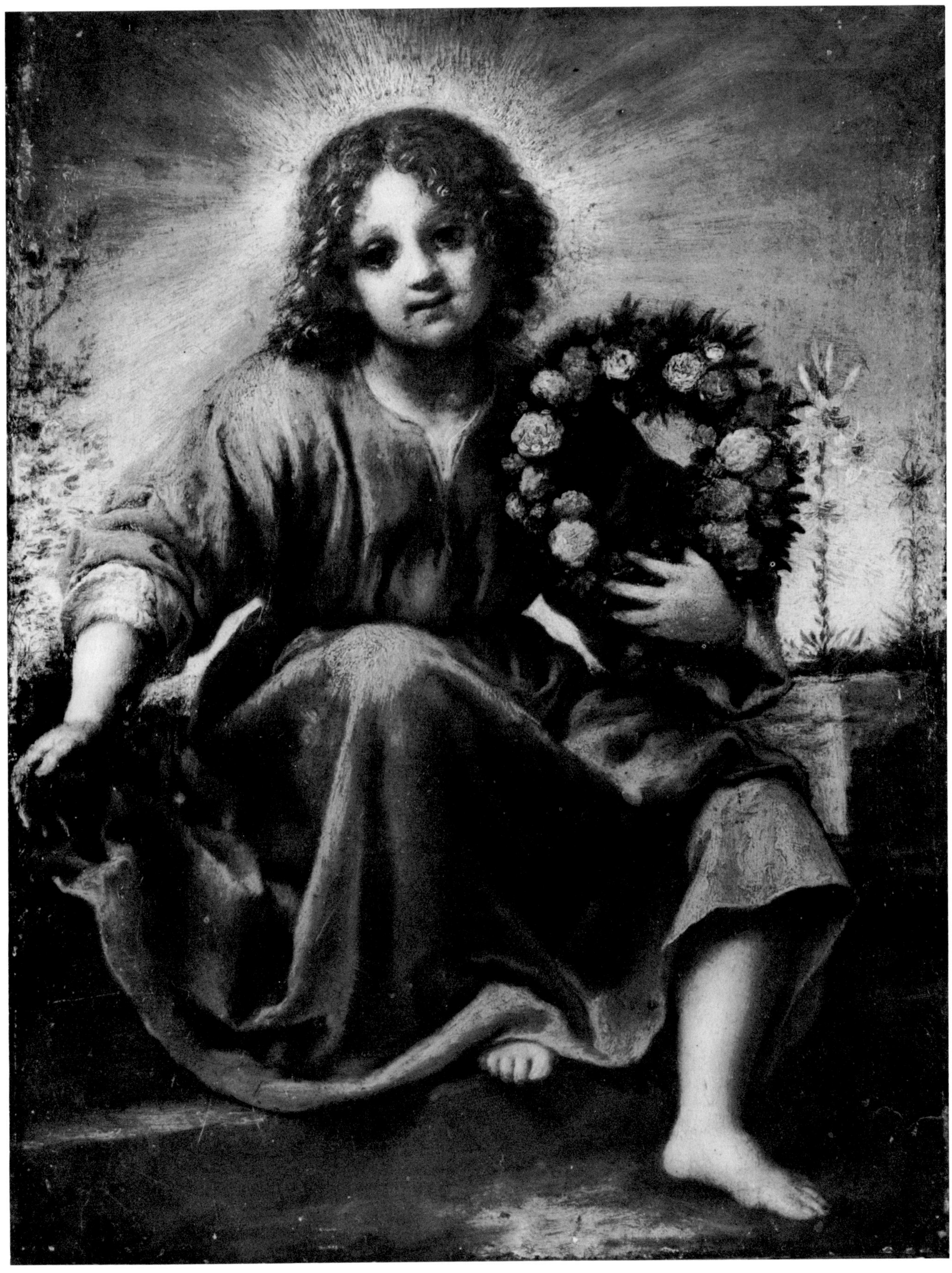

Gaspard Dughet

Rome 1615–1675 Rome

Gaspard Dughet was born of French parents in Rome, where he spent the whole of his life. In 1630 his sister married Nicolas Poussin; for at least the three years following Dughet studied painting from the great Frenchman and even adopted his surname. A corpus of Poussinesque landscapes ascribed by Anthony Blunt to the Silver Birch Master may be Dughet's earliest works, but they remain controversial.

By 1635 Dughet was already a specialist in landscapes. His initial development was much influenced by the direct observation of nature as well as the asymmetrical compositions and genre subjects of such Dutch Italianates as Both and Swanewelt.

Baldinucci reports a visit to Florence during the 1640s. Between 1647 and 1650 Dughet painted a series of frescoes in S. Martino ai Monti, wherein the landscape settings overshadow the figured episodes. This commission inaugurated the second of Dughet's three phases of development. His naturalistic bias was supplanted by a classical balance, openness, and clarity observed from Domenichino's landscapes, not to mention the contemporary works of Claude and Poussin.

In the Sala di Pussino of the Palazzo Doria, Dughet painted in 1635 the landscapes for a series of religious scenes with figures by Il Borgognone. Dughet's decorative genius launched a Roman vogue for landscape murals in private residences, including the Palazzi Bernini, Muti, Costaguti, and Colonna.

In the Sala degli Ambasciatori of the Quirinal Palace, Dughet provided the landscape backgrounds to the oval frescoes of Filippo Lauri and Lazzaro Baldi. The next year he worked extensively on the decoration of the ill-fated Palazzo Pamphili, Valmontone.

After 1660, Dughet began his third manner, which may be compared to Rosa for its admission of picturesque motifs of countryside and copses shrouded in romantic mist. During this period Cardinal Omodei commissioned pendant altarpieces from Dughet and Rosa (Brera, Milan). In many of the richly colored landscapes of his late years, Dughet employed Filippo Lauri (1623–94) to paint the figures.

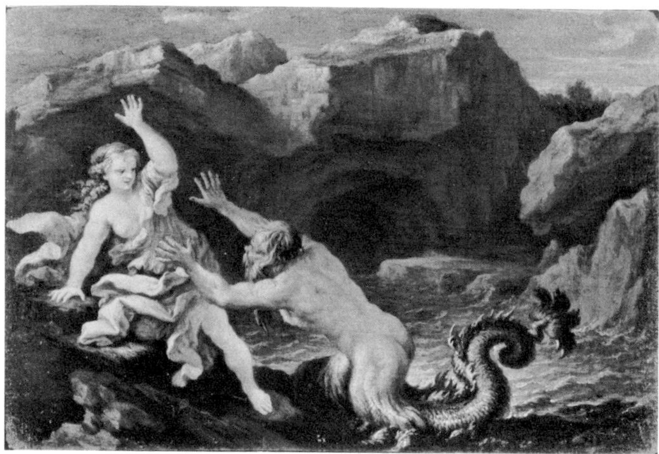

Fig. 11 Filippo Lauri (1623–94): *Glaucus and Scylla,* oil on canvas. Brinsley Ford collection, London

20 *Hagar in the Wilderness*

Oil on canvas. 96.5 × 130.8 cm. Ca. 1653–56.

Provenance: Maréchal Sebastiani, sale, Paris, 24 November 1851, lot 172; Thomas J. Bryan, New York; New York Historical Society, New York, sale, Parke-Bernet, New York, 2 December 1971, lot 112.

References: White, 1853, p. 107; *Catalogue of the Gallery of the New York Historical Society,* 1893, no. 405; *Catalogue of the Gallery of the New York Historical Society,* 1915, no. B-229.

Private collection, New York

When Hagar was lost in the wilderness of Beersheba with her dying son, Ishmael, she was succored by an angel who pointed out the water from a miraculous spring with which to revive the child (Genesis 21:15–20).

The three figures of the angel, Hagar, and Ishmael in this impressive landscape were tentatively attributed to Filippo Lauri when the picture was in the Bryan Collection at the New York Historical Society. Comparison with other works by Lauri, such as his *Glaucus and Scylla* (fig. 11), fully confirms this observation. What is more, in the course of restoration, fragments of the initials "F. L." (Lauri's typical signature) were noticed;[1] unfortunately the foliage behind Hagar has not yielded this prize on the occasion of this exhibition, despite a thorough search.

Although Dughet and Lauri often collaborated on easel paintings after 1670, the style of this landscape would indicate a date close to their first collaboration in fresco, 1657, or perhaps slightly earlier. The clear, beige-blond tonality and the strictly planar features of this landscape belong to Dughet's most classical period, dated to ca. 1653–56 by Marie-Nicole Boisclair.[2] Poussin's heroic landscapes of *St. Matthew* (Gemäldegalerie, Berlin-Dahlem) and *St. John on Patmos* (Art Institute of Chicago) anticipate many features in this work by Dughet.

Another painting of this view by Dughet has been at

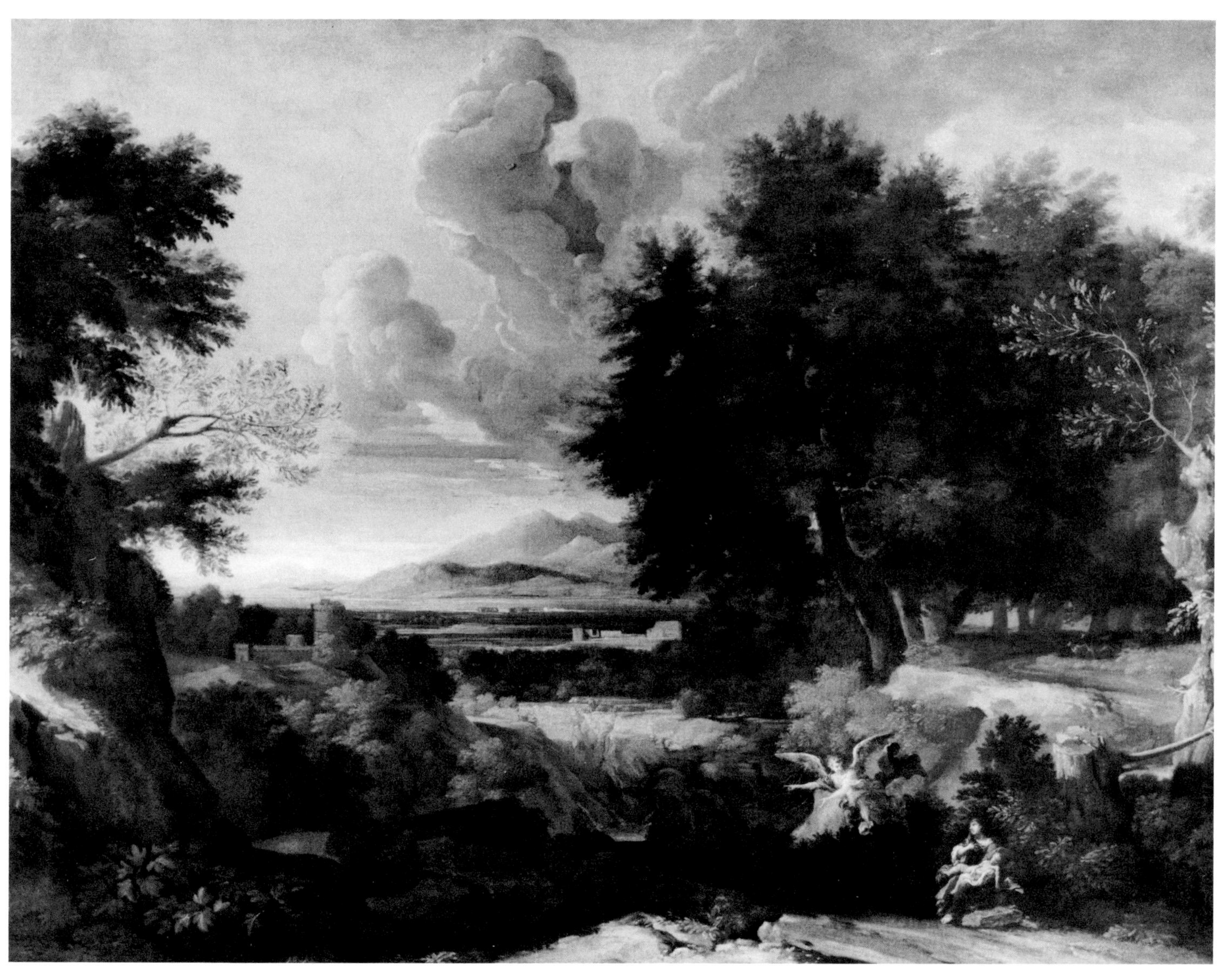

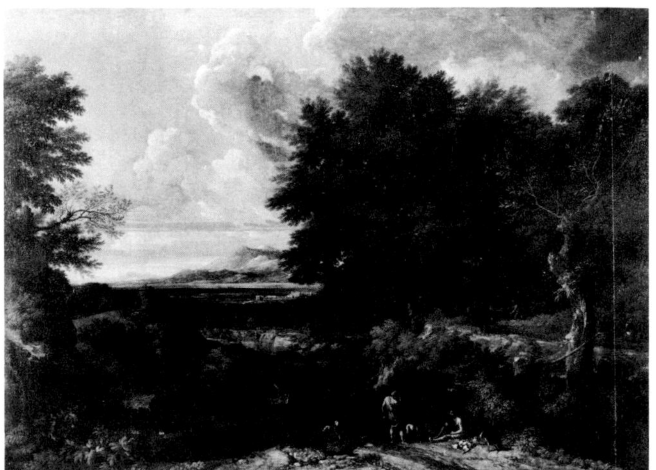

Fig. 12 Dughet: *Landscape with Figures,* oil on canvas. Stourhead House, Mere, Wiltshire

Stourhead, Wiltshire, since the eighteenth century (fig. 12). The Stourhead picture hangs with a pendant of *Eurydice;* its own subject is not specified.[3] In both canvases the figures are attributable to Dughet himself. Marie-Nicole Boisclair would date the Stourhead version to ca. 1659[4] (i.e., subsequent to the date proposed here for the *Hagar in the Wilderness),* which would accord with its more atmospheric and detailed handling. The painting at Stourhead is considerably larger than the present picture and shows an extended view to the right.[5]

NOTES

1 By Miss Gabrielle Kopelman, New York, who kindly informed me of her discovery.

2 Boisclair, "Gaspard Dughet: une chronologie révisée," 1976, p. 39.

3 The Stourhead paintings are known to me through photographs at the Frick Art Reference Library, New York.

4 Boisclair, "Gaspard Dughet: une chronologie révisée," 1976, p. 42 n. 54.

5 It measures 152.4 × 215 cm. as opposed to 96.5 × 130.8 cm.

Domenico Fetti

Rome ca. 1589–1623 Venice

Although Fetti has sometimes been considered a follower of Caravaggio, his short but prolific career represents in actuality what avenues were open to a Roman painter who belonged to neither the Caravaggesque nor Carraccesque camps. Fetti studied in Rome under Ludovico Cardi, called Il Cigoli (Baldinucci) and was trained as well in an "accademia" in the house of Andrea Commodi, another Florentine in Rome (Mancini). The single documented painting from Fetti's Roman period (an altarpiece now in the Walters Art Gallery, Baltimore) combines Cigolesque tonalities with motifs observed from Rubens's high altarpiece of 1608 in the Chiesa Nuova, Rome. The Venetian roots of Orazio Borgianni's style were also an early influence.

From 1613 to 1622 Fetti was painter to Duke Ferdinando Gonzaga in Mantua. As superintendent of the famous Gonzaga gallery of old masters, Fetti had ample opportunity to study the paintings of Veronese, Titian, and Bassano. Fetti's copy of Titian's *Tribute Money* (also in the Walters Art Gallery) evinces a visit to the d'Este collections in Ferrara. In 1621 Fetti was sent to Venice in search of new acquisitions. The next year he fled to Venice following an altercation with a nobleman; there he contracted a fever from which he died on 16 April 1623.

21 *Salvator Mundi*

Oil on panel. 59.7 × 43.8 cm. Ca. 1614.

Provenance: Private collection, England.

Private collection, New York

Christ in glory with cherubs holds an orb surmounted with a cross, the sign that he is Salvator Mundi. This theme is traditionally treated as a bust-length icon of hierarchic frontality. Fetti's energetic and immediate interpretation is a precocious example of Early Baroque style.

Although dates are exceedingly scarce for Fetti's oeuvre, this *Salvator Mundi* may be placed in the artist's first Mantuan years, ca. 1614.[1] The influence of Cigoli has been almost wholly supplanted by renewed studies of Rubens, who had left many works in Mantua in 1604–6. Christ's broad brow and heavy-lidded eyes are unmistakably Rubensian, no less so than the coursing vitality of his figure, the monumentality of which threatens to burst the limits of this small panel. Fetti's paintings of female martyrs in the Palazzo Ducale, Mantua (dated 1613) display these identical qualities.[2]

Fetti habitually executed several versions of his favorite compositions, which were mostly cabinet pictures for

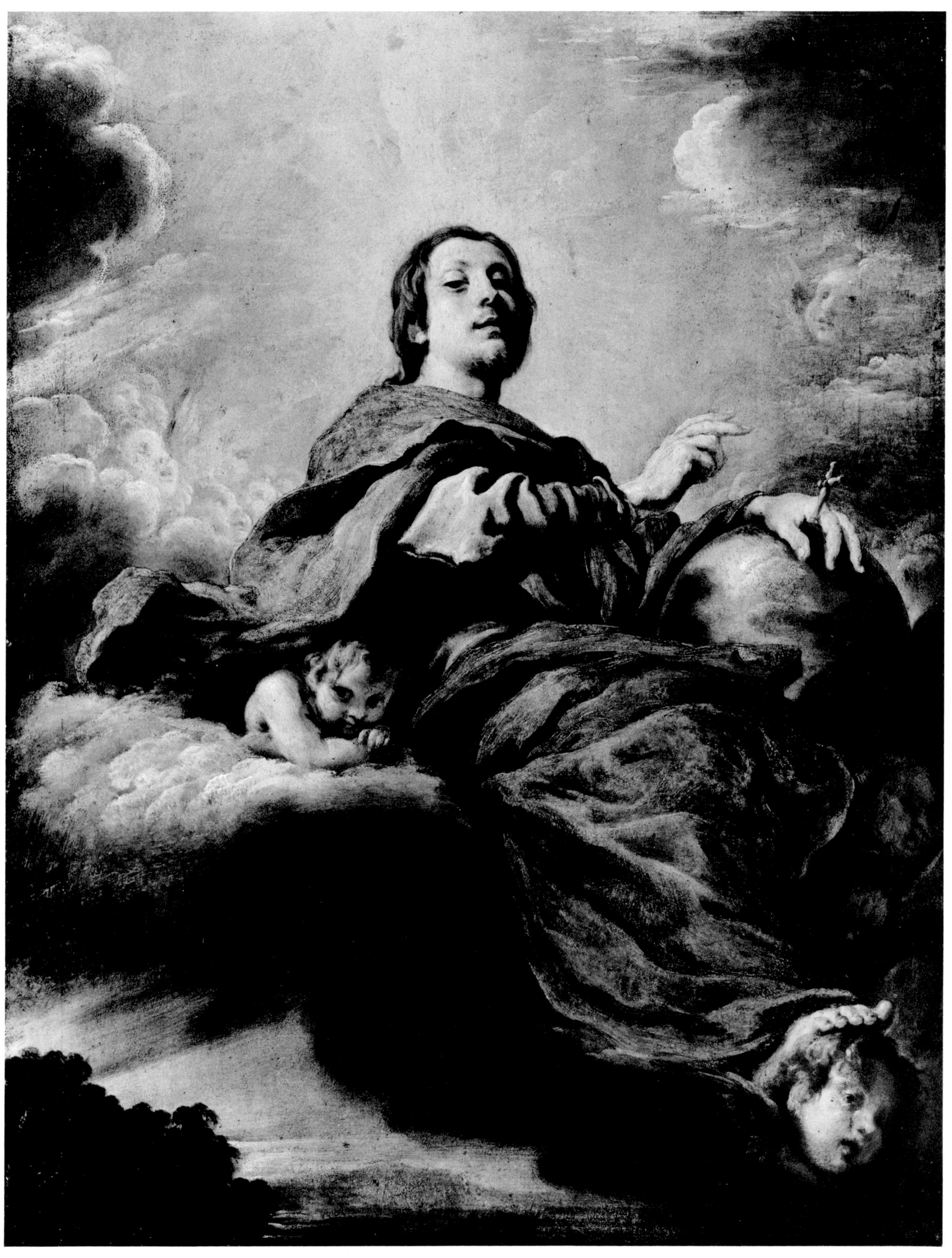

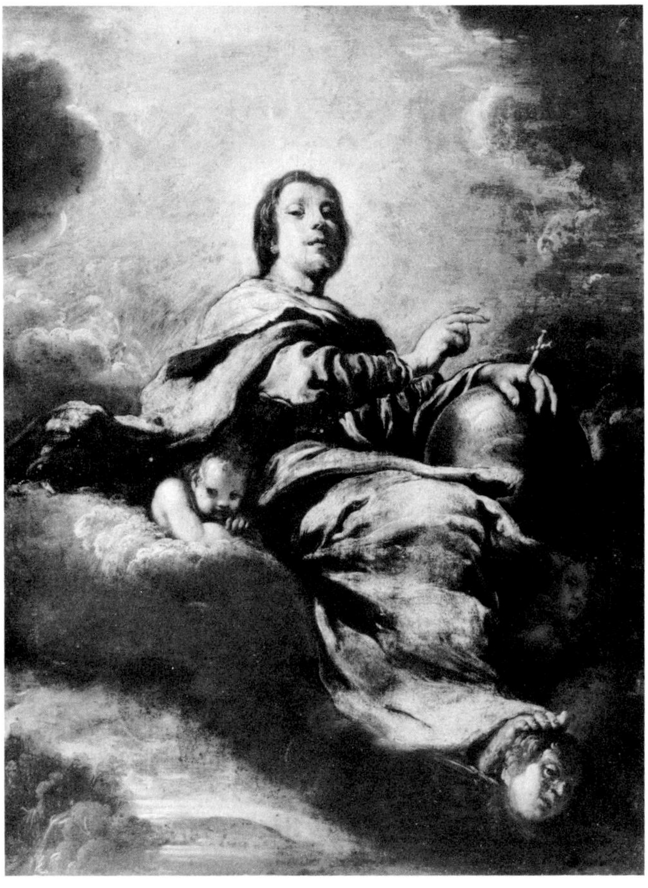

Fig. 13 Attributed to Fetti: *Christ the Redeemer in Glory,* oil on panel, 60.95 × 45.1 cm. Museo Tadini, Lovere (113)

private patrons, and they were frequently copied as well. A version of this *Salvator Mundi* in the Museo Tadini, Lovere (fig. 13), has been judged a contemporary, autograph replica by Jürgen Lehmann,[3] and an anonymous copy by Eduard Safarik[4] and Pamela Askew.[5] Judging from a photograph of the Lovere painting, if it is by Fetti the de-emphasis on weighty, tangible figures and the increased action of light upon the surfaces would suggest a subsequent stage in the artist's development.

NOTES

1 A dating of ca. 1613–15 was suggested to me by Jürgen Lehmann (letter, 19 June 1979); Eduard Safarik proposes a date in the artist's Venetian period, i.e., his last three years (letter, 29 June 1979).
2 Paccagnini, 1956, figs. 313–18.
3 Letter, 19 June 1979.
4 Letter, 29 June 1979.
5 Letter, 25 October 1979.

22 *St. Simeon*

Oil on panel. 17.78 × 17.35 cm. Ca. 1621.

Provenance:[1] Possibly De la Roque, Paris (1745); possibly Crozat, Baron de Thiers (1755); possibly Hermitage, St. Petersburg (1774); private collection, Venice.

References:[2] *Catalogue des tableaux du cabinet de M. Crozat, Baron de Thiers,* 1755, p. 63: "le Vieillard Saint Siméon tenant l'Enfant Jesus entre ses bras, demi-figure par le Feti: sur bois, de 6 pouces e demi"; *Catalogue,* Hermitage, 1774, no. 911; Mireur, 1911, p. 146, in reference to the De la Roque picture: "Saint Siméon tenant l'Enfant Jesus (7 p.[ouces] en carré. 252 fr."; Stuffmann, 1968, p. 116, no. 15, as the Hermitage painting, identical to no. 25 in the Tronchin inventory, 1771, of the Crozat de Thiers collection.

Robert and Bertina Suida Manning, New York

The Lord had revealed to Simeon, whom Fetti has portrayed as a temple priest, that he would live to see the Christ (Luke 2:25–35). At the presentation of the infant Jesus in the temple of Jerusalem, the aged Simeon received the Child in his arms and foretold his mission. Fetti has depicted this event in a most original fashion, since the prophet Simeon is almost exclusively represented within the context of the ceremony of the Presentation in the Temple. Instead, Fetti adapted his composition from the precedent of a somewhat less rare subject, St. Joseph and the Infant Christ, in which St. Joseph cradles the Child in his arms. In this affectionate pose Simeon lifts up his eyes in thanksgiving.

The painting is in Fetti's late style,[3] when Rubensian physicality has given way to an incessant, nervous play of light dissolving the outlines of the forms. The insubstantial, flattened features of the Child's face are found, for example, in the face of the angel in the upper left of the *Martyrdom of SS. Fermo and Rustico* (Wadsworth Atheneum, Hartford), which Pamela Askew has dated after Fetti's Venetian visit of 1621.[4]

NOTES

1 The information on the history of this picture was kindly brought to my attention by Pamela Askew (letter, 25 October 1979) and also Eduard Safarik (letter, 29 June 1979). The questions remain as to whether these descriptions refer to the present picture or to a version in the Hermitage (the existence of which has been impossible to ascertain), or indeed whether the Manning and the Hermitage pictures are one and the same. Safarik saw the Manning picture in Venice "some years ago."
2 See note 1, above.
3 Eduard Safarik (letters, 29 June and 16 September 1979) and Pamela Askew (letter, 25 October 1979) both expressed this same view to me. Jürgen Lehmann (letter, 20 August 1979) dates the painting ca. 1615/16.
4 Askew, 1961, p. 249.

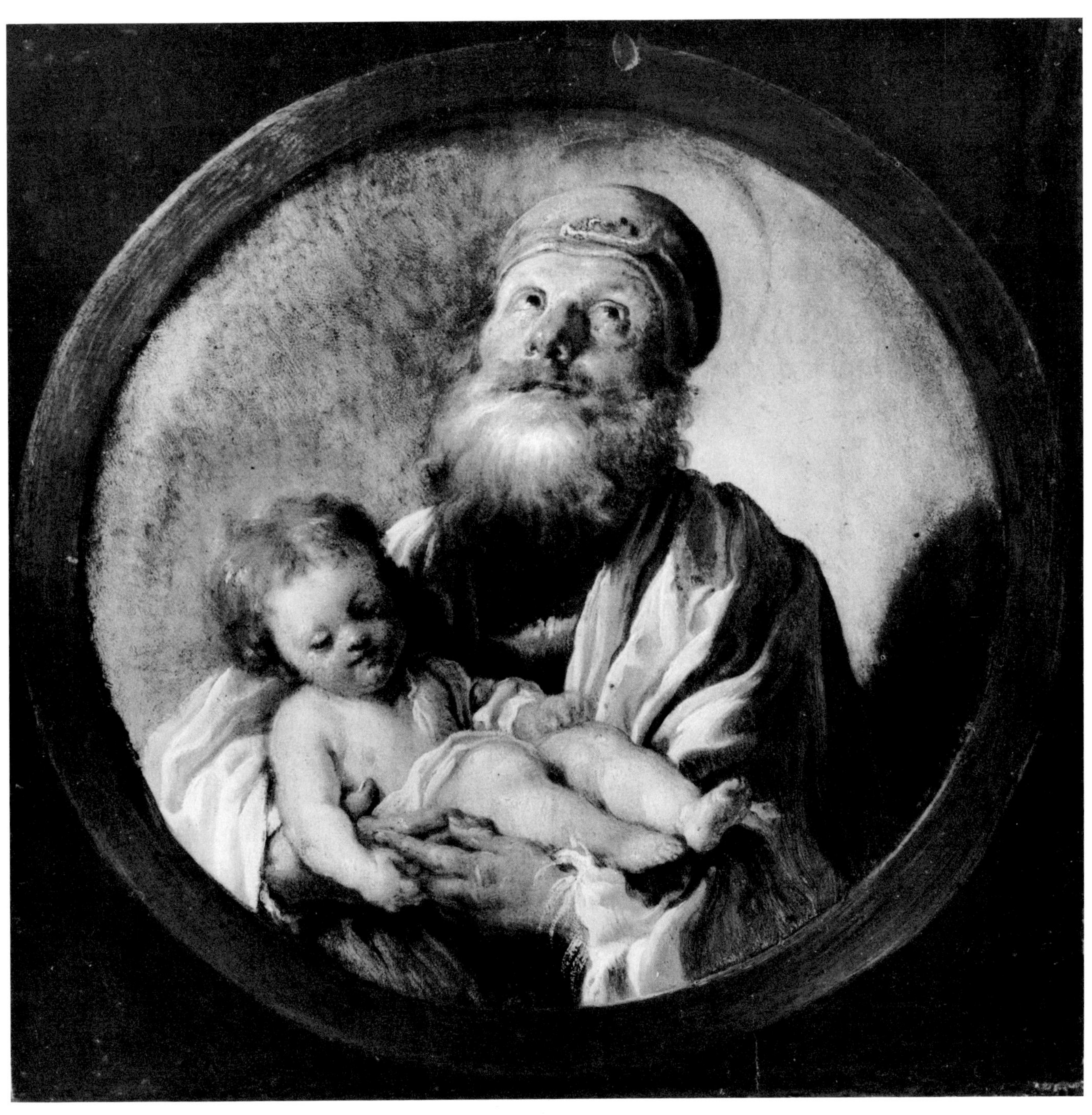

Girolamo Forabosco

Padua 1604/5–1679 Padua

Born in Padua, Forabosco entered the Venetian school of his compatriot Alessandro Varotari, called Il Padovanino. With other pupils of Padovanino, Forabosco was directed to find his pictorial models in the Venetian Renaissance, especially the work of Titian. Forabosco's paintings have in fact been mistaken for sixteenth-century works by Titian or Lorenzo Lotto, another source of inspiration. His presence in Venice is documented for the years 1634–39, although he may have arrived as early as 1627.

Forabosco's small oeuvre was divided between portraiture and paintings of Old Testament or classical histories. Dated works are almost nonexistent. As regards his gift for portraiture, it is worth noting that in 1675 Boschini wrote to Don Leopoldo Medici his belief that Forabosco was a pupil of Tiberio Tinelli, the foremost portraitist in Venice early in the century.[1] After 1630 Bernardo Strozzi influenced Forabosco technically in his predilection for thickly applied pigment.

After an unspecified period of activity in his native Padua, the artist returned to Venice in 1654. His two paintings for the church of S. Niccolò da Tolentino probably date after this juncture. To the presence of Guido Cagnacci in Venice during the 1650s can be attributed the appearance of something like Bolognese refinement in some of Forabosco's later pictures. About 1670 he painted his masterpiece, an enormous *Family Miraculously Saved from the Shipwreck* (parish church, Malamocco), which delightfully juxtaposes portraiture, incidents of genre, and celestial visions to proto-Rococo effect.

23 *Judith with the Head of Holofernes*

Oil on canvas. 109 × 134 cm.

Reference: Safarik, 1973, p. 363 n. 52.

Mr. and Mrs. Paul H. Ganz, New York

As related in the Apocryphal Book of Judith (13:1–12), Judith was a beautiful Hebrew widow, who by her courage and resourcefulness delivered her besieged city, Bethulia, from the Assyrians. Posing as a deserter, she entered the camp of Holofernes, general of the Assyrian forces. Holofernes, inflamed by her beauty, brought Judith to his tent for the night. When Holofernes fell asleep, Judith cut off his head. The confused Assyrians were easily put to flight.

Forabosco's reading of this story stresses the truly epic dimensions of the heroine. A favorite Baroque theme, most often the erotic aspect or the gruesome exertion of decapitation is afforded center stage. This picture by Forabosco exemplifies a major current of Baroque sensibility, one that is implicit even in the derivation of the word "Baroque," i.e., eccentric, bizarre. Judith's immense figure expresses the *terribilità* of her adventure more immediately even than her horrible trophy (of which the ugliness is less disturbing for being dead than is the head of the crone in Judith's employ).

The impassive, somewhat vulnerable expression of the heroine occurs frequently in Forabosco's portraiture. In fact, an old but not contemporary copy of Judith's head and shoulders was acquired in 1926 by the Detroit Institute of Arts as a portrait by Paris Bordone.[2] Hermann Voss subsequently provided Forabosco's name.

NOTES

1 See Safarik, 1973, p. 362 n. 37.

2 *Portrait of a Young Woman*, 32¾ × 27¾", acc. no. 26.105.

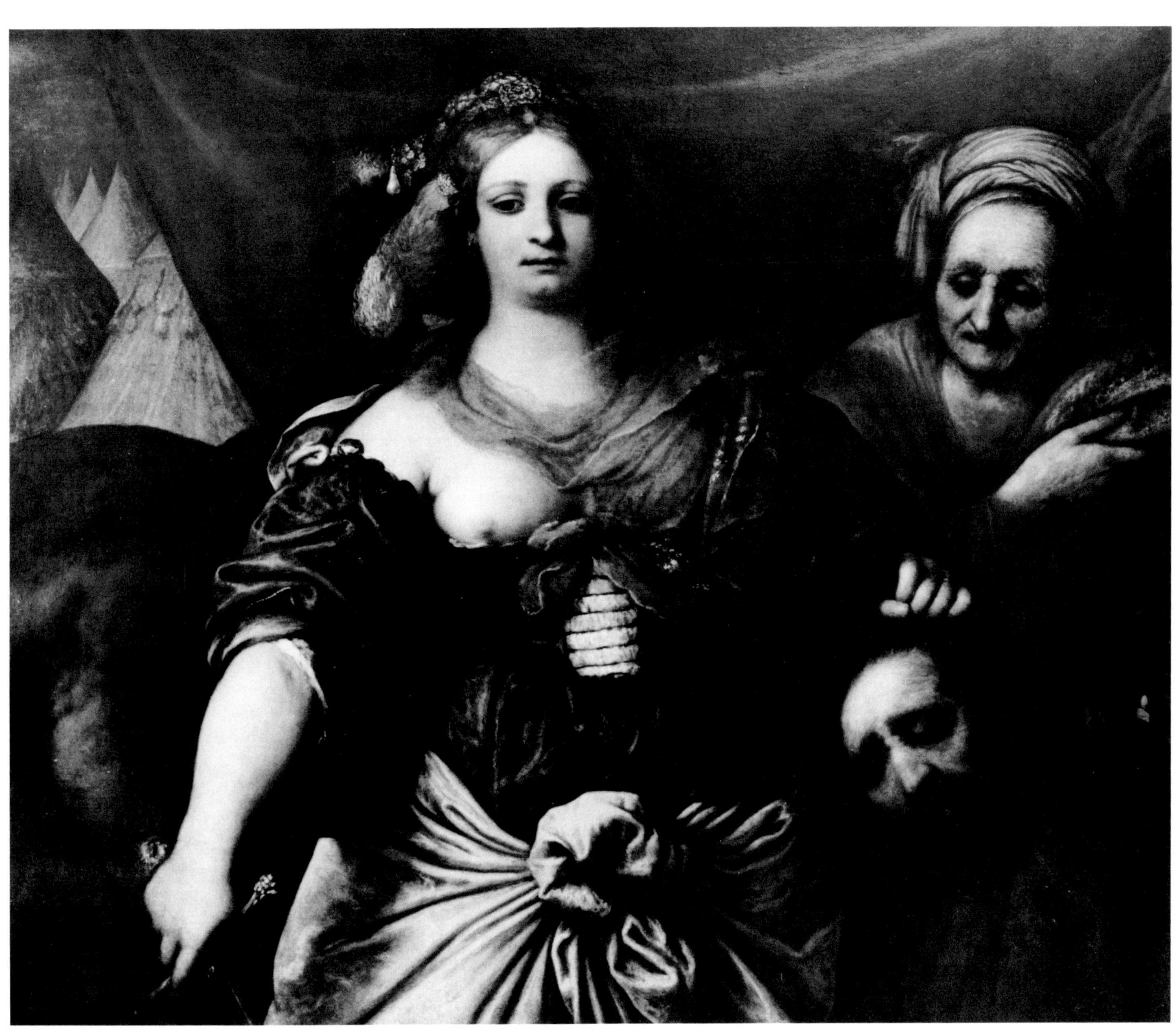

Francesco Fracanzano

Monopoli 1612–ca. 1656 Naples

The shadowy careers of Francesco Fracanzano and his elder brother, Cesare (ca. 1605–53) constitute the thorniest problems in Neapolitan seicento studies. Francesco's name in particular has become associated with a rough-and-tumble strain of Riberism, which persisted in Neapolitan *botteghe* throughout the century. Some of the hands confused with Francesco's have been with time defined as distinct enigmae, for example, the so-called Master of the Annunciation to the Shepherds. A few altarpieces of sure attribution to Cesare Fracanzano indicate that his abiding aspiration was to an ill-suited decorousness of Bolognese derivation.

The even rarer certain works of Francesco reveal a greater talent, who was more than a distorted mirror of Jusepe de Ribera, presumably his master. Francesco seems to have arrived in Naples from Puglia at an early age. His greatest paintings are, remarkably, the achievements of a young man: a series of stories of St. Gregory of Armenia for a chapel in the church of that saint, datable to 1635. Three years earlier Francesco had married the sister of Salvator Rosa, who, his junior by only three years, studied with him for a period. In 1647 Francesco signed the *Ecce Homo* exhibited here, which informs us that the artist's development did not stray from the path laid down at the start.

24 *Ecce Homo*

Oil on canvas. 75.55 × 63.8 cm. 1647.

Signed and dated: Francesco Fracanzano 1647.

Provenance: J. Weitzner, New York; Mr. and Mrs. Paul H. Ganz, New York.

References: Gilbert, 1961, no. 20, repr.; Manning, *Neapolitan Masters,* 1962, no. 13, repr.; Causa, 1972, pp. 933 and 976, no. 74; Schleier, 1975, p. 32.

Mr. and Mrs. Morton B. Harris, New York

After Christ had been whipped and in mockery dressed in a robe and crowned with thorns, he was brought before Pilate for judgment. The sight of Jesus moved the Roman governor to exclaim, Ecce Homo (Behold the Man), in an appeal to the compassion of the populace (John 19:5).

Were this *Ecce Homo* not clearly dated 1647 by the artist, we would assume a much earlier date for it. The diminutive scale of the figures, their exaggerated expressions, and the delicate tints favored by Fracanzano all bear witness to the resiliency of the Mannerist tradition in Naples. The wavering outlines of the gesticulating actors call to mind the drawing style of a Mannerist such as Belisario Corenzio, who lived until 1643.

Fracanzano's knobby facial types remain constant from his S. Gregorio Armeno canvases of 1635. However, the broad pictorialism and the sense for monumentality of those early works raise the possibility that the mannered qualities of this *Ecce Homo* stem in part from the taste of the patron who commissioned the picture. Still, a good measure of stylization is noticeable even in a Caravaggesque *Denial of St. Peter* convincingly ascribed to Fracanzano by Roberto Longhi.[1]

NOTE

1 Longhi, 1969, fig. 33. The painting was formerly in the Boblot collection, Paris; a photograph is in the Frick Art Reference Library, New York, under Strozzi.

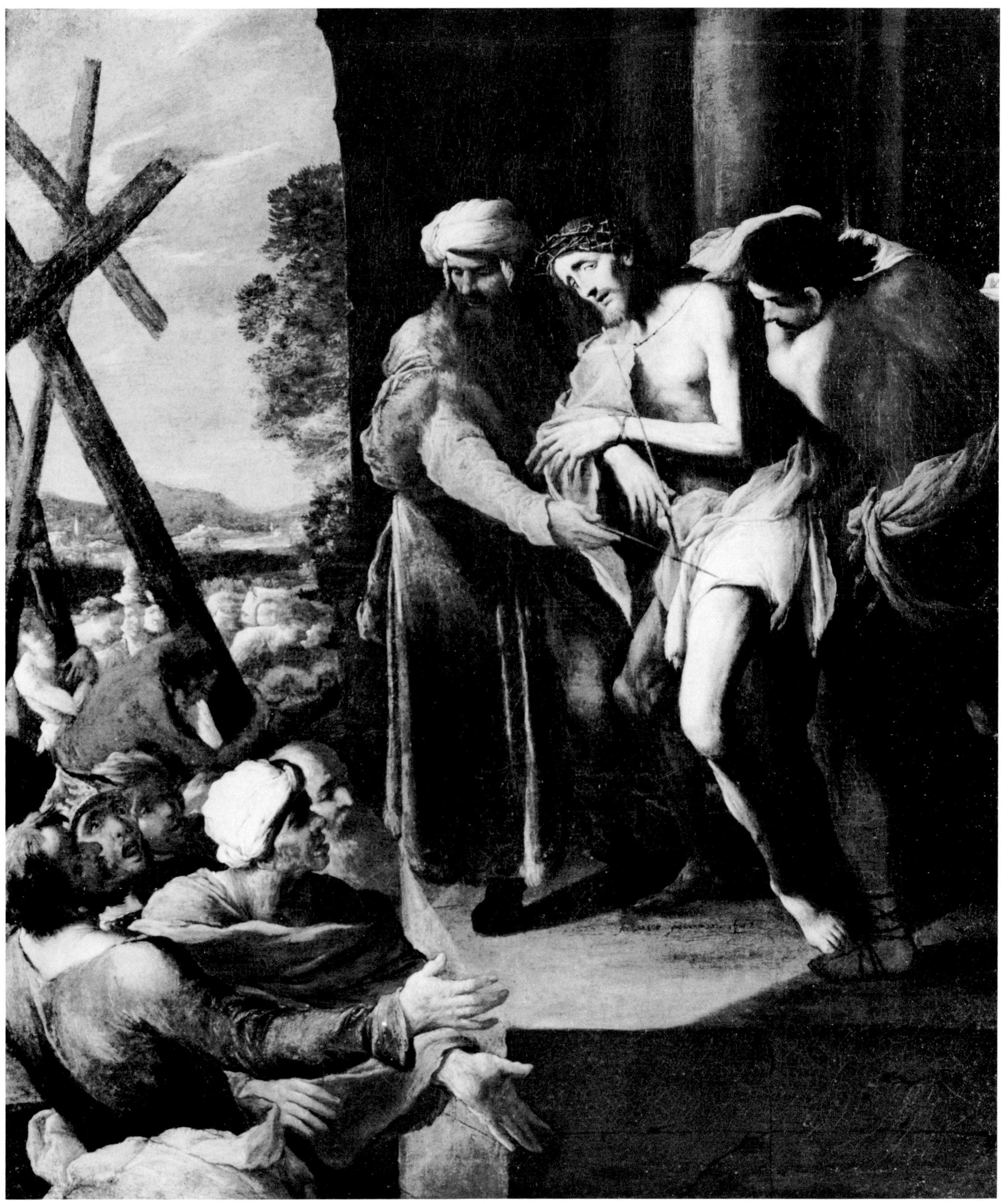

Luca Giordano

Naples 1634–1705 Naples

Luca Giordano was aptly nicknamed "fa presto" for his extraordinary speed of execution. A child prodigy, Giordano's imaginative powers never failed him in his long career; he was indubitably the most prolific painter who ever lived. With his travels and enormous production Giordano single-handedly brought the Neapolitan school of painting to international prominence. His Late Baroque style laid the groundwork for the most decorative aspects of the Rococo.

The young Giordano played an important role in the workshop of Jusepe de Ribera during the last few years of the master's life. Despite the depth of his involvement in *riberismo,* Giordano's personal sensibility for thundering action and dramatic chiaroscuro emerged clearly from the start. He loved the very substance of oil pigments, and he laid them on with brio.

After the death of Ribera in 1652 Giordano traveled to Rome to study the Renaissance masters—and also Pietro da Cortona. He proceeded to Venice, where he painted several altarpieces in his dashing Riberism, most notably a *Deposition* for S. Maria del Pianto (now in the Galleria dell'Accademia, Venice).

Giordano's first public commission was in 1654 in Naples for two paintings, still indebted to Ribera, in S. Pietro ad Aram. As though it had taken him some moments to collect his impressions (or courage), not until 1655, in the *S. Nicola da Bari* altarpiece (S. Brigida, Naples), did Giordano allow the colorism of Venice and the expansive vitality of Pietro da Cortona to pour out onto the canvas.

The artist escaped the plague of 1656 in Rome; no doubt he was chagrined to discover upon his return to Naples that Mattia Preti had captured the most prestigious commissions in the meantime. On Preti's example Giordano launched in 1658, with two altarpieces in Sant'Agostino degli Scalzi, an explosively Venetian-influenced phase of development, lasting until the early 1660s. The tonalities of this *maniera dorata* derived from the late Titian and Veronese, while his new breadth of composition was inspired by Preti, Lanfranco, and Rubens. During the same period, as Oreste Ferrari has noted Giordano had frequent recourse to satisfy the continuing Neapolitan taste for *Riberismo.*

About 1665 Giordano passed through Florence en route to Venice. His *Assumption* in S. Maria della Salute, Venice, is dated 1667, in which year he was again present in Naples. The ensuing decade encompassed a transitional period, during which he made Cortona's formal vocabulary his own. Some extraneous observations made in Venice, as of the contemporary Pietro Liberi, had to be discarded. The triumphant culmination of this phase was the allegorical fresco of 1683 in the vault of the Palazzo Medici-Riccardi in Florence.

In his full maturity Giordano, with a populous workshop, continued to cover the walls of the Neapolitan churches at an unslackened pace. He departed Naples in 1692 at the invitation of Carlos II to conquer the field in Spain. The chief legacy of Giordano's productive decade as principal painter at the Spanish court were his ebullient frescoes that seem to open windows into the solemn Escorial. Upon his return to Naples he painted with undiminished powers his fresco of the *Triumph of Judith* in the Cappella del Tesoro in the Certosa di S. Martino.

25 *A Miracle of St. Gregory of Armenia*

Oil on canvas. 61.5 × 48.4 cm. Ca. 1679.

Provenance: A. Busiri Vici, Rome.

Reference: Ferrari and Scavizzi, 1966, II, p. 96, III, fig. 170.

Private collection, New York

St. Gregory the Illuminator (257?–337?) is the apostle and patron saint of Armenia. He was tortured for his Christianity by King Tiridates, who imprisoned him in a vile pit for fifteen years. Eventually, as a punishment for his wickedness, Tiridates was possessed by a devil and turned into a boar. The sisters of the monarch learned from a vision that only the prayers of Gregory could save their brother. After exorcising the evil spirit, St. Gregory began to proselytize; under the rule of the converted Tiridates, Christianity became the national religion of Armenia.

Luca Giordano painted the fabulous episode of Tiridates with the head of a boar in preparation for one of an extensive cycle of frescoes in the Neapolitan church of S. Gregorio Armeno. Roberto Pane has associated Giordano's work in S. Gregorio Armeno with the church's reconsecration in October 1679, one century exactly after its original consecration.[1] Giordano contributed the principal part of the church's redecoration; it was his first commission for a fresco cycle in his native city. He painted scenes from the life of St. Gregory of Armenia on the interior facade, on both sides of the nave between the windows, and in the cupola; Benedictine subjects were placed in the choir.

These works were immediately acclaimed in Naples and the church must have shone with color during its second century; a cleaning is now quite in order. The artist's technique in fresco is notably fluent. The scenes

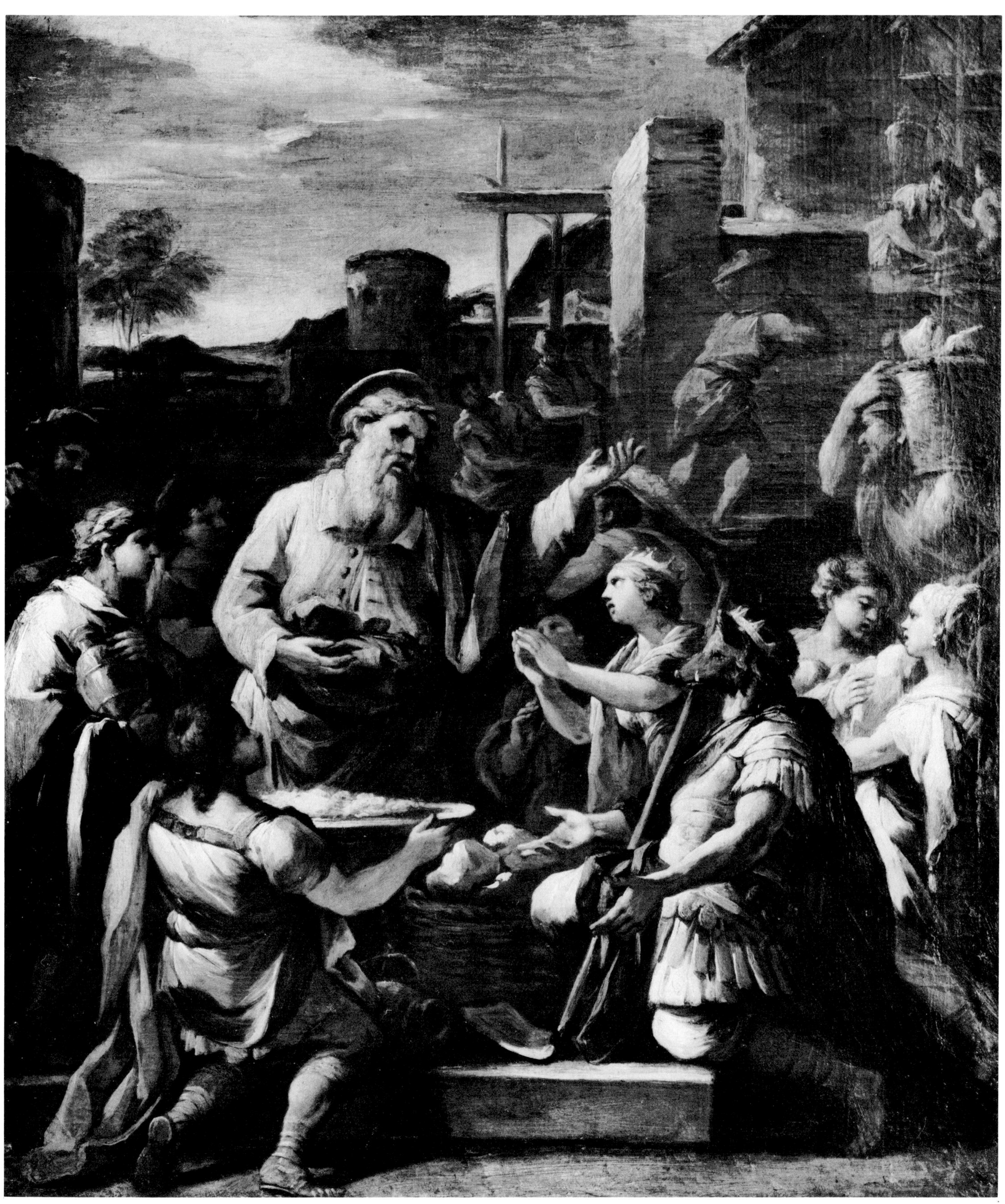

were evidently planned to combine as an ensemble, and the large, expansive figures constitute Giordano's most intelligent emulation of Cortona to date.

The style of this handsome bozzetto reveals little of this development, which would indicate that it was painted in the earliest stage of planning and not during the course of the undertaking. Its dignified, highly legible expression follows quite closely in fact the "devout" style that Ferrari and Scavizzi have identified for the artist's fresco series of 1677 at the Benedictine monastery of Montecassino.[2] In view of these considerations and also of the picture's markedly "finished" character, it seems reasonable to propose that the painting's purpose was more than a sketch, that it served Giordano to illustrate to the Benedictines his ideas for the decorations; perhaps it was even the piece submitted to secure the commission.[3] Only one other bozzetto (a much slighter work) is known for the artist's frescoes in S. Gregorio Armeno.[4]

NOTES

1 Pane, 1957, pp. 100–101 n. 7. See also Ferrari and Scavizzi, 1966, I, p. 84, and II, pp. 95–96.

2 Ferrari and Scavizzi, 1966, I, p. 83.

3 This might be true as well for Mattia Preti's *Martyrdom of St. Catherine* (exhibited here as no. 36), apparently his unique sketch for the paintings for S. Pietro a Maiella in Naples.

4 Ferrari and Scavizzi, 1966, II, p. 96, and III, fig. 171.

Giovanni Francesco Barbieri, called Guercino

Cento 1591–1666 Bologna

Although he apprenticed with a minor local painter, Guercino is properly considered to have been self-taught. His artistic formation was a perfect reflection of his geographic situation mid-way between Ferrara and Bologna. Ludovico Carracci's altarpieces in Cento (1591; now Museo Civico) and in Bologna introduced Guercino to enraptured emotion and fluid brushwork. Scarsellino was the young Guercino's medium to the sensuous visions of Ferrarese painting and the luminous naturalism of the great Venetians.

After 1613, the date of his first important public commission, Guercino's talent towered over the local school and began to attract wider notice. Cardinal Alessandro Ludovisi called him to Bologna for several works in 1617. He made study visits to Venice in 1618 and to Ferrara (presumably not his first) in 1619 and 1620. For S. Gregorio, Bologna, Guercino painted in 1620 a fully Baroque altarpiece of the *Investiture of St. William of Aquitaine* (Pinacoteca, Bologna), which marked the culmination of his first period.

In 1621 the Bolognese Pope Gregory XV summoned Guercino to Rome for two eventful years (until 1623). His fresco of *Aurora* in the newly acquired casino of the pope's nephew excited attention by the drastic contrast of its exuberant luminism to the classicizing serenity of Guido Reni's *quadro riportato* of the same subject (1613/14). Before departing Rome Guercino painted his immense altarpiece of the *Burial of S. Petronilla* for St. Peter's (now in the Musei Capitolini, Rome), in which he made notable accommodations to the stately style of Rome.

The energetic *luminismo* of Guercino's Roman works would have tremendous import for such artists as Mola and Preti. Ironically, after his return to Cento, Guercino's own style progressively evolved towards the classicism of Annibale Carracci and Domenichino, and ultimately, Reni. He remained in Cento to preside over a growing studio, except for a sojourn in Piacenza in 1626/27 to paint frescoes in the Duomo.

After the death of Reni in 1642, Guercino moved to Bologna to assume the leadership of the local school. His rather staid version of the refined classicism of Reni's late style found innumerable champions among the neoclassical painters of the next century.

26 *Landscape with Tobias and the Angel*

Oil on copper. 33.7 × 44.5 cm. Ca. 1617/18.

Provenance: Possibly Prince Maffeo Barberini, Rome (d. 1685, inv. 1686).[1]

Reference: Sutton, 1978, no. 37, fig. 6.

Robert and Bertina Suida Manning, New York

The subject is taken from the Apocryphal Book of Tobit (6:2–9). Tobias, accompanied by the Archangel Raphael (of whose identity he is unaware), made an arduous journey to Media to collect a debt owed to his father, the blind Tobit. While bathing in the Tigris, Tobias was attacked by a great fish; however, Raphael called to him to haul the fish onto the land. Later, on Raphael's instructions, the youth would use the fish's heart and liver to exorcize an evil spirit from his wife, Sarah, and its gall to cure his father's blindness (see no. 40).

Guercino is only known to have painted landscapes during his early activity in Cento. One of his first recorded commissions was to paint a series in fresco of decorative landscapes for the Palazzo Pannini (1615–17; now Pinacoteca, Cento). His landscapes in oil were directly inspired in their small scale, chromatic richness, and intimate charm by the example of Scarsellino.[2] This delightful *Landscape with Tobias and the Angel,* discovered only recently, pertains to this aspect of the painter's development.

Denis Mahon has proposed to date this picture to ca. 1617/18,[3] based on comparison with Guercino's *Landscape with a Concert Party* (Uffizi, Florence) and *Landscape with Bathing Women* (Boymans-van Beuningen Museum, Rotterdam). Indeed, the Ferrarese palette and costume style may be compared to a *St. Sebastian with Two Angels* by Guercino on copper, signed and dated in Cento in 1617.[4]

NOTES

1 The present picture may be identified with a reference in an inventory published by Lavin, 1975, VII.inv.86.496: "Un Paesino in Rame, con due figurine cioe l'Angelo, e Tubia largo p.i 1. alto p.i 1/2 in circa con cornicetta d'Ebano nero, mano del Guercino da Cento."

2 See Mahon, 1937, pp. 177–89, for the fundamental study of Guercino's relationship to Scarsellino.

3 See Sutton, 1978, no. 78.

4 Whitfield, 1973, no. 31, repr.

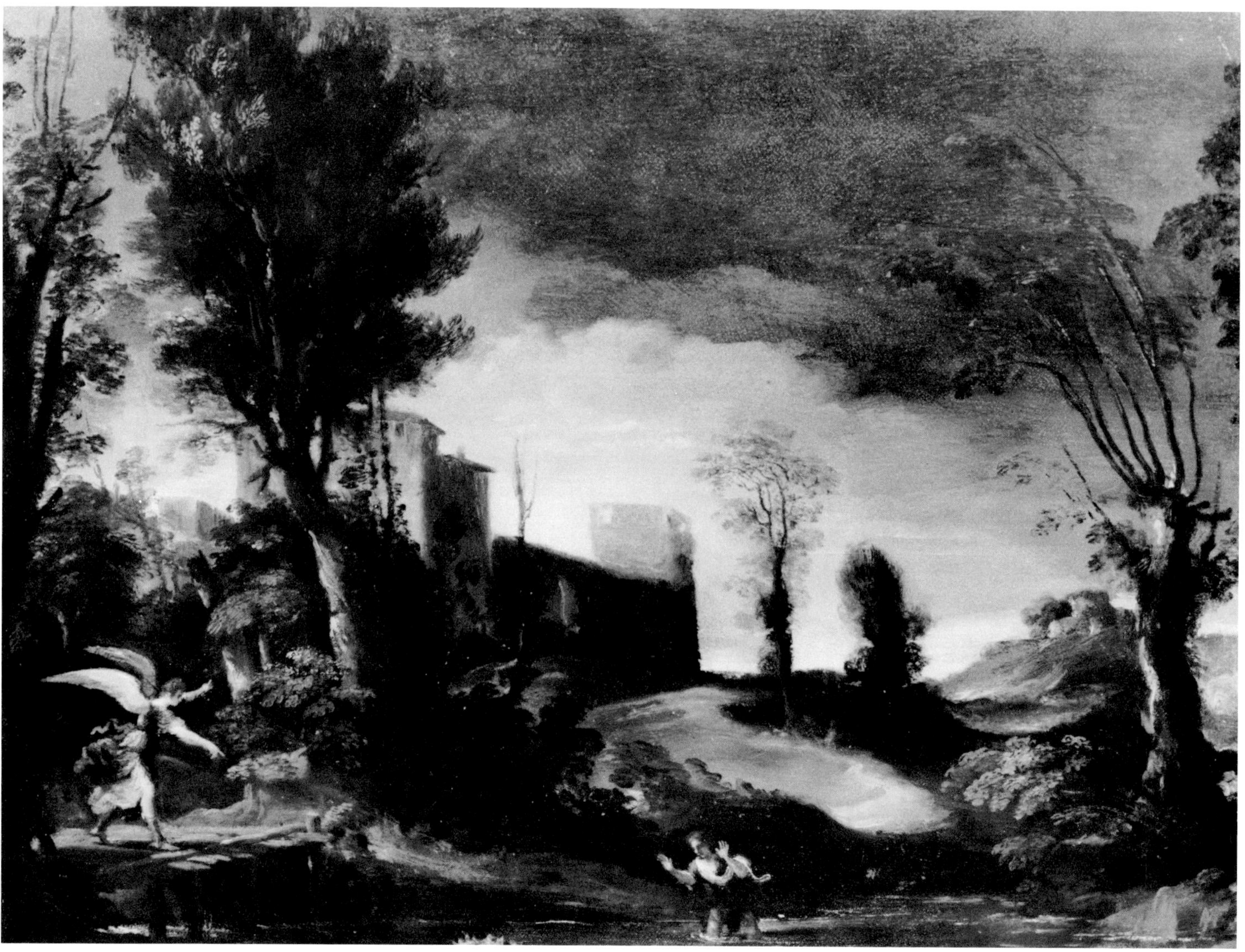

Giovanni Lanfranco

Parma 1582–1647 Rome

Giovanni Lanfranco studied under Agostino Carracci in Parma, then entered the Roman workshop of Annibale Carracci after Agostino's death in 1602. The young Parmese became an indispensable assistant to Annibale, and his participation is documented in all of the more important fresco cycles executed by the Bolognese school in Rome during the first decade. Domenichino was Lanfranco's bitter rival for primacy amongst the heirs to the Carraccesque tradition, a competition that Lanfranco had won by the 1620s.

After the death of Annibale, Lanfranco returned to Parma and Piacenza (1610–12), as if to affirm his roots in the energized figures and charged emotionalism of the great Antonio Correggio. Lanfranco's fresco of 1616 in the Bongiovanni chapel in S. Agostino, Rome, introduced Correggesque illusionism to seventeenth-century vault decorations. He painted his masterpiece in this mode in the vast cupola of S. Andrea della Valle (1625–27), an instant triumph that clinched his ascendancy amongst Roman painters.

In 1633/34 Lanfranco traveled to Naples, where eminent Roman painters were often invited to execute monumental commissions. In the next twelve years he completed four major cycles of frescoes in the most prominent churches of the city: the Gesù Nuovo (1635–37), the Certosa di S. Martino (1637/38), SS. Apostoli (1638–46), and the Cappella di S. Gennaro in the Duomo (1641–43). This outpouring of genius was largely ignored by Ribera and Stanzione, the leaders of the Neapolitan school, but Mattia Preti found it a revelation in 1656, and Preti explained Lanfranco, as it were, to the generations of Giordano and Solimena. Lanfranco died in Rome, where he had returned in 1646 to fresco the apse of S. Carlo ai Catinari.

27 *Noli Me Tangere*

Oil on copper. 23 × 19.5 cm. Ca. 1646.

Provenance: Duke Antonio Farnese, Palazzo del Giardino, Parma (d. 1731, inv. 1708, 1731, 1736); transferred with the Farnese collections to Naples, 1734–36; Carlo di Borbone (Charles VII), Naples; sale, Sotheby & Co., London, 6 December 1972, lot 59.

References: Volkmann, 1767, p. 200; Schleier, 1979, pp. 2–15, fig. 2.

Richard L. Feigen, New York

On the first day of the week after the Crucifixion of Christ, Mary Magdalen visited his sepulchre, which she found empty. As she stood weeping, Christ appeared to her, but Mary, supposing him to be a gardener, did not recognize him until he spoke her name. He then said, "Touch me not [Noli me tangere], for I am not yet ascended to my father" (John 20:17).

Lanfranco painted this diminutive *Noli Me Tangere* as a pendant to a picture of the *Mystic Marriage of St. Catherine,* now in Louisville, Kentucky (fig. 14), as Erich Schleier has recently discussed in depth.[1] Both themes concern holy women who were particularly devoted to Christ. Schleier has traced the provenance of these gem-like pendants to the Farnese Palazzo del Giardino in Parma early in the eighteenth century. The pictures are listed as a pair in several early inventories and were undoubtedly brought to Naples (where seen by Volkmann) with the whole of the Farnese collections in 1734–36 by Carlo di Borbone, King of Naples as Charles VII. The two paintings probably left the Farnese-Bourbon collections and Naples during the upheavals of 1798/99, as did many others.

A two-sided sheet of studies by Lanfranco (Windsor Castle)[2] for this *Noli Me Tangere* was pointed out by Philip Pouncey in the catalogue of the painting's London sale in 1972. While Anthony Blunt and H. L. Cooke erred in relating the drawing to Lanfranco's *Annunciation* in the Hermitage, Leningrad, they rightly referred the style of the draftsmanship and the paper employed to Lanfranco's late period.[3] Schleier has upheld the late style of the New York and Louisville paintings, noting that the artist's development in his Neapolitan years does not admit datings to specific years for most of his paintings on canvas or copper. It may be remarked that the expressive liberties that Lanfranco allows himself in his anatomical draftsmanship does evoke the late style of the series of canvases that he (and assistants) painted for the Duomo at Pozzuoli during the 1640s.

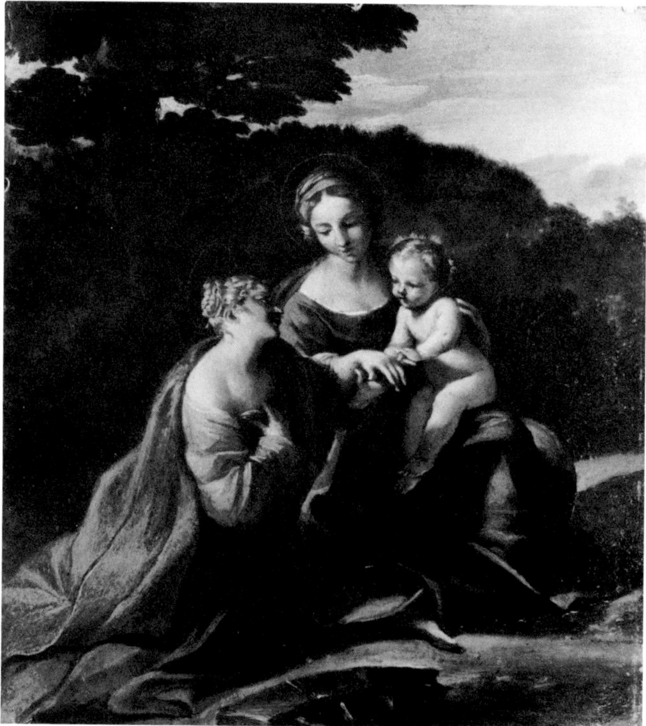

Fig. 14 Lanfranco: *Mystic Marriage of St. Catherine,* oil on copper. J. B. Speed Art Museum, Louisville (66.45)

NOTES

1 Schleier, 1979, pp. 2–15, on whose text this entry is based.
2 Royal Collections, Windsor Castle, no. 5709r (for the Magdalen) and no. 5709v (for the Christ, substantially changed); see Schleier, 1979, figs. 4 and 5.
3 Blunt and Cooke, 1960, p. 46, no. 187.

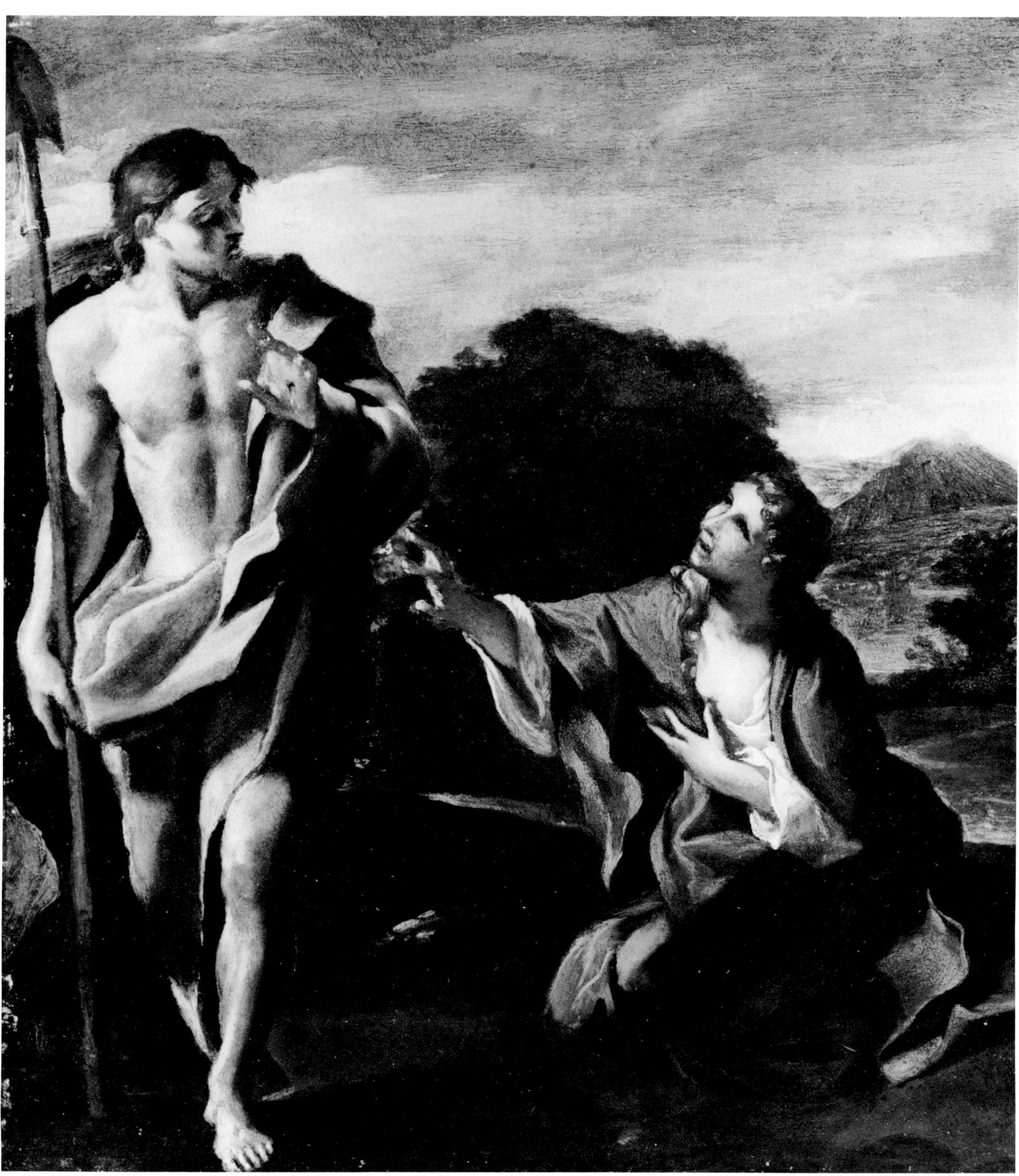

Giovanni Battista Lupicini

Florence ca. 1575–before 1648 Florence

The career of G. B. Lupicini has not yet been reconstructed. Baldinucci writes only that Lupicini, a pupil of Cigoli, was especially esteemed for his copies after older masters; on a 1625 commission to Pisa for that purpose, he chose the young Cesare Dandini to assist him. A signed *Martha Reproving Mary* in the Kunsthistorisches Museum, Vienna (fig. 15), and an altarpiece in S. Domenico, Pistoia, are the touchstones for attributions to Lupicini. The records of the Accademia del Disegno in Florence indicate that he died before 1648.

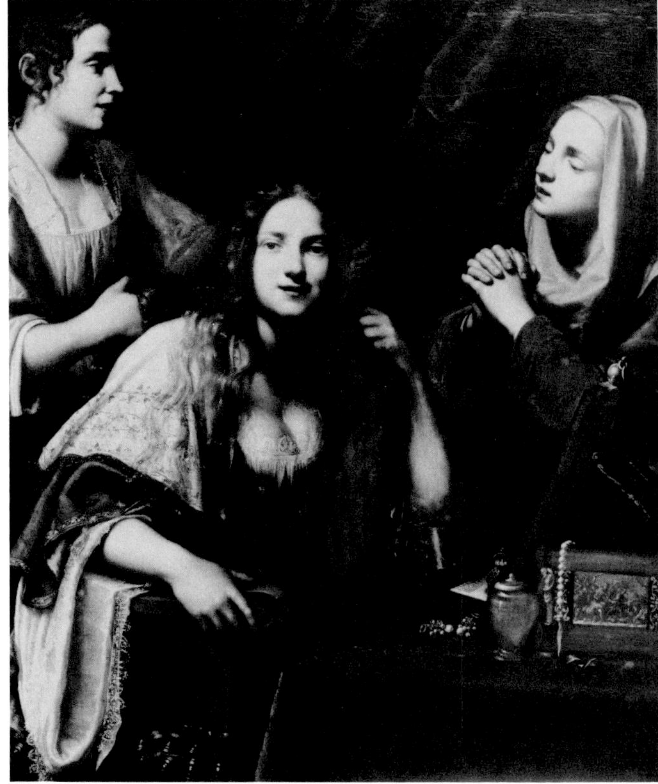

Fig. 15 Lupicini: *Martha Reproving Mary,* oil on canvas. Kunsthistorisches Museum, Vienna (364)

28 *The Repentant Magdalen Contemplating the Cross*

Oil on canvas. 52.05 × 39.35 cm.

Provenance: P. & D. Colnaghi and Co., London.

Reference: McCorquodale, *Painting in Florence 1600–1700*, 1979, no. 34, repr.

Mr. and Mrs. Morton B. Harris, New York

A native of Magdala, a village on the Sea of Galilee, Mary Magdalen was born of a prosperous family, sister to the virtuous Martha. According to her legend, Mary wasted her father's inheritance and lapsed into sinfulness and idle vanity. After her repentance Mary Magdalen became one of Christ's most devoted followers. She is believed to have passed the last thirty years of her life in the wilderness of Provence in meditation, penitence, and sorrow for her early sins.

This sensitive representation of the humble Magdalen was recently added to Lupicini's oeuvre by Charles McCorquodale. The full, rounded features of her face and the artist's keen eye for distinguishing textures do accord convincingly with the signed picture in Vienna (fig. 15) as well as the *Allegory of Painting* (Kress Collection, Columbia, South Carolina, Museum of Art and Science) attributed by Gerhard Ewald.[1]

Lupicini evidently inherited his master's naturalistic aspirations, which he fulfilled with a refreshing directness of observation that belies his activity as a copyist. Until further works come to light, it will not be feasible to address the artist's development.

NOTE

1 Ewald, 1965, p. 308, fig. 15. See also Shapley, 1973, p. 85.

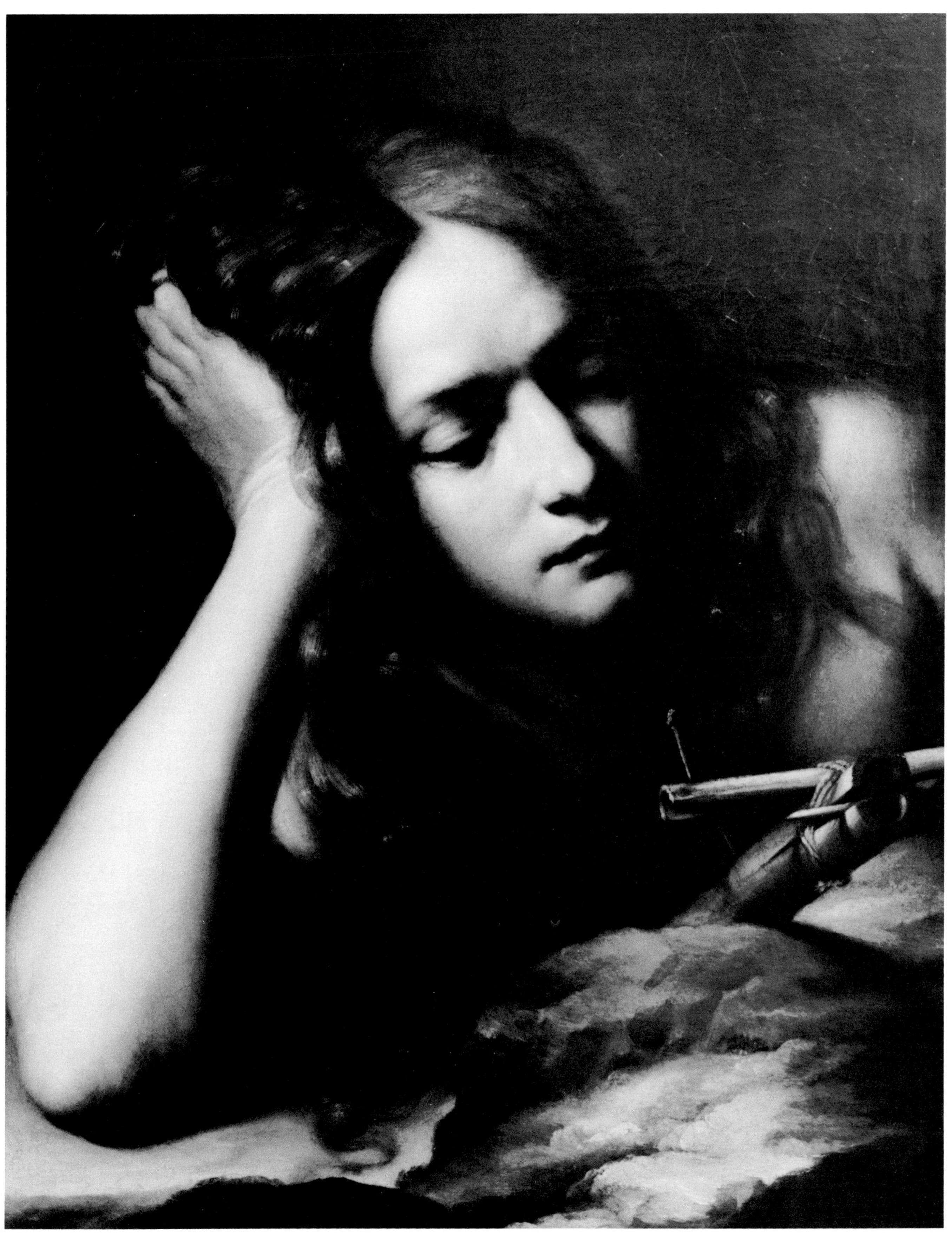

Bartolomeo Manfredi

Ostiano ca. 1587–1620/21 Rome

Very few particulars concerning the life and career of Bartolomeo Manfredi have come down to us. Mancini (ca. 1620) listed him among the close followers of Caravaggio, and noted that Manfredi, then thirty-three or -four years of age, was already commanding high fees for his pictures from patrons in Rome and Florence. He seems never to have executed a public commission. According to the same source, Manfredi was born in Ostiano (Mantua), but came to Rome following brief studies in Milan, Cremona, and Brescia. Baglione reported that Manfredi entered the Roman studio of Cristoforo Roncalli, called Il Pomarancio, before the latter's departure in 1606. A highly stylized *Punishment of Cupid* (Art Institute of Chicago) attributed to Manfredi by most scholars testifies to a grounding in Roman Late Mannerism. Manfredi lived in the parish of S. Andrea delle Fratte between 1616 and 1619. He must have died prematurely thereafter, since Baglione discusses his lifetime within the pontificate of Paul V (1605–21).

Manfredi's interpretation of Caravaggism attained such immediate currency among his fellow Caravaggists that within a century his works had been completely subsumed within the oeuvre ascribed to Caravaggio himself. It has only been disentangled by modern-day scholars, especially Voss, Longhi, and Nicolson. Manfredi fashioned his style from Caravaggio's early genre paintings and the most naturalistic, violent, and also monumental implications of Caravaggio's first tenebrism, above all the St. Matthew cycle in the Contarelli Chapel, S. Luigi dei Francesi. Among the prominent adherents to the *methodus Manfrediana,* as Sandrart termed this speciality in nocturnal tavern scenes or secularized religious subjects, were Valentin, Honthorst, Renieri, and the young Preti.

29 *Christ Crowned with Thorns*

Oil on canvas. 82.6 × 110.5 cm. Ca. 1620.

Provenance: Mr. and Mrs. Paul H. Ganz, New York.

References: Brejon, 1979, p. 309, fig. 44; Nicolson, 1979, p. 79.

Private collection, New York

Prior to the recent publication of this *Christ Crowned with Thorns,* its composition was known through several copies.[1] Arnauld Brejon has observed aptly that Manfredi's reduction of the narrative to its essential elements—Christ tormented and mocked by a single captor—evokes Caravaggio's aspirations to express the universal through simplified pictorial means.[2] Manfredi evidently reached this solution via a series of paintings. The pose of Christ is identical to a three-quarter-length figure of Christ in another *Christ Crowned with Thorns* by Manfredi, likewise published by Brejon.[3] The latter canvas is upright in format and depicts two tormentors; from the photograph the textures of fabric and flesh appear to be described with greater specificity than in the present version, which therefore must have been executed subsequently.[4] However, the dim fluorescence of the surfaces in the New York picture is anticipated in the broad handling of Manfredi's *Christ Crowned with Thorns* in the Florentine Galleries, which must be earliest of all, if we are right in ascribing to relative inexperience the additive arrangement of the figures.[5]

The posture of Christ's head forced to one side and below his shoulder is a typically Caravaggesque metaphor for extreme duress, although the pose does not appear in any known treatment by Caravaggio of this particular theme.[6] Manfredi's success with this concep-

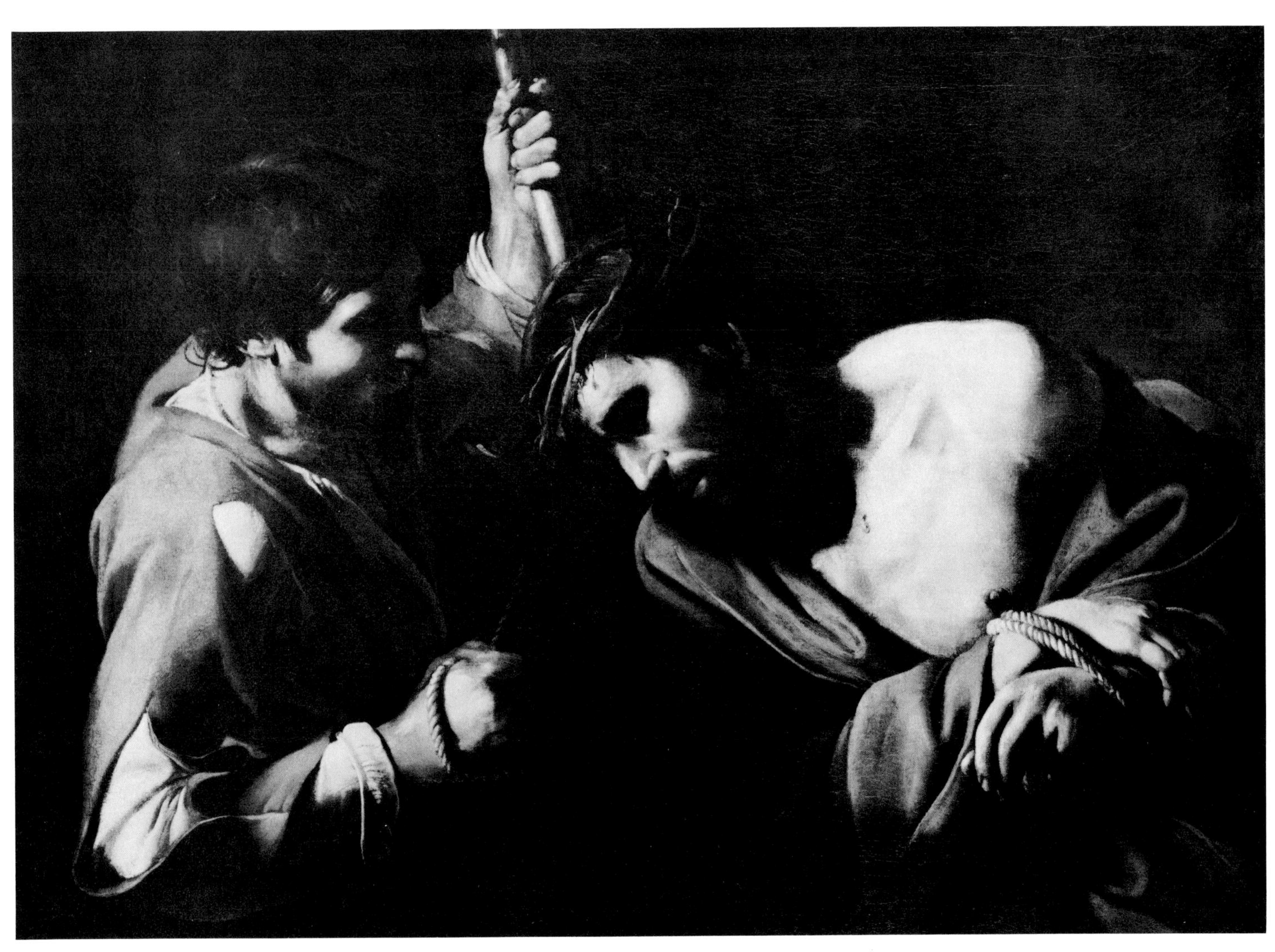

tion is evinced through his own replicas, such as this one, and through its frequent adoption in Caravaggesque paintings, as by Terbrugghen, Baburen, and Riminaldi, to name only three interesting examples.[7]

NOTES

1 Moir, 1976, p. 146 n. 245 (item vi), cites four copies "probably after a lost original by Manfredi": (1) Christ Church, Oxford (88.5 × 108.1 cm.), repr. in Byam Shaw, 1967, no. 138, fig. 102; (2) Bennington Museum, Bennington, Vermont (80 × 114 cm.), repr. in Moir, 1976, fig. 83 (subsequently sold at Christie's, New York, "Important Paintings by Old Masters," 11 January 1979, lot 147); (3) known from a photograph in the archives of Thomas Agnew & Sons, London (82 × 113 cm.); (4) sale, American Art Galleries, New York, 21–22 March 1922, lot 26 (80 × 115.5 cm.), to R. Pearsons.

2 Brejon, 1979, p. 309.

3 Ibid., fig. 49. The painting is in a private collection in Italy.

4 It should be noted that the New York painting has undergone extensive restoration.

5 See Borea, 1970, no. 7, repr. p. 137.

6 Following Longhi, 1943, p. 18, a *Christ Crowned with Thorns* in the Kunsthistorisches Museum, Vienna, has been regarded as a good copy of a lost Caravaggio by numerous scholars. See Moir, 1976, p. 146 n. 245, fig. 76. In the Vienna composition a seated Christ leans his head below his proper left shoulder. His pose in the paintings discussed in this entry should not be mistaken as a simple reversal of the Vienna design, be it Caravaggio's or not. Manfredi has quite originally construed Christ's torso in these works as a pyramid of which the rounded shoulder is the apex.

7 The paintings of *Christ Crowned with Thorns* by Terbrugghen (Regional Art Museum, Irkutsk) and Baburen (Provincialaat der Minderbroeders, Weert) are both illustrated in Vsevolozhskaya and Linnik, 1975, fig. 109 and facing page. See also Brejon, 1976, p. 309. Riminaldi adapted this pose with remarkable sensitivity for his *Martyrdom of St. Cecilia* (Florentine Galleries), which was painted for the Pantheon in Rome; see Borea, 1976, no. 15, repr. pp. 146–47.

Pier Francesco Mola

Coldrerio 1612–1666 Rome

P. F. Mola was the son of G. B. Mola, an architect and author of a guide book, who brought his family from the canton of Ticino to Rome before 1616. Mola studied first with Prospero Orsi and Cavalier d'Arpino, but his attention seems to have been diverted immediately by the Venetian-influenced manner of landscape painting that became current in Rome during the latter 1620s. Bologna and Venice were the focal points of Mola's lengthy passages north of Rome, 1633–40 and 1641–47. Two years' experience in the workshop of Francesco Albani were crucial in his development, as Albani himself remarked in a letter of 1658. However, in the absence of dates amongst his juvenilia, scholars disagree as to whether Mola stayed with Albani at the onset of his travels or after his frescoes of 1641/42 in his native Coldrerio (which reveal his inexperience in monumental compositions).

Upon his return to Rome, Mola was already a master of lush, evocative landscapes and he was rapidly gaining confidence as a figure painter. His imposing *Barbary Pirate* in the Louvre is signed and dated 1650. The next five years witnessed increasingly important public commissions, culminating in his masterpiece in fresco, the *Meeting of Joseph and His Brothers* of 1656/57 in the Palazzo del Quirinale. In 1659 Mola sued Prince Don Camillo Pamphili over the payment for his nearly completed fresco in the Stanza dell'Aria of the Palazzo Pamphili at Valmontone. As the suit dragged on to an unsuccessful verdict in 1664, Mola's health declined. (In the meantime, the fresco had been replaced in 1661 by one of Mattia Preti's.) Mola was elected Principe of the Accademia di San Luca in 1662, but he had to step down the next year because of illness. He had numerous pupils, about whom, with the partial exception of Antonio Gherardi, we know hardly more than their names. In Mola's mature style an absorbing tension exists between his sturdy figures (inspired by Albani, Lanfranco, and Guercino) and his dramatic, luxuriant landscapes, as if the two aspects of his art vie for preeminence without either party clearly winning out.

30 *St. John the Baptist Preaching in the Wilderness*

Oil on canvas. 73.65 × 99.05 cm. Ca. 1650–55.

Provenance: Baron de Breteuil (d. 1713); Duc d'Orléans, Palais Royale (by 1729); Louis-Philippe-Egalité (1792); Vicomte Edouard de Walkuers (1792); Laborde de Méréville, London (1792); Duke of Bridgewater, Earl of Carlisle, and Earl Gower, London (1798/99); Earl Gower (later Marquis of Stafford), Cleveland House; Duke of Sutherland, Stafford House, sale, Christie's, London, 11 July 1913, lot 70; Thomas Agnew & Sons, London; Ugo Ojetti, Florence.

References: Dubois de Saint-Gelais, 1727 , p. 398; *Recueil d'estampes d'après les plus beaux tableaux et d'après les plus beaux dessins qui sont en France* [*"Recueil Crozat"*], 1729 (engraving by J. P. le Bas); Couché, 1786–1806 (engraving by R. de Launay); London, Bryan's Gallery, 1798/99, no. 81; Britton, 1808, pp. 20–22, no. 13; Ottley, 1818, no. 31, repr.; Buchanan, 1824, I, p. 108; J. Young, 1825, I, no. 70, pl. XXI; Waagen, 1854–57, II, pp. 65 and 492; Stryienski, 1913, pp. 86 and 174, no. 300, repr. p. 78; Florence, Palazzo Pitti, 1922, p. 131, no. 691, pl. 64; Ojetti, Dami, and Tarchiani, 1924, repr. p. 209; Voss, 1924, p. 560, fig. 282; Nugent, 1930, II, pp. 219–21, repr. p. 220; Rudolph, 1969, p. 24; Cocke, 1972, pp. 21–23, 38, 43, 45–46, 53, pl. 51; Rudolph, 1972, p. 352 n. 16; Sutherland Harris, 1974, p. 291.

Private collection, New York

The theme of the ministry of St. John the Baptist in the wilderness of Judea (Matthew 3:1–4) was evidently sympathetic to Mola, for he treated it on several occasions with notable success.[1] The present *St. John the Baptist Preaching in the Wilderness* has been admired in distinguished collections since the turn of the eighteenth century. However, its whereabouts have not been known to scholars since its inclusion in the famous exhibition of seicento paintings at the Palazzo Pitti in 1922.

As Richard Cocke has pointed out, Mola derived the pose of the Baptist as well as the general arrangement of the figures from Albani's painting of the same subject now in the Musée des Beaux-Arts, Lyons.[2] Comparison of the pictures shows that Mola has characteristically enhanced the role of the figures in relation to their setting; the expressions are more vividly described and differentiated than Albani's. In this manner Mola's mature works defy simple categorization as "landscapes with figures."

Stella Rudolph has convincingly dated this picture to the period between 1650 and 1655, i.e., between Mola's *Barbary Pirate* and the *St. Michael* in S. Marco, Rome, of about 1655.[3] Cocke prefers a date in the latter 1640s.[4]

Two compositional studies by Mola in pen and ink in the Cabinet des Dessins du Louvre have been related with the present *St. John the Baptist* by Cocke;[5] several other associations of Mola's drawings for the painting are unpersuasive.[6] Attention should also be drawn to a variant (reversed) on copper of the Lyons *St. John the Baptist* by Albani, which was formerly in the collection of the Marquis of Lansdowne (Bowood Hall, Wiltshire).[7] From the photograph, certain features of this painting, for instance the augmented scale of the figures, are analogous to Mola's transformation of the same model.

NOTES

1 See Cocke, 1972, nos. 19 and 35, for pictures of this theme in London and Paris.

2 Ibid., pp. 23 and 46.

3 Rudolph, 1972, p. 352 n. 16.

4 Cocke, 1972, p. 46. Sutherland Harris, 1974, p. 291, rightly questions Cocke's argument that the New York picture might have been painted for G. B. Costaguti because a Mola drawing in the Teyler Museum, Haarlem (inv. no. K.I. 78) has a sketch of a *St. John the Baptist Preaching* on the verso and a study for the Costaguti Bacchus and Ariadne on the recto.

5 Cocke, 1972, pls. 49 and 50. The two Louvre drawings are: inv. no. 8.405, ink and wash, 16 × 17.6 cm.; inv. no. 8.406, ink over black chalk, 20.7 × 27.6 cm.

6 I doubt the associations with this painting of the drawings in the Teyler Museum, Haarlem (inv. no. K.I. 78 verso), in the Ecole des Beaux-Arts, Paris (inv. no. 205) and in the Gurney collection, New York; see Cocke, 1972, pls. 46, 47, and 48. A head study in the Incisa collection, Rome, is not at all close; see Martinelli, 1958, p. 106, pl. XLIX, fig. 10.

7 Known to me only from a photograph in the Frick Art Reference Library, New York, under "Albani: supply." It is listed in Waagen, 1854–57, III, p. 165.

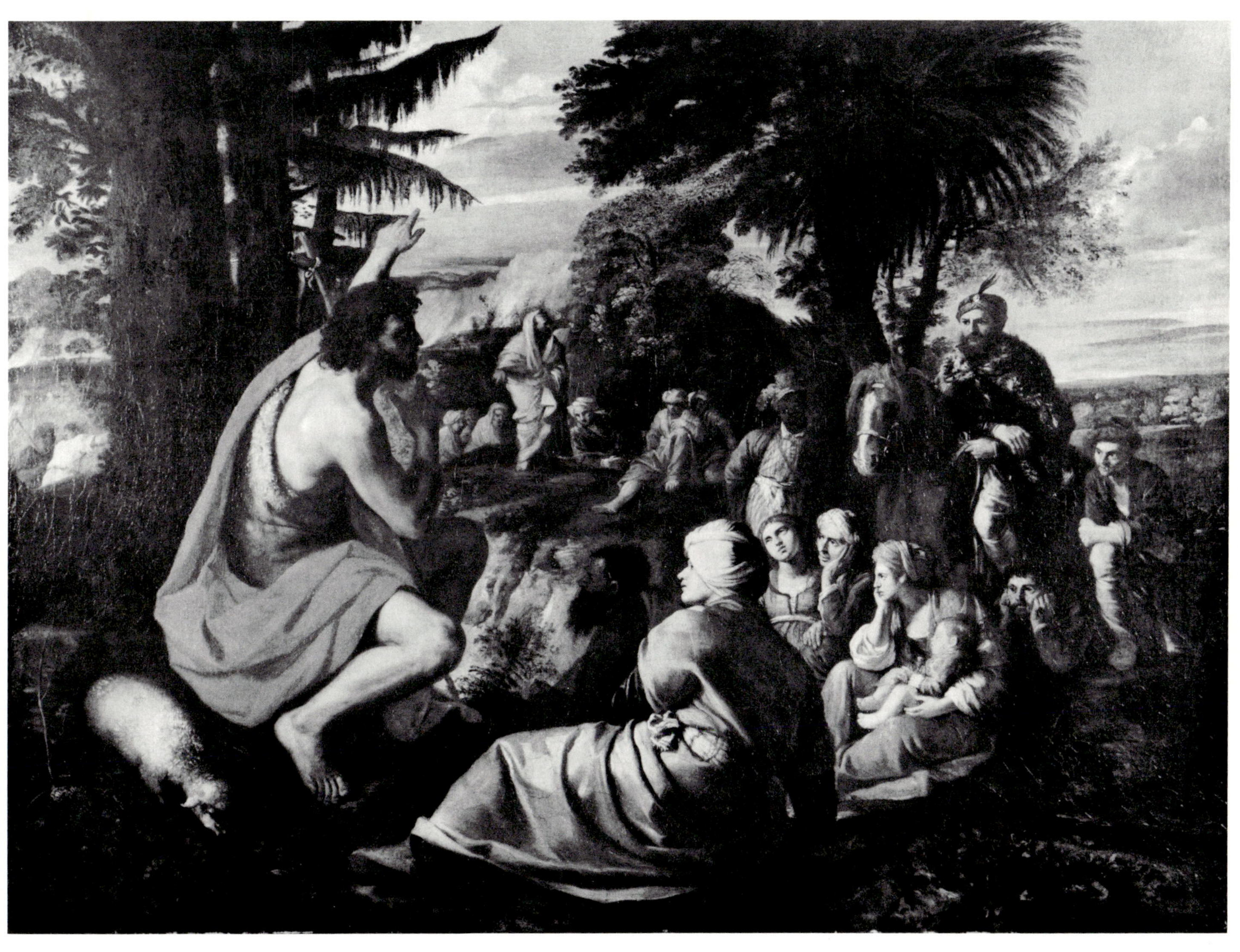

Giovanni Battista Passeri

Rome 1610/16–1679 Rome

Giovanni Battista Passeri was a Roman pupil of Domenichino, to whose memory he remained always devoted. Passeri's artistic, as opposed to literary, activity is only now being reconstructed. In 1634 he was working alongside G. A. Canini in the Villa Aldobrandini, Frascati. He was admitted to the Accademia di San Luca by 1638 (he was Principe in 1663) and in 1641 into the honorific society of the Virtuosi del Pantheon. With two assistants Passeri painted frescoes in the Palazzo Doria al Collegio Romano during the summer of 1661. Scattered references to lost altarpieces in Rome, Naples, and near Viterbo (1665) tantalize, but tell us little. A signed painting in the National Gallery, Dublin, and a signed drawing in the British Museum testify to his interest in northern-influenced landscape.

Passeri has achieved lasting recognition for his scrupulous compilation of artist's biographies, *Vite dei pittori, scultori ed architetti che anno lavorato in Roma morti dal 1641 al 1673* (first published in 1772), which he composed as a sequel to Baglione's *Vite.* Notwithstanding his classicist bias, Passeri's lives are notable for the tolerance and perception of the author's judgments, rather in contrast to the disputative Baglione.

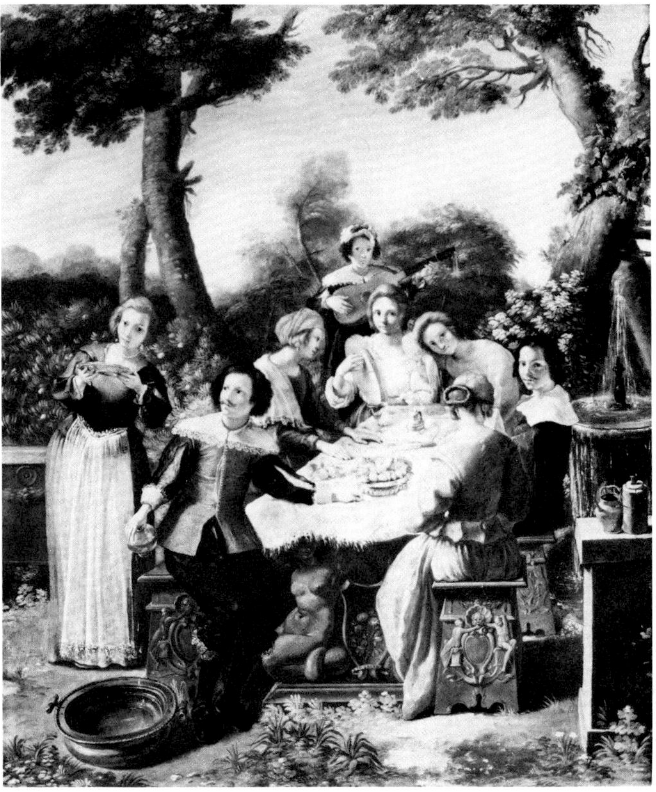

Fig. 16 Passeri: *Party Feasting in a Garden.* Oil on canvas. National Gallery of Ireland, Dublin

31 *Musical Party in a Garden*

Oil on canvas. 73.65 × 99.05 cm.

Robert and Bertina Suida Manning, New York

At a charming taverna, dappling in the warm Roman sun, a musical banquet is taking place. A properly attired gentleman at the far right gestures as if to direct the viewer's attention. Evidently this gathering is imbued with some emblematic significance; what it might be eludes us at present. The juxtaposition of ancient to modern dress is confusing: is this a theatrical performance of some sort or do the antique actors serve a symbolic function? Sir Ellis Waterhouse has suggested that the statue in the courtyard may be a figure of Hygeia and that the subject would therefore concern the healthy mores of the ancients.[1]

The attribution of this *Musical Party in a Garden* to G. B. Passeri is assured by comparison with the artist's sole recognized painting, the signed *Party Feasting in a Garden* in Dublin (fig. 16). As it happens, the Dublin picture represents festivities that are similarly invested with moralizing content, specifically a *vanitas* theme.[2]

As a more ambitious conception, this *Musical Party in a Garden* affords us our first good glimpse into the artistic career of Passeri. It is surprising that this admirer of Domenichino should paint such casually arranged scenes of open debt to the genre pictures of the *Bamboccianti.* Then again, Passeri's *Vite* were notably sympathetic to their rustic style. Of course, Passeri addressed himself to lofty issues only, but he took no less delight in the sensuous pleasures of the Italian countryside. His somewhat unstable figures do not betray particular devotion to Domenichino's academy; perhaps they emulate the suppleness of Lanfranco's mature Roman style of draftsmanship.

NOTES

1 In a letter of 24 September 1979.

2 The table is set next to an antique sarcophagus inscribed, "CADUN[T]/ET REMANENT" (they fall, they remain).

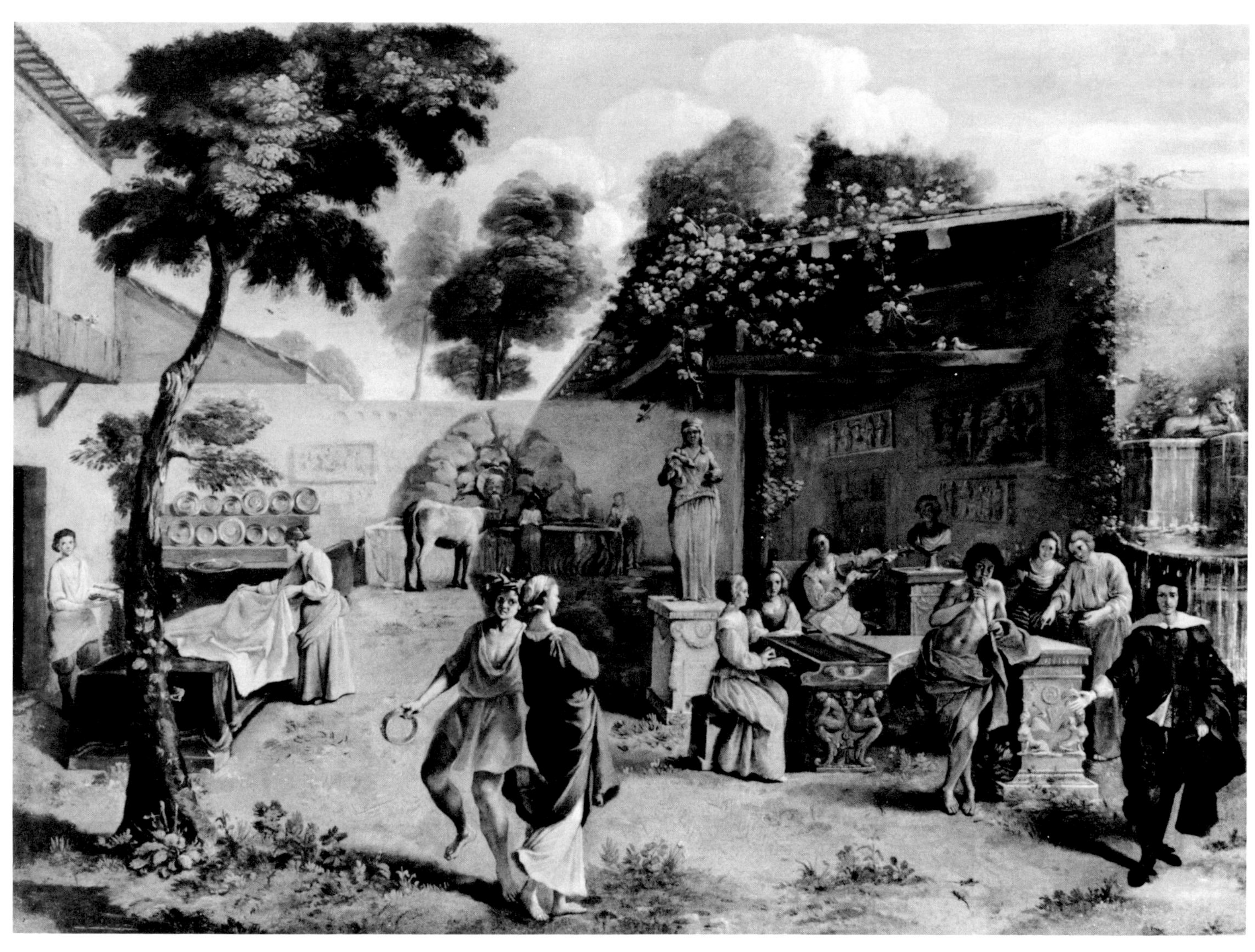

Simone Pignoni

Florence 1611–1698 Florence

Pignoni received his first instructions from Fabrizio Boschi, and thereafter Domenico Passignano, a more important master. His course was decisively influenced by the art of Francesco Furini, his senior by only a few years, into whose circle Pignoni entered. During the 1640s Pignoni's emulations of Furini are practically indistinguishable from their prototypes.

Like Furini, Pignoni specialized in nude or provocatively dressed saints or allegorical figures of three-quarter length. He wrapped these voluptitudes in a Venetian-inspired *sfumato* that softens the forms enticingly.

The chronology of these commissions for private collectors remains to be established. In his later manner much of the *sfumato* is dispelled in favor of weightier nudes derived from Reni and other Bolognese. Pignoni's major public commissions occurred toward the end of his career in two altarpieces in SS. Annunziata (1671) and S. Felicita (1682). He was the master of the prolific Giovanni Camillo Sagrestani.

32 *The Penitent Magdalen*

Oil on canvas. 85.1 × 69.8 cm.

Provenance: Sestieri, Rome.

References: Nissman, 1969, no. 56, fig. 30; Minault, 1972, p. 44, repr.

Howard and Shirley G. Hibbard

The Magdalen is represented at the moment of her repentance and rejection of mortal vanity, of which the skull before her is a symbol.[1] In treating this rare episode, Pignoni permits himself a double-edged approach to the theme of *vanitas*: even as the Magdalen discards her fine apparel, the viewer's attention is inevitably drawn to just those pleasurable vanities of the flesh she renounces.

Pignoni painted this canvas with his most appealing Furinesque bravura. The saint's eyes and parted lips are dissolved in shadow. Her softened features and the deep colors of her dress anticipate the decorative style of Pietro Dandini and other Late Baroque Florentines. When the whirlwind Luca Giordano visited Florence, he sowed the ground of Venetianism that Pignoni and Furini had prepared.

NOTE

1 For the story of St. Mary Magdalen, see no. 28.

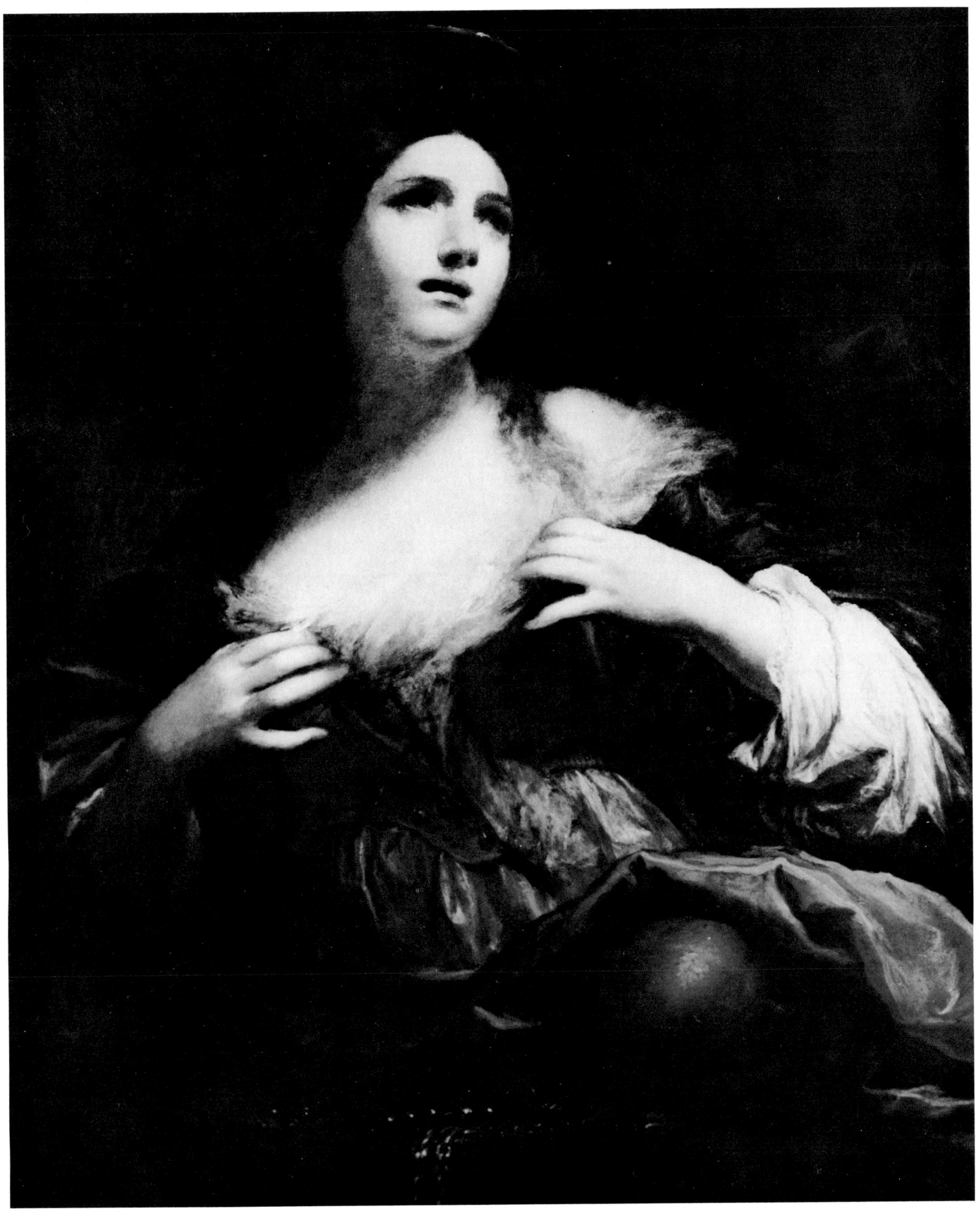

Domenico Piola

Genoa 1627–1703 Genoa

Domenico Piola was the leading painter of the Baroque in Genoa, where he passed his long, extraordinarily productive life. His masters proper were his short-lived brother, Pellegro, and A. Cappellino, but he soon taught himself to paint in the manner of G. B. Castiglione with deceptive fidelity. Piola's first dated work was his *Decollation of St. James* of 1647 (Oratorio di S. Giacomo della Marina, Genoa). By 1651 he had executed a fresco for a chapel in S. Domenico (now destroyed). Piola's activity in countless churches and palaces in Genoa has left numerous dated works.

Upon the death of Valerio Castello in 1659, Piola completed a fresco left by that master whose verve had impressed him deeply. Piola's mastery of the fresco medium led him, in friendly rivalry with his son-in-law, Gregorio de' Ferrari, to elevate the art of fresco decoration in Genoa to heights not attained elsewhere. Piola derived his grand manner from Pietro da Cortona; Gregorio imported a Correggesque luminosity and sweetness from four years' study in Parma, between 1669 and 1673.

In 1684/85, after Genoa was bombarded by the French, Piola made a working tour to Milan, Bologna, Piacenza, and Asti. He was paid in 1688 for frescoes in two salons of the Palazzo Brignole, Genoa. Still active in 1700, he participated in the competition to decorate the Sala del Maggior Consiglio of the Palazzo Reale (Ducale).

Acclaimed in his patria, the fame of this great artist seems hardly to have extended abroad. A satisfactory monograph on the artist has yet to be written.

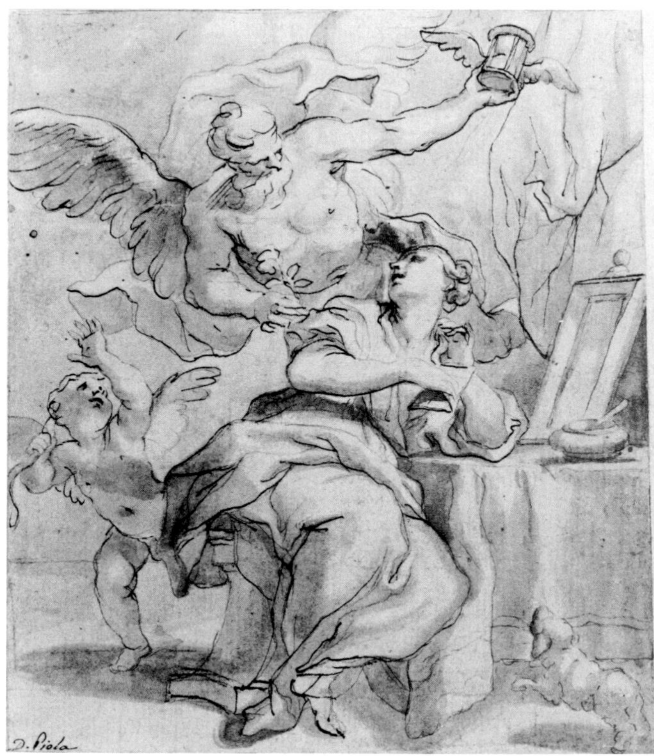

Fig. 17 Piola: *Allegory of Time,*
ink and wash over black chalk on paper.
Staatsgalerie, Stuttgart (6426)

33 *Allegory of Youth*

Oil on canvas. 152.4 × 113 cm.

Provenance: J. Weitzner, New York.

References: Manning and Manning, 1962, no. 47, repr.; Manning, *Genoese Painters,* 1964, no. 65; Bruno, 1971, p. 285.

Robert and Bertina Suida Manning, New York

Piola's theme is the ephemera of beauty and all worldly vanity. An allegorical figure of Time interrupts a young maiden at her toilette to proffer a flower, yet another symbol of the inevitable decay of beauty. The cupid who flees at the sight of Time refers to the inconstancy of love, another preoccupation of the Baroque Age.

This painting has been dated to the artist's full maturity by Robert and Bertina Suida Manning.[1] Indeed the soft, full drapery style may be found in Piola's works of the 1680s and somewhat earlier. The influence of Van Dyck noted by the same writers is especially pronounced in the features of the personification of Time.

A preparatory study by Piola for this *Allegory* is preserved in the drawings cabinet at Stuttgart (fig. 17). The Stuttgart drawing depicts the figures in full-length and adds such details as the little dog. The drawing has a finished quality and certain variations in pose, which might indicate that Piola made it as a distinct composition, perhaps as a reprise of this painting.

NOTE

1 Manning and Manning, 1962, no. 47.

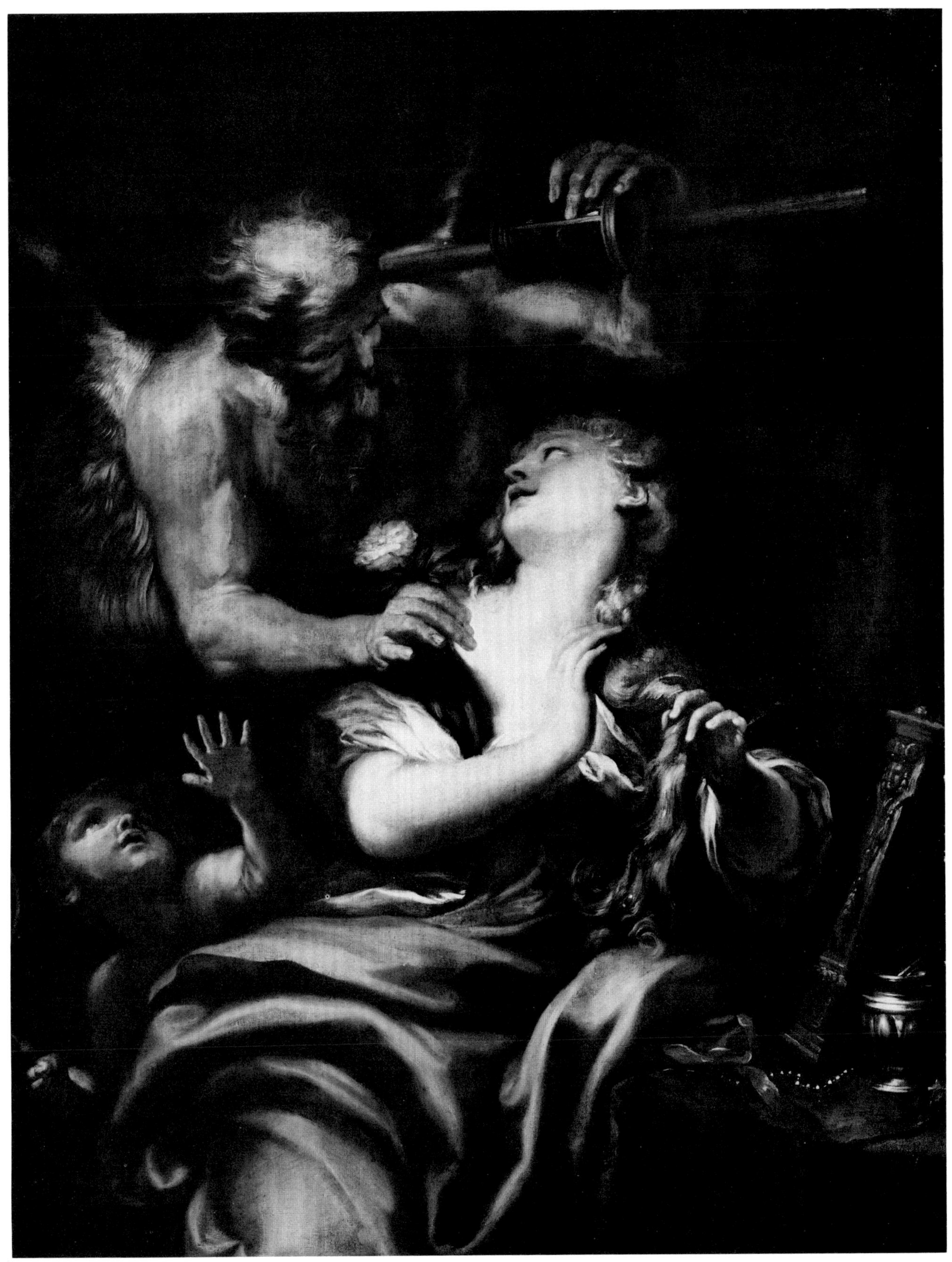

Giacomo del Po

Rome 1652–1726 Naples

Giacomo del Po was the son and pupil of a Sicilian painter and engraver, Pietro del Po. His father was active in Naples (1644–47), then passed to Rome. Of Giacomo's Roman activity we know only that he was admitted into the Accademia di San Luca in 1674 and the Congregazione dei Virtuosi in 1680; he painted altarpieces for two churches, Sant'Angelo in Pescheria and S. Marta al Collegio Romano (now lost).

After his relocation to Naples in 1683, del Po's first documented works were a series of paintings in Sant'Antonino, Sorrento, one of which he dated 1685, another 1687. These pictures do not reveal any particular influence of Baciccio, whose manner del Po, in his mature style, is usually considered to have introduced to Naples.

The last decade of the century witnessed the maturation of this slow developer. He executed numerous altarpieces for Neapolitan churches (Sant'Agostino degli Scalzi, 1693), gradually distancing himself from *Giordanismo* to pursue his own rather extravagant mode of expression. Presumably also during the 1690s, while Giordano was absent in Spain, del Po established his reputation as a specialist in secular decorations in the *palazzi* of the nobility. De Dominici mentions many such schemes; those in the Palazzo De Matteis are notable survivals.

After the death of Luca Giordano, del Po was fully occupied as the principal alternative to Solimena. Indeed, his frenetic, tortuous figures could hardly be more opposed to the increasingly serious conceptions of the *caposcuola.* De Dominici describes del Po as an arrogant personality who was always quick to criticize his colleagues.

As an indication of his copious production it will suffice to note that in the first decade of the century alone the artist placed works in the Duomo of Sorrento, in S. Pietro a Maiella (an *Assunt à,* ca. 1705), and in S. M. di Ognibene (ca. 1706) and S. Caterina a Formiello (ca. 1706), not to mention one of his masterpieces, the *Triumph of St. John of the Cross,* with other paintings in S. Teresa agli Studi (1708).

Following this period the artist's style succumbed to the general turning of the school towards classicism. The rich chiaroscuro of his first maturity was replaced by a brighter, less saturated palette.

34 *Gates of Hell*

35 *Sleep of Adam and Eve*

Oil on canvas. Each 126 × 101 cm. Ca. 1703–8.

Provenance: Thomas Agnew & Sons, London (1966).

References: London, Thomas Agnew & Sons, 1966, nos. 42 and 26; Vitzthum, 1970, pp. 28–31; "Giacomo del Po," 1974, fig. 179 (*Sleep of Adam and Eve*); Rabiner, 1978, pp. 39 and 40 n. 3.

Mr. and Mrs. Paul H. Ganz

The subjects of this pair of paintings by Giacomo del Po are taken from John Milton's epic *Paradise Lost* (1667). As Walter Vitzthum observed, Milton is a most unlikely inspiration for a Neapolitan painter at the turn of the eighteenth century.[1] The first translation of *Paradise Lost* into Italian was not published until 1729. However, the artist knew the illustrations to the London editions of 1688 (for the *Gates of Hell*) and 1705 (for the *Sleep of Adam and Eve*) as they are the sources, after much modification, for these two compositions.[2] The *Gates of Hell* depicts the dramatic encounter in the poem's second book between Satan and Death, with Sin in between them. Milton describes the sleep of Adam and Eve prior to the Fall in the fourth book. Vitzthum did not rule out the possibility that this series once included other scenes.

One of the few known drawings by del Po is a sizable study for this *Gates of Hell* (Achenbach Foundation for Graphic Arts, California Palace of the Legion of Honor, San Francisco).[3] When the drawing was exhibited in Canada in 1970, the identification of its Miltonian subject was credited to Harry Dillow.[4] Elizabeth Gardner later related the drawing to the painting in the Ganz collection.[5]

Vitzthum dated these canvases to del Po's maturity, comparable in style to his paintings of 1708 in S. Teresa agli Studi and 1712 in the sacristy of S. Domenico Maggiore, Naples. This view has been accepted by Donald Rabiner, who would specify the period of ca. 1703–8, before del Po largely ceased to employ the deep greens that so enrich the *Sleep of Adam and Eve.*[6]

NOTES

1 Vitzthum, 1970, pp. 28–31.

2 Ibid., figs. 2 and 3. These are engravings after some listless designs of J. B. Medina and J. Goeree, respectively; that del Po saw their latent pictorial possibilities bespeaks his genius.

3 In black chalk, 328 × 241 mm.; ibid., fig. 4.

4 Montreal, Musée des Beaux-Arts, 1970, no. 72.

5 Vitzthum, 1970, p. 30.

6 Rabiner, 1978, p. 39.

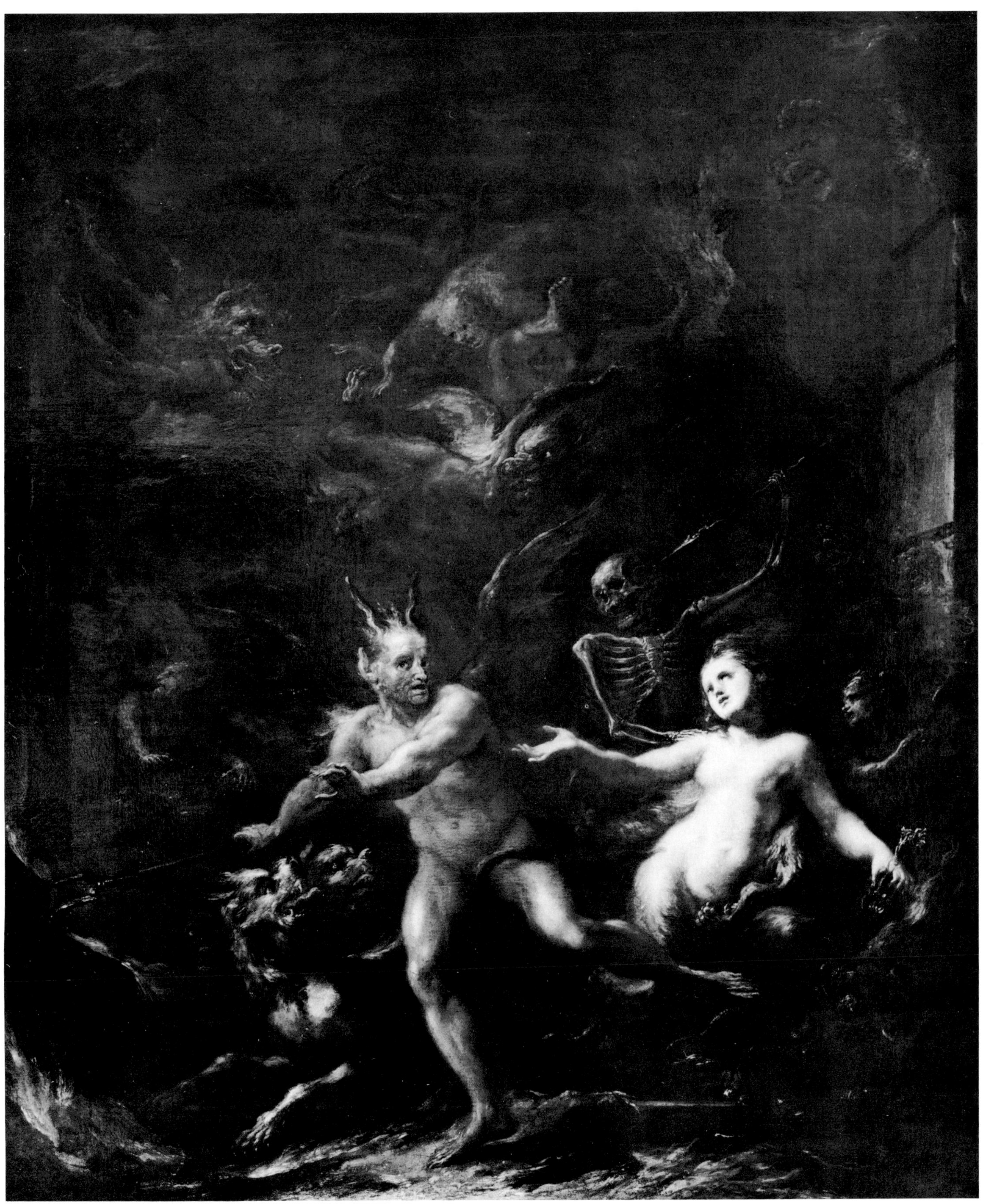

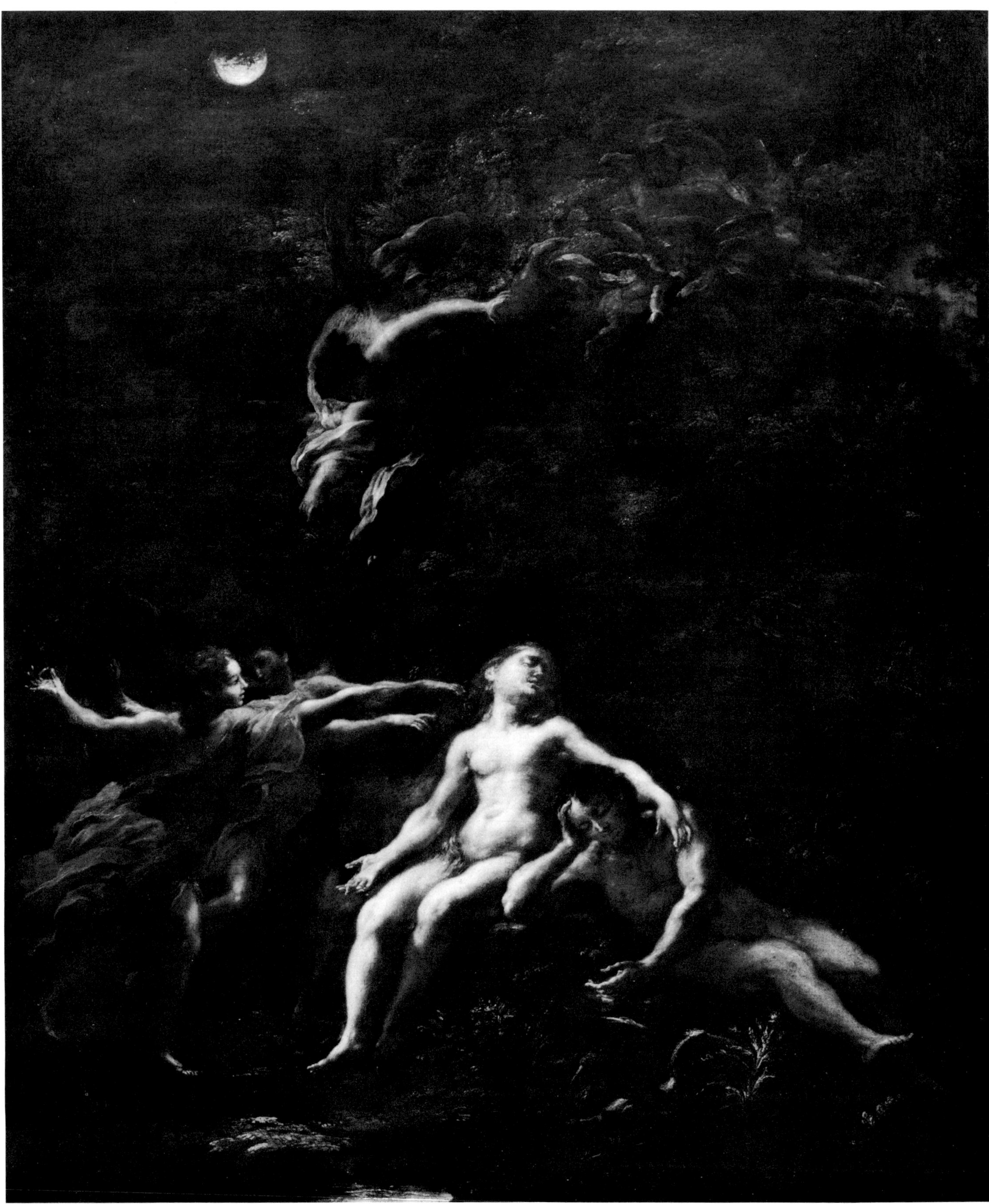

Mattia Preti

Taverna 1613–1699 Malta

Although Preti was trained and won his first honors in Rome, he is chiefly associated today with the Neapolitan school of painting, whose course he decisively affected. By 1633 Petri had left his native Calabria and was living in Rome with his elder brother, Gregorio, a painter of much less attainment. Preti's juvenilia adhere to the *methodus Manfrediana,* perhaps an inauspicious direction by this date. However, before the end of the 1630s the young artist had broadened his Caravaggesque base with observations of the neo-Venetian exercises of Andrea Sacchi and Nicolas Poussin, as evidenced by his altarpiece of *St. Andrew* (Hofkirche, Lucerne) datable to this period. In 1641 Pope Urban VIII elevated Preti to *cavaliere d'obbedienza* in the Order of St. John of Jerusalem (the Knights of Malta), hence his sobriquet "Il Cavalier Calabrese." About 1642 Mattia and Gregorio Preti painted pendant frescoes on the interior facade of S. Carlo ai Catinari, Rome.

Undocumented journeys north of Rome during the mid-1640s were determinative for Preti's mature style. Preti's ponderous, yet energetic figures emulate Guercino and Lanfranco (this last was a recurrent inspiration for him). From Venice Preti drew a lifelong admiration for the dignity and splendid pomp of Paolo Veronese.

When his three great frescoes of the *Martyrdom of St. Andrew* (1650/51) behind the high altar of S. Andrea della Valle were compared unfavorably with Domenichino's frescoes overhead, Preti seems to have lost his taste for Rome. After a sojourn in Modena (ca. 1653–55), he was called in 1656 to Naples to paint ex-voto frescoes on the city gates. His ten canvases for the ceiling of S. Pietro a Maiella were a revelation to the young Luca Giordano and, subsequently, Francesco Solimena.

After a short visit to Malta in 1659 Preti took an active interest in his future in the Order of St. John. At the end of 1660 he left Naples for Rome, where, besides politicking, he painted an ebullient replacement to P. F. Mola's *Allegory of Air* in the Palazzo Pamphili, Valmontone (1661). With papal dispensation in hand, Preti's rank was raised to *cavaliere di grazia* in Malta in September of 1661. He immediately undertook the painted decorations of the vault and apse of the Conventual Church of St. John, Valletta (1661–66), which proved to be his masterpiece. For the remainder of his long life Preti lived on Malta, placing altarpieces in seemingly each of the island's myriad churches and dispatching as many canvases to patrons abroad, especially in Naples.

36 *Martyrdom of St. Catherine*

Oil on canvas. 101.6 × 75.1 cm. 1657–59.

Provenance: David M. Koetser, New York.

References: Manning, *Neapolitan Masters,* 1962, no. 21; Detroit Institute of Arts, 1965, no. 152, repr.; New York, Knoedler & Co., 1967, no. 21, repr.

Robert and Bertina Suida Manning, New York

St. Catherine of Alexandria was a third-century martyr renowned for her learning. When the wife of the tyrant Maximin II became one of her converts to Christianity, Catherine was sentenced to die on the sharp points of four revolving wheels. A miraculous fire from heaven exploded the wheels, however, and Catherine was finally martyred by beheading.

In this masterly sketch one senses the imperturbable serenity of the maiden even while the executioner swings his arm back to begin his lightning stroke of death. Preti's particular genius lay in the exposition of just such breathless drama and complex states of mind. The physicality of the figures makes the action seem immediate; the jagged, striking chiaroscuro is a metaphor for the psychological tension.

This bozzetto was preparatory to a painting in a series that was Preti's principal legacy to Naples. Between May 1657 and February 1659 Preti painted ten large canvases and supervised their installation in the Gothic church of S. Pietro a Maiella.[1] Set into the carved and gilt ceilings of the nave and transept were five scenes of the life of St. Peter Celestine and five of the life of St. Catherine of Alexandria. In each ceiling, the canvases followed the scheme of tondo, oblong, octagonal, oblong, and tondo. With characteristic enthusiasm Roberto Longhi termed this ensemble the Raphaelesque *stanze* of the seicento.[2]

The octagonal painting in the crossing above the high altar depicts the *Martyrdom of St. Catherine* (fig. 18), for which the Manning picture is the study. No other bozzetti nor any drawings are known for this commission. The artist altered his conception significantly between bozzetto and final version, and not merely with respect to the format. The sweeping sense of space, which is so marvelous in this small sketch, was abandoned in the ceiling picture. In the S. Pietro a Maiella cycle in general Preti eschewed High Baroque illusionism in favor of an emphasis on decorative pattern. By arranging brightly colored forms across the picture surface with a mind to their ornamental values, Preti was laying down the tenets of the Late Baroque style pursued by Luca Giordano. Perhaps the only grain of truth in De Dominici's thoroughly discredited account of this commission is the statement he ascribes to Giordano to the effect that the S. Pietro a Maiella paintings should serve as a "school for studious youth."[3]

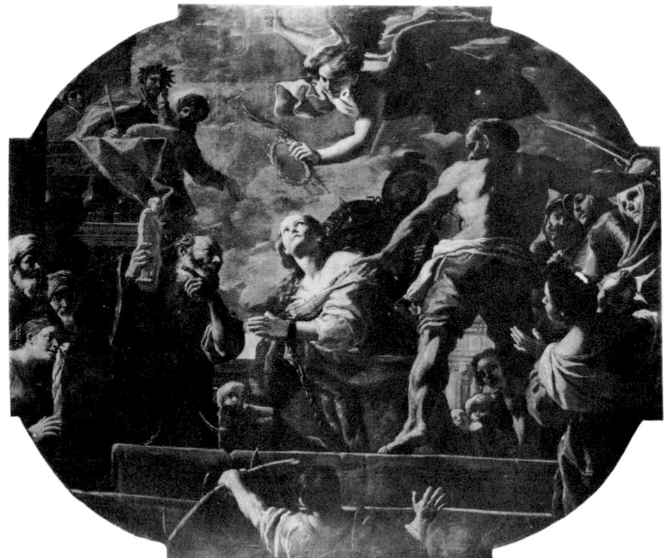

Fig. 18 Preti: *Martyrdom of St. Catherine,* oil on canvas. S. Pietro a Maiella, Naples.

During his visit to Malta in 1659 Preti ingratiated himself with the Italian knights by painting an altarpiece of the *Martyrdom of St. Catherine* for their national church, S. Caterina d'Italia.[4] Although he changed the pose of the executioner, in other respects the Maltese version evokes the bozzetto more than the ceiling canvas.

NOTES

1 See De Conciliis and Lattuada, 1979, pp. 294–301, for the full documentation and illustrations of the entire series.

2 Longhi, 1913, pp. 29–45.

3 De Dominici, 1742/43, III, p. 352.

4 Spike, "Mattia Preti's Passage to Malta," 1978, fig. 13.

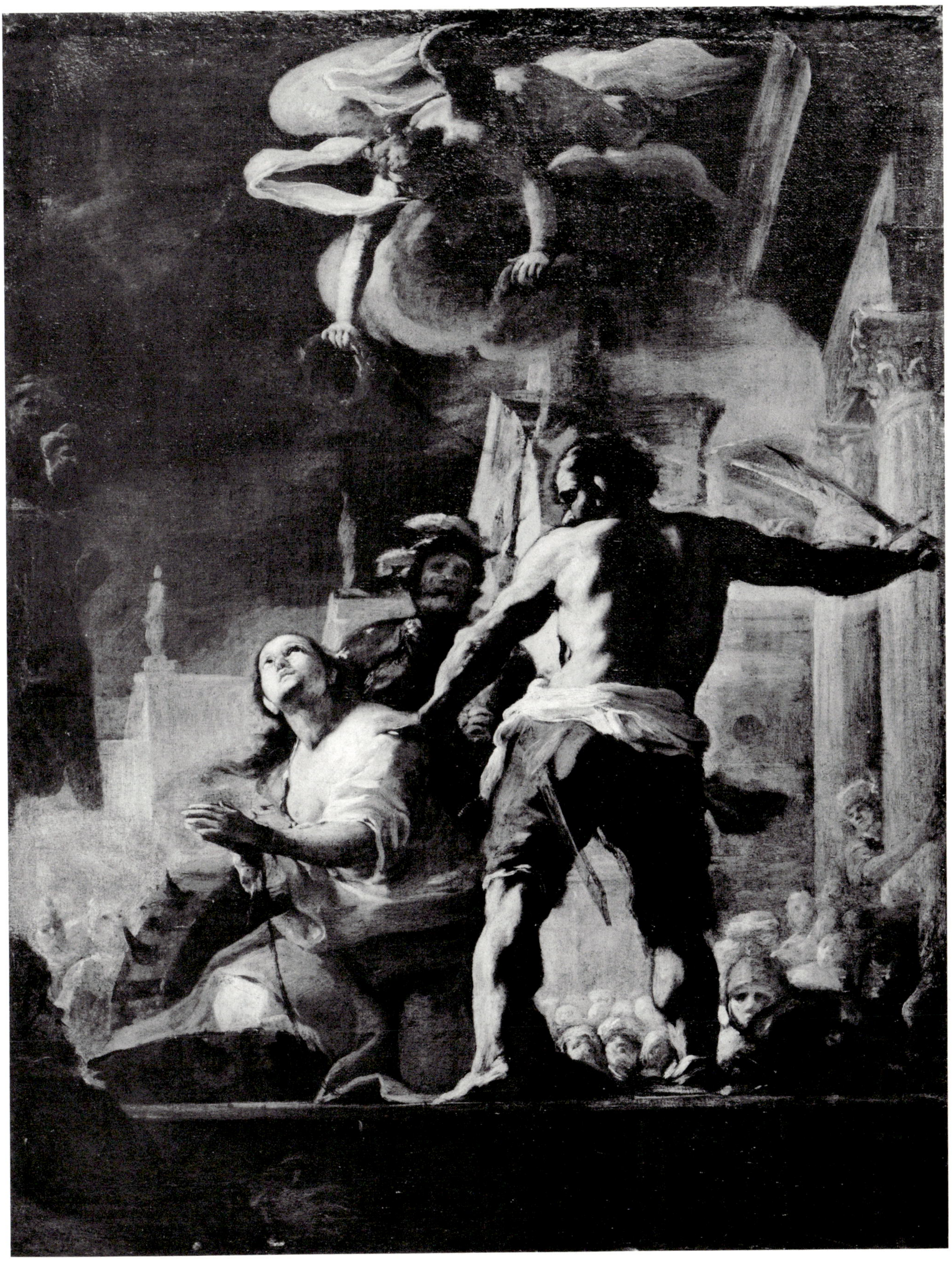

37 *Decollation of S. Gennaro*

Oil on canvas. 153.05 × 200 cm. Ca. 1685.

Provenance: Marchese Gagliano; Avvocato Angelo Cecconi, Florence.

References: Marangoni, 1921, pp. 368–70, repr. p. 367; Florence, Palazzo Pitti, 1922, no. 798; Ojetti, Dami, and Tarchiani, 1924, repr. p. 235; Frangipane, 1929, p. 81; Nugent, 1930, II, p. 88, repr. p. 89; Refice Taschetta, 1959, pp. 65–66, fig. 44; Longhi, 1961, p. 508.

Private collection, New York

S. Gennaro (St. Januarius), a third-century bishop of Benevento, was martyred in the persecution of Diocletian. After being thrown to the wild beasts in the amphitheater at Pozzuoli, who refused to touch him, he was beheaded. A woman named Eusebia collected his blood in a vial, which is kept in the cathedral of Naples. The blood liquifies miraculously eighteen times during the year.

A Neapolitan patron could be deduced for Preti's *Decollation of S. Gennaro* from the *terribilità* of the interpretation even if the subject were not one of that city's patron saints.[1] Before Preti's arrival in Naples, the Spaniard Jusepe de Ribera had cultivated the local taste for explicit depictions of the agony and pathos of martyrdom. Although such themes were rare in Preti's career prior to 1656, Ribera's success was not lost on him. Preti was called on so often for his dramatic paintings of martyrdoms (of St. Bartholomew especially, who was flayed alive) that to this day his reputation rests chiefly on them.

This *Decollation of S. Gennaro* was last exhibited publicly in the landmark sei-settecento show at the Palazzo Pitti in 1922, where it made a powerful impression.[2] Until recent documentary discoveries,[3] the chronology of Preti's paintings presented insoluble problems; earlier commentators on this painting assumed reasonably enough that it dated from Preti's Neapolitan years, 1656–60.[4] There was once a prevalent tendency to date every important work by this great artist to that brief epoch.

However, a dating to the middle of the 1680s is indicated for this *S. Gennaro* on the basis of comparison with Preti's Passion cycle on the ceiling of the oratory of the Decollation, St. John's, Valletta (1683),[5] and his *St. Sebastian* sent to S. Domenico, Taverna, in 1687. A masterpiece, and not of the artist's most famous period, the New York painting must be considered a persuasive argument for the re-evaluation of his under-appreciated years in Malta. In his late style the master reduced his art to its essentials. The imposing figures are daringly modeled in only the broadest aspects, while the palette is restricted to a few expressive tones. The startling interjection of two arresting passages of lilac (Eusebia's dress) and gold (the bishop's cope) invokes an aura of poignancy and mystery to this day of doom.

NOTES

1 In fact De Dominici, 1742/43, III, p. 347, describes a similar *Decollation of S. Gennaro* by Preti as in the house of the Marchese di Genzano in Naples. See also note 2, below.

2 The notable exception was the young Roberto Longhi, who in 1922 jotted in his catalogue the opinion that the picture is a copy (Longhi, 1961, p. 508). As it happens, a copy of this painting was on the Roman art market in 1979, reputedly with a Neapolitan provenance.

3 For documents concerning Preti's Neapolitan chronology, see Spike, "Mattia Preti's Passage to Malta," 1978, pp. 497–507, and De Conciliis and Lattuada, 1979, pp. 294–301. Documents on Preti's Maltese chronology may be found in Spike, 1979, p. 10, as well as in appendix II in this author's dissertation (1979), on deposit in Widener Library, Harvard University.

4 Refice Taschetta, 1959, pp. 65–66, was the most recent.

5 Spike, "The Church of St. John," 1978, p. 627, fig. 110.

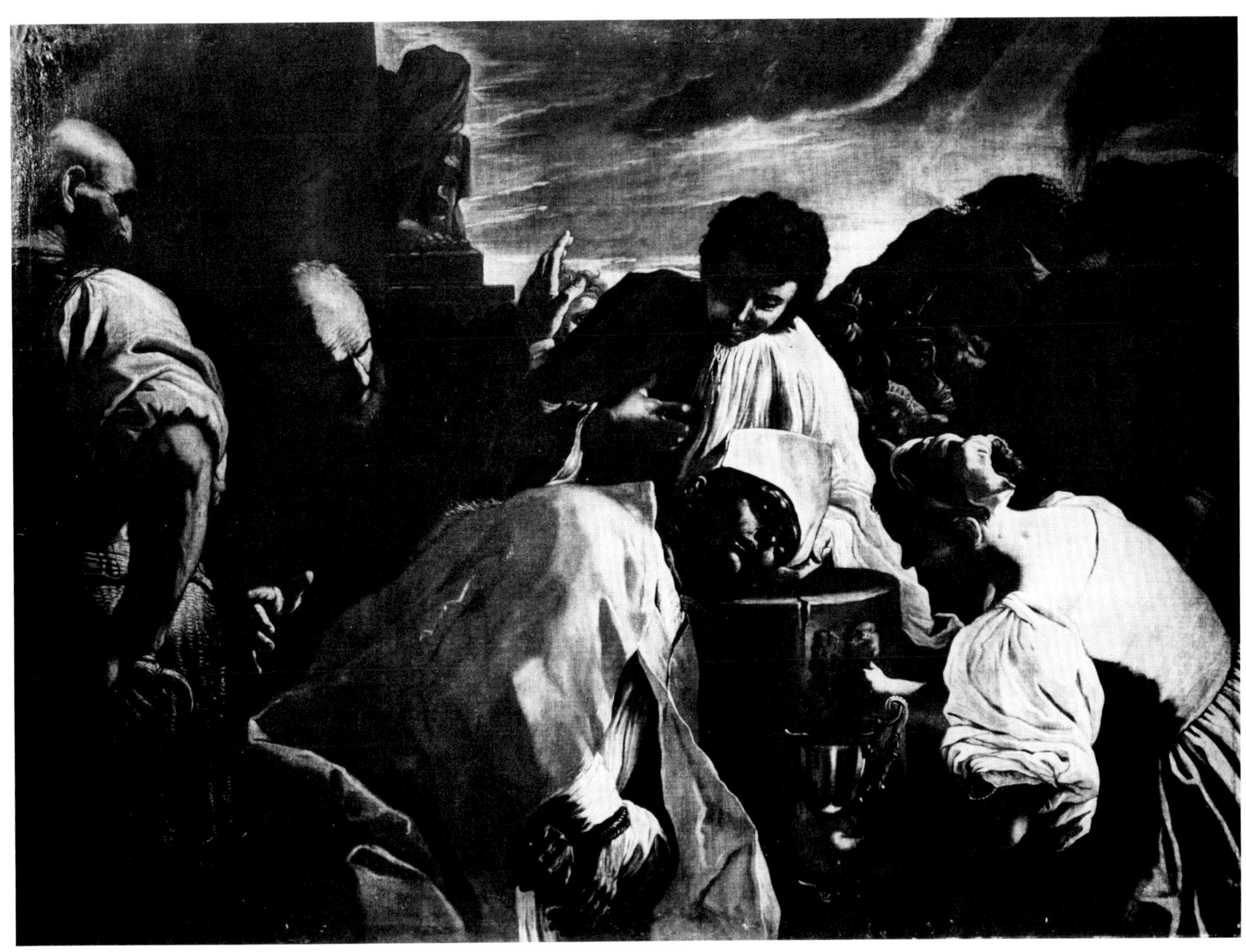

Sebastiano Ricci

Belluno 1659–1734 Venice

Sebastiano Ricci deserves to be considered the founder of the triumphant Venetian school of painting in the eighteenth century. His virtuoso talent enabled him to absorb an extraordinary range of influences, most especially the decorative pyrotechnics of Luca Giordano and the sublime grandeur of Paolo Veronese (which Ricci made into something quite different).

After studies in Venice with Francesco Cervelli and probably Mazzoni, Ricci removed himself to Bologna to take in some refinement in the school of G. G. dal Sole. During extensive activity for the Farnese in Parma and Piacenza (1685–88), Ricci thoroughly investigated the art of Correggio. Duke Ranuccio II Farnese supported Ricci's studies in Rome from 1691 until 1697, when Ricci went to Milan. His frescoes in the dome of S. Bernardino, Milan (1695–98), reflect his study of Correggio and Cortona. In Venice for the ensuing twelve years, save for sojourns in Vienna (1701–3), Bergamo (1704), and Florence (1706/7), Ricci achieved full maturity as evinced in the luminous, excited frescoes in the Palazzo Marciale, Florence. With lightning brushwork, he set out to enliven his neo-cinquecentesque prototypes. In London (1712–16) and Paris (1716) during the second decade, Ricci was highly appreciated by such connoisseurs as the Earl of Burlington. His scintillating canvases after his final return to Venice belong fully to the Rococo, and were formative influences on Giovanni Battista Tiepolo.

38 *Flora*

Oil on canvas. 125.7 × 152.4 cm. Ca. 1712–16.

References: Manning, 1961, no. 37, repr.; Milkovich, 1965/66, no. 5, repr.; Daniels, *Sebastiano Ricci,* 1976, no. 274, repr.; Daniels, *L'opera completa di Sebastiano Ricci,* 1976, no. 306, repr.

Robert and Bertina Suida Manning, New York

Ovid (*Fasti* 5.200–206) informs us that the nymph Chloris was seduced by Zephyrus, the West Wind, who thereafter married her and named her Flora, goddess of flowers and spring. Flora was among the most ancient of Roman deities; in time the celebrations of her feast became notorious for their indecency. Flora's association with the voluptuous character of Venus gave rise to the legend that Flora had been a courtesan who had left her fortune to the Roman people.

In typically lush fashion Sebastiano Ricci has painted an episode of Flora and Zephyrus without especial concern for narrative content. It is hard to interpret Zephyrus's gesture as he appears while Flora is arranging some flowers. At one point in this picture's history his figure was painted out.[1] The scattered placement of diverting figures across the picture surface is characteristic of Late Baroque style, which places a premium on decorative values.

A date in the early eighteenth century is clearly in order: during the first decade, according to Michael Milkovich, but in Ricci's English sojourn, 1712–16, in the opinion of Jeffrey Daniels. The many similarities to the artist's canvases for Burlington House, Royal Academy,[2] as well as the evocation of classical sculpture in Flora's pose make the inclusion of this *Flora* amongst Ricci's English activity most likely. The flowers do not appear to be the work of a specialist-collaborator, as Daniels has suggested.[3]

NOTES

1 The figure of Zephyrus re-emerged after cleaning by the present owner, who reports that the painting bore an attribution to Fragonard before it was acquired by him.

2 See Daniels, *Sebastiano Ricci,* 1976, figs. 165–68.

3 Ibid., no. 274.

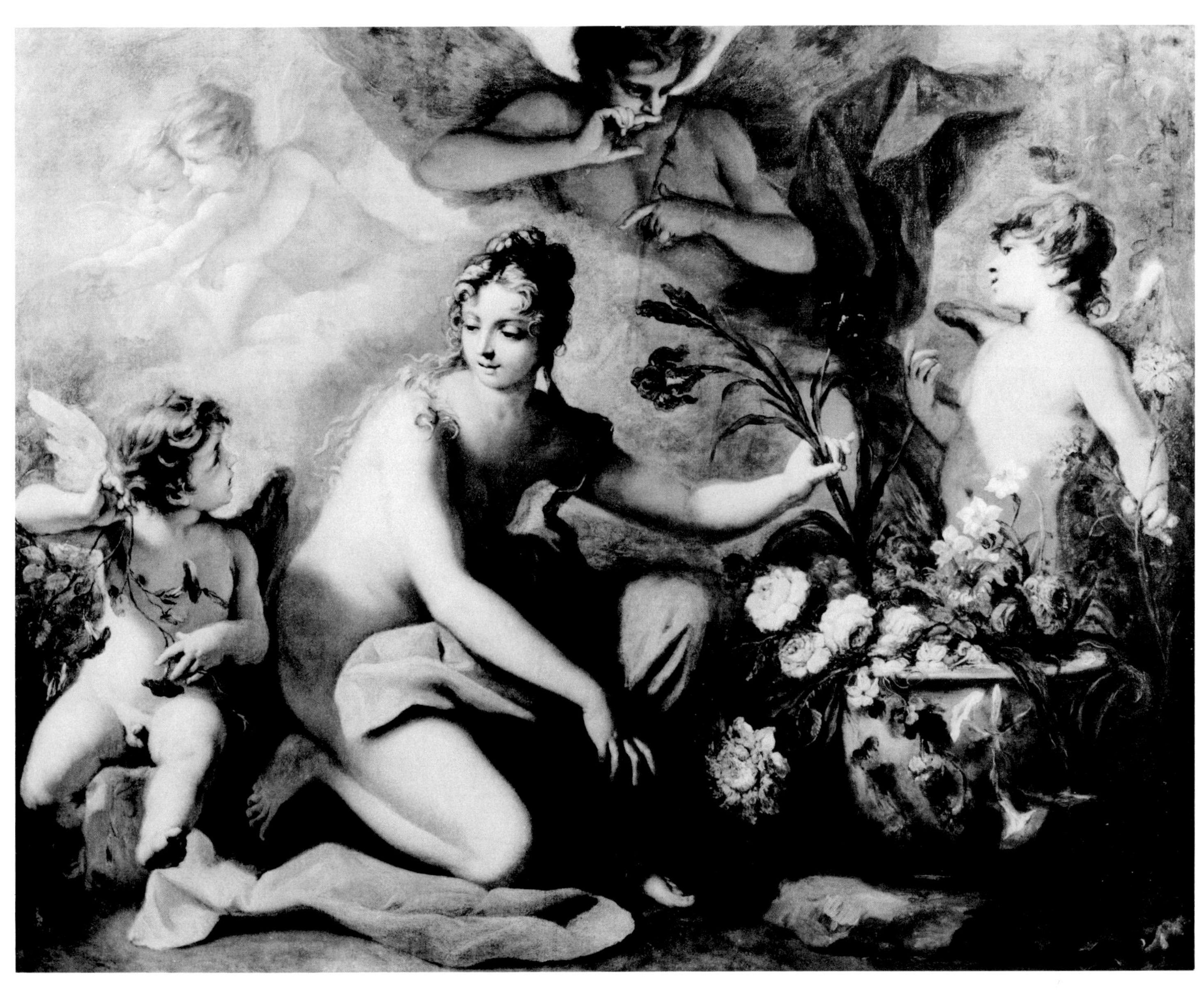

Giovan Francesco Romanelli

Viterbo ca. 1610–1662 Viterbo

A native of Viterbo, G. F. Romanelli was active in the Roman studio of Pietro da Cortona by 1631. Passeri reports that Romanelli studied with Domenichino before the latter's departure for Naples in 1631. However, Romanelli's earliest-known work, an *Adoration of the Shepherds* fresco in the Palazzo Barberini of 1631/32 (first attributed by Briganti), is wholly in the manner of Cortona, under whose auspices he was working. Romanelli's hand in this fresco can be differentiated from Cortona's only by his characteristically sweet expression and his already distinctive typology of sharply linear facial features.

Within a few years, Romanelli's relations with Cortona broke irrevocably: it seems that while Cortona was in Florence, Romanelli and a fellow pupil attempted to supplant their master in the commission for the vault of the salone Barberini. By that time the young artist had already won the patronage of Cardinal Francesco Barberini, nephew of Pope Urban VIII; indeed, on 30 May 1638 Romanelli was elected to a term as Principe of the Accademia di San Luca in Rome.

Prestigious commissions followed in unbroken sequence. Between 1637 and 1642, Romanelli executed frescoes in the Sala della Contessa Matilda in the Vatican Palace. These frescoes evince an impressive development in the artist's style away from strict dependence on Cortona; the narratives unfold at a measured pace across a stagelike space reminiscent of Domenichino and Raphael before him. Romanelli has struck a highly original accommodation of Cortona's vivacity with the classical balance of the Carraccesque tradition in Rome, of which Andrea Sacchi, another Barberini favorite, was the most influential heir of Romanelli's generation.

Upon the death of Urban VIII, Francesco Barberini withdrew to Paris, whence Romanelli was called in 1646 to paint fresco decorations in the palace of Cardinal Mazarin. Following his return to Rome in 1647, Romanelli again did not want for commissions. His frescoes in the Palazzo Lante date from 1653. Louis XIV called him once more to Paris in 1655 for frescoes in the Louvre. In 1657 Romanelli returned to Viterbo. Before his death in 1662, he painted several altarpieces for the Duomo and other churches in his native city.

Although Romanelli left no direct followers other than his short-lived son, Urbano (1650–82), his works exerted considerable influence on younger Roman painters, especially Carlo Maratti and his circle. His paintings in France were admired by the local painters of the next century.

39 *St. Thomas of Villanova Giving Alms*

Oil on canvas. 66.05 × 48.9 cm. Ca. 1660.

Provenance: Possibly Cardinal Carlo Barberini, Rome, 1663;[1] Cardinal Antonio Barberini, Rome, 1671;[2] Cardinal Carlo Barberini, Rome, 1692;[3] Hazlitt Gallery, London, 1962.

References: London, Hazlitt Gallery, 1962, no. 21, pl. 10a; Detroit Institute of Arts, 1965, no. 36, p. 52 repr.; Lavin, 1975, p. 515.

Private collection, New York

Born into a pious family, St. Thomas of Villanova (1488–1555) joined the Augustinians in 1516 and took his vows the following year. He was preacher to the court of Charles V, and in 1544 he was raised to the archbishopric of Valencia. His unceasing generosity to the poor of his see earned him the epithet "Thomas the Almoner." Saint Thomas was canonized by Pope Alexander VII on 1 November 1658.

The date of the saint's canonization points to the likely moment for Romanelli's altarpiece of *St. Thomas of Villanova Giving Alms* in S. Agostino, Rome, for which the present canvas is a sketch in oils, or bozzetto. (According to Jacob Hess, the altarpiece now in place is an excellent old copy, and Romanelli's original painting is preserved in poor condition in the convent of S. Agostino.[4]) A dating subsequent to the artist's second return from Paris is confirmed by the earliest reference to this altarpiece: in the Roman guidebook compiled between 1660 and 1663 by Fioravante Martinelli, the painting is remarked as newly installed.[5]

The tempered emotion of Romanelli's late works is quite unlike Cortona's unrelenting exuberance. The symmetrical composition revolves slowly about the central actor, St. Thomas—a pictorial idea derived from Sacchi.[6]

A number of variations between this bozzetto and the altarpiece may be noted. Romanelli reversed the architectural backdrop so that the saint's miter should

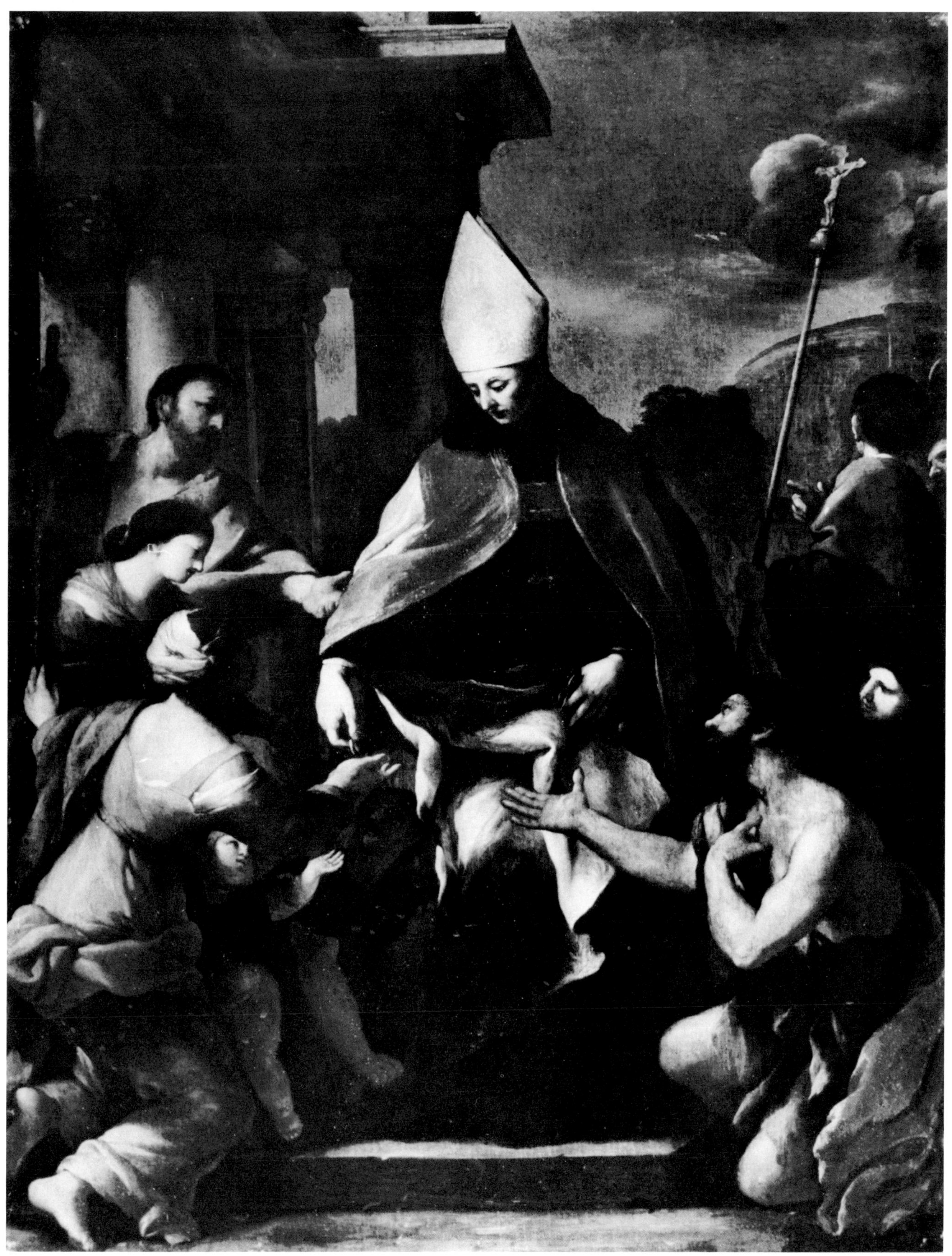

stand out against the open sky, and to strengthen the diagonal axis that directs our attention upon St. Thomas. In addition, the group of women at left has been completely redrawn. The bristling movement amongst the almsmen in the bozzetto gives way in the final version in favor of especial prominence for the mother and child and the man kneeling in the foreground, who take on enhanced roles as archetypal recipients of St. Thomas's charity.

NOTES

1 Lavin, 1975, p. 515, suggests that this bozzetto may be identified with an inventory reference (VI.inv.63.21) to an unattributed painting of this subject, listed without dimensions, which was amongst the contents of Cardinal Carlo Barberini's Casino alle Bastione, Rome, in 1663.

2 Ibid.; this bozzetto is clearly the picture of the same subject by Romanelli (3 × 2 palmi in size) that was in the inventory (IV.inv.71.355) taken after the death of Cardinal Antonio Barberini.

3 Ibid.; the bozzetto appears among the possessions in the legacy of Cardinal Carlo Barberini (VI.inv.92-04.19).

4 See Waterhouse, 1976, p. 109. The sacristy altarpiece is illustrated as an original work by Voss, 1924, p. 269, who also assigns the commission to the master's late years (p. 549).

5 Martinelli, "Roma ornata dall' Architettura, Pittura e Scoltura," in D'Onofrio, 1969, p. 11: "Il quadro ad olio di S. Tomaso da Villanova della cappella nuova e del Romanelli."

Romanelli's altarpiece in S. Agostino escaped the attention of G. B. Mola in his guide to Rome (1660, rev. 1663, published for the first time in 1966), which omission further attests to its late date.

6 See, for example, Sacchi's *St. Anthony of Padua Reviving a Dead Man* of 1632/33 in S. Maria della Concezione, Rome, which, however, is less severely centralized in arrangement; repr. in Sutherland Harris, 1977, fig. 61.

Salvator Rosa

Arenella (Naples) 1615–1673 Rome

With Claude Lorrain and Gaspard Dughet, Salvator Rosa completes the triumvirate of landscape painters in Baroque Italy. Rosa's subjects are the wild reaches of unrestrained nature, where hermits, philosophers, and other fugitives from civilization take precarious shelter. His proto-Romantic conceptions of nature, necromancy, and artistic genius (these last influenced by G. B. Castiglione) struck sympathetic chords in later centuries, even while appreciation in general for the Baroque declined. The nineteenth century saw in Rosa's life and art the stuff of legend, as if his paintings and etchings of *banditti* were somehow autobiographical.

In Naples Rosa was trained in the circle of Ribera (his brother-in-law was Francesco Fracanzano) and he practiced his lifelong propensity to improvise rapid sketches in oil from nature. His early drawing style bears out De Dominici's assertion of studies alongside Micco Spadaro in the workshop of Aniello Falcone. Rosa won early recognition for his emulations of Falcone's "battlepieces without heroes" (i.e., amongst unidentified combatants).

In 1635 Rosa abandoned Naples (returning only once, in 1637) for the greater challenges of Rome. The Neapolitan Cardinal Ferdinando Brancaccio obtained commissions for him in Viterbo, including an *Incredulity of St. Thomas* (1638/39), which he based on a Caravaggesque altarpiece by P. P. Bonzi.

The landscapes and genre paintings of Rosa's first decade of activity bore witness to the currency in Rome of the northern traditions of such artists as Paul Bril and Pieter van Laer, called Bamboccio. For Claude, Rosa observed how atmosphere may be painted to seem charged with light. The artist's efforts at self-promotion through satiric wit liberally dispersed only brought him the enmity of Bernini, the undisputed czar of artistic policy under the Barberini papacy.

Prudently, Rosa accepted a Medici invitation to relocate in Florence, where he stayed from 1640 to 1649. By this time he had renounced the *Bamboccianti* and dedicated himself to themes derived from classical history and stoic philosophy. His first satires in verse were acclaimed. A literary academy devoted to erudite discussion, theatricals, and banqueting convened at his house. In Florence too Rosa met his life's companion and frequent model, Lucrezia.

When Rosa ventured again to Rome, his artistic and literary prowess sufficed to withstand the criticism of his numerous enemies. Not a little resentment stemmed from his highhanded dealings with clients. He resisted suggestions as to subject matter, and in the last decade of his career he all but ceased painting his prized landscapes in favor of highly dramatic, sometimes jejune figural compositions. Rosa and Lucrezia took marriage vows ten days before his death.

40 *Angel Departing the House of Tobit*

Oil on paper. 135 × 96 cm. Ca. 1662.

Provenance: M. Sestieri, Rome.

References: Salerno, 1963, p. 140, no. 72, repr.; Edinburgh Festival Society, 1972, no. 99, repr.; Salerno, 1975, no. 207, repr.; Mahoney, 1977, p. 578.

Private collection, New York

The Book of Tobit (see no. 26) relates the eventful journey taken by Tobias and his companion, the angel Raphael (in human guise). Upon his return to the house of his parents, Tobias was able to cure his father Tobit's blindness with the gall of a fish that Raphael had directed him to catch. In this large painting on paper Rosa has depicted Raphael's dramatic revelation of his true nature and his re-ascent into heaven. The central figure, Tobit, stares fixedly with his regained sight.

This *Angel Departing the House of Tobit* was the final stage, or modello, in the preparation of one of five chapel paintings executed by Rosa about 1662 (fig. 19).[1] The artist was anxious to have his works on public view in a Roman church, and in 1659 he first mentioned his idea for a cycle of paintings on biblical themes of divine deliverance or resurrection.[2] The plan was postponed for lack of funds until 1662 when, according to Baldinucci, Rosa completed the series for his friend Carlo de' Rossi.[3] De' Rossi did not install them in his chapel in Santa Maria in Montesanto, Rome, until 1677, after Rosa's death.[4] All five of the paintings were removed in 1802 and eventually found their way to the Musée Condé, Chantilly.[5]

The existence of numerous preparatory drawings,[6] not to mention this elaborate modello itself, testifies to Rosa's abiding concern for this project. These paintings inaugurated the final phase of his career, in which full-length figures displaced the landscape backgrounds. Michael Mahoney has deduced from his researches into Rosa's drawings that the artist initially intended to paint the *Angel Leaving Menoah and His Wife* before turning to this episode from Tobit.[7]

NOTES

1 The *Angel Departing the House of Tobit* was paired with a *Raising of Lazarus; Jeremiah Freed from the Pit* with *Daniel in the Lion's Den*. The altarpiece was the *Resurrection of Christ* (see note 5, below). In a letter transcribed by Rinaldis, 1939, letter 110 bis, Rosa notes that the *Jeremiah* was exhibited in August 1662.

2 Ibid., letter 73.

3 Baldinucci, 1847, V, p. 465.

4 See Salerno, 1975, no. 173, and M. Mahoney, "Salvator Rosa: Drawings" in Kitson, 1973, no. 72.

5 Mahoney, 1977, p. 578 n. 5. Mahoney (in Kitson, 1973, no. 72), believes that the Chantilly *Resurrection of Christ*, painted on panel, is a copy after Rosa; Salerno, 1963, no. 100b, writes that the painting is an autograph canvas.

6 See Mahoney, 1977, esp. nos. 66.18–33.

7 Ibid., nos. 66.17–19, repr.

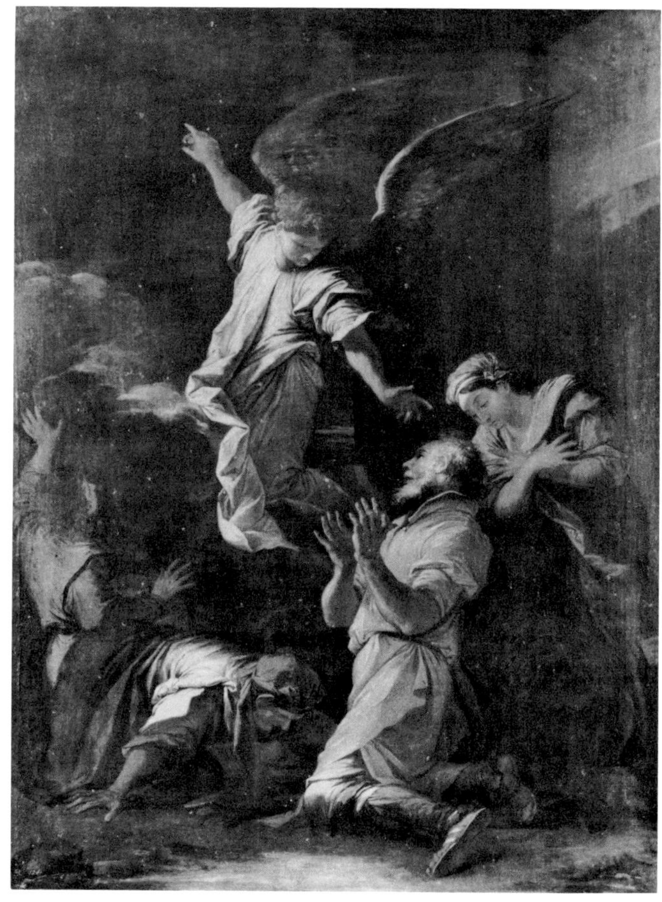

Fig. 19 Rosa: *Angel Departing the House of Tobit*, oil on canvas, 135 × 100 cm., ca. 1662. Musée Condé, Chantilly

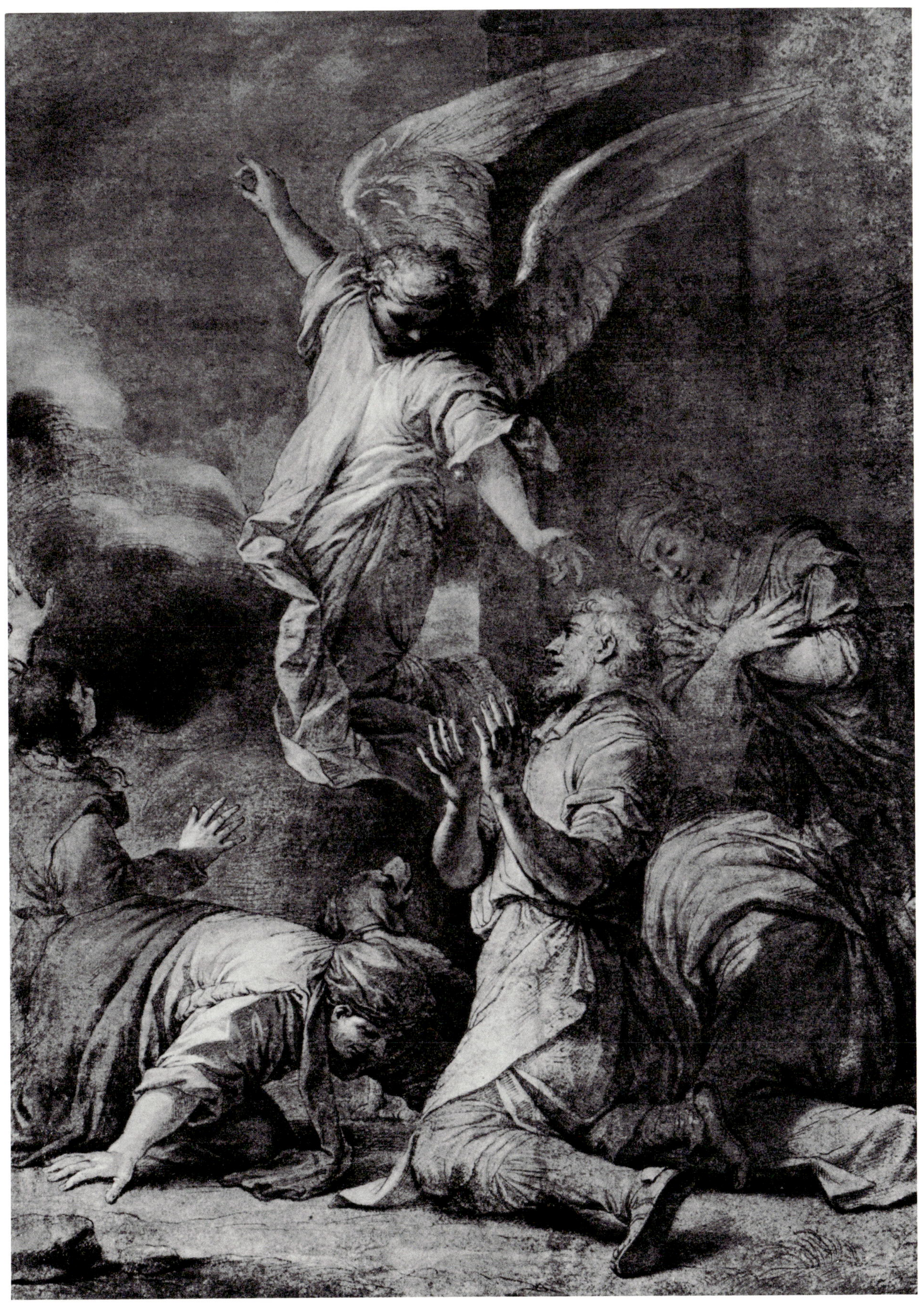

41 *Christ Tempted by Satan*

Oil on canvas. 46 × 36 cm. Ca. 1665–70.

Provenance: Earl of Jersey, Osterley Park;[1] Sir William McLaren, St. John's College; Heim Gallery, London; Viancini, Venice, from whom purchased in 1968.

References: London, Heim Gallery, 1967, no. 6, repr.; Salerno, 1975, no. 225 (as *Two Philosophers in Discussion*), repr.

Private collection, New York

During Christ's retreat into the wilderness for forty days of fasting and meditation, Satan appeared to him in the guise of a hermit, saying "if thou be the son of God, command that these stones be made bread." But Christ "answered and said, It is written, Man shall not live by bread alone, but by every word that proceedeth out of the mouth of God" (Matthew 4:3–4).

Among the most appealing of Rosa's late works are his figure paintings on a small scale, which resemble sketches for their quick, firm strokes. Luigi Salerno convincingly associates this *Christ Tempted by Satan* with paintings datable to the latter 1660s, not long in fact after his *Pindar and Pan* of ca. 1666 (see no. 42).[2] Similarly emphasized hands and brows are present in two pendants (each 65 × 49 cm.) at Chatsworth of *Jacob Wrestling with the Angel* and *David and Goliath*.[3] These unpretentious pictures fairly pulse with activity, while the artist's preoccupation with gesture often leads to histrionics in his major compositions of these years.

Salerno's misreading (on the basis of a photograph) of the subject as two disputative philosophers was induced by the singularity of Rosa's interpretation.[4] Christ's usual attitude in this episode is one of rejection: Rosa has taken to heart the didactic quality of the text and represented Christ in the act of explication.

NOTES

1 The picture was not included in the London sales from the collection of the Earl of Jersey in 1930 and 1949. In a letter of 26 September 1953 in the files of the Frick Art Reference Library, New York, the Earl of Jersey notes that the painting was probably sold either in 1946/47, when he left Osterley Park to live in Jersey, or in 1934, when he had a sale of pictures and furniture at Middleton Park, Middlesex.

2 Salerno, 1975, no. 225.

3 Ibid., nos. 228 and 229, repr.

4 Ibid., no. 225.

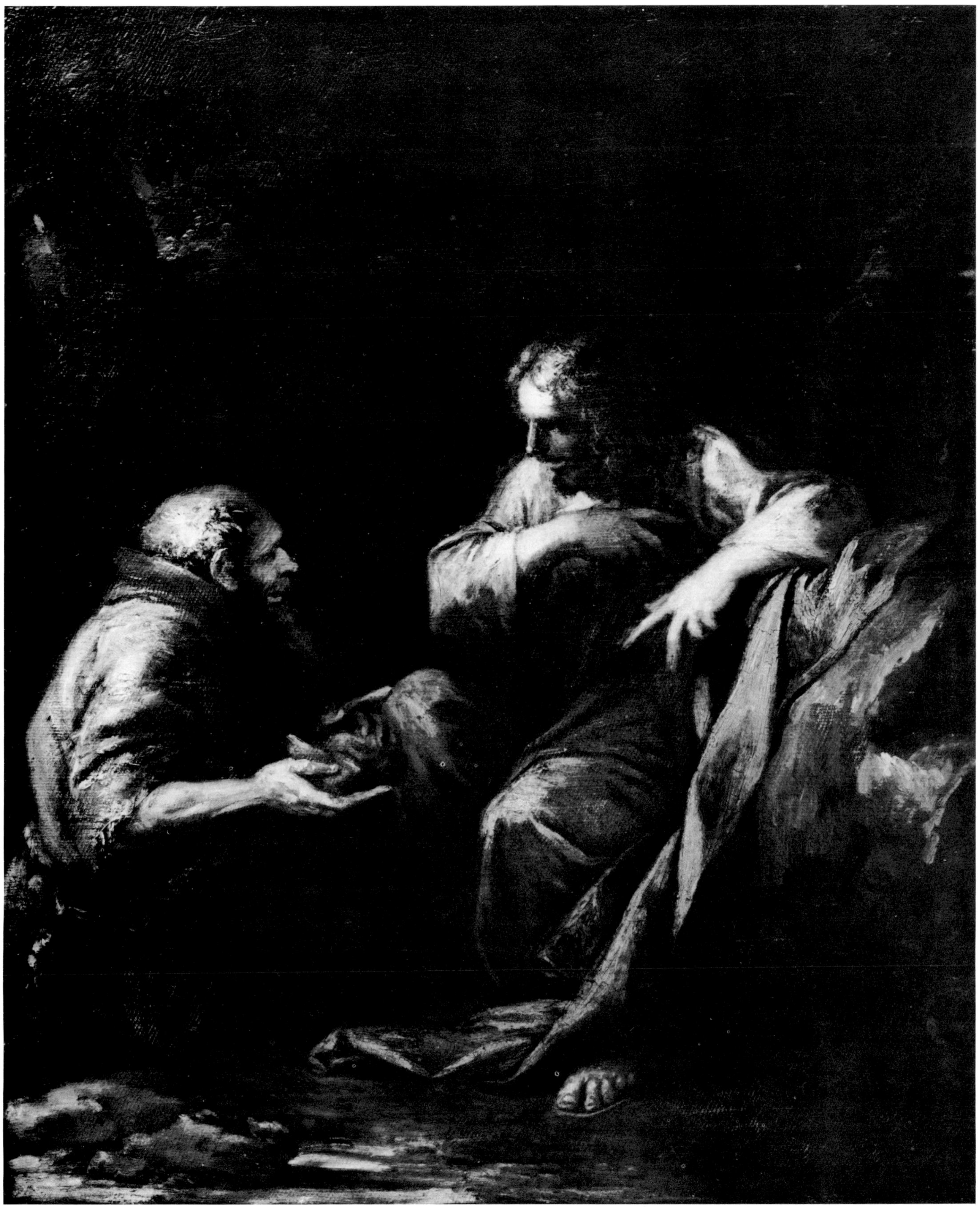

42 *Pindar and Pan*

Oil on canvas. 97.8 × 75.9 cm. Ca. 1666.

Provenance: J. R. Bell, Sussex; Brian Koetser Gallery, London.

References: Nicolson, 1966, p. 211, fig. 55; exh. cat., Brian Koetser Gallery, London, spring 1966, no. 26; New York, Knoedler & Co., 1967, no. 10, repr.; Salerno, 1970, p. 62, fig. 46; H. Langdon, "Salvator Rosa: Paintings," in Kitson, 1973, p. 35; Salerno, 1975, no. 207, repr.; Mahoney, 1977, pp. 668–69, fig. 78.14A; Wallace, 1979, p. 104 n. 24.

Private collection, New York

Rosa's absorption in classical learning led him to mine his favorite authors for new themes, seemingly unconcerned as to their pictorial potentialities. It is a measure of his genius that Rosa was able to translate literary allusions into compelling images as often he did. Plutarch's reference to the love of Pan (god of the Arcadian flocks) for the poetry of Pindar must have implied to Rosa that artistic inspiration bespeaks a heightened state of spirituality.[1]

This bozzetto, rare in Rosa's oeuvre, depicts god and poet in animated dialogue. Rosa sent a large painting of *Pindar and Pan*[2] along with two other erudite subjects to an exhibition on 29 August 1666 in the Roman church of S. Giovanni Decollato.[3] The sketch most likely was executed shortly before that event, although Rosa substantially modified his conception of Pindar in the final version.

In October 1666 Rosa wrote to his friend Giovan Battista Ricciardi that the three new works were the best that he had painted up to that time.[4] However, as Carla Lord and Mary Lea Gibson observed upon the exhibition of the New York bozzetto in 1967, the excitement that Rosa had instilled into this intellectual discourse was dissipated in the final canvas wherein Pindar's expression has become introspective and his gestures more restrained.[5]

Michael Mahoney has associated six drawings in Leipzig with this composition.[6] Two of these drawings test various possibilities for the postures finally settled on in this bozzetto.[7]

NOTES

1 From Plutarch's *Life of Numa* according to Rosa himself in a letter to G. B. Ricciardi transcribed by Limentani, 1950, no. XL. Rosa notes with pride that he is the first painter to select the theme.

2 Now in Ariccia (near Rome), Chigi collection; see Salerno, 1963, no. 87, repr.

3 Limentani, 1950, no. XXXIX.

4 Ibid., no. XL.

5 New York, Knoedler & Co., 1967, p. 15.

6 Mahoney, 1977, nos. 78.13–18. The identifications of drawings nos. 78.16–18 are problematic.

7 Ibid., nos. 78.13–14.

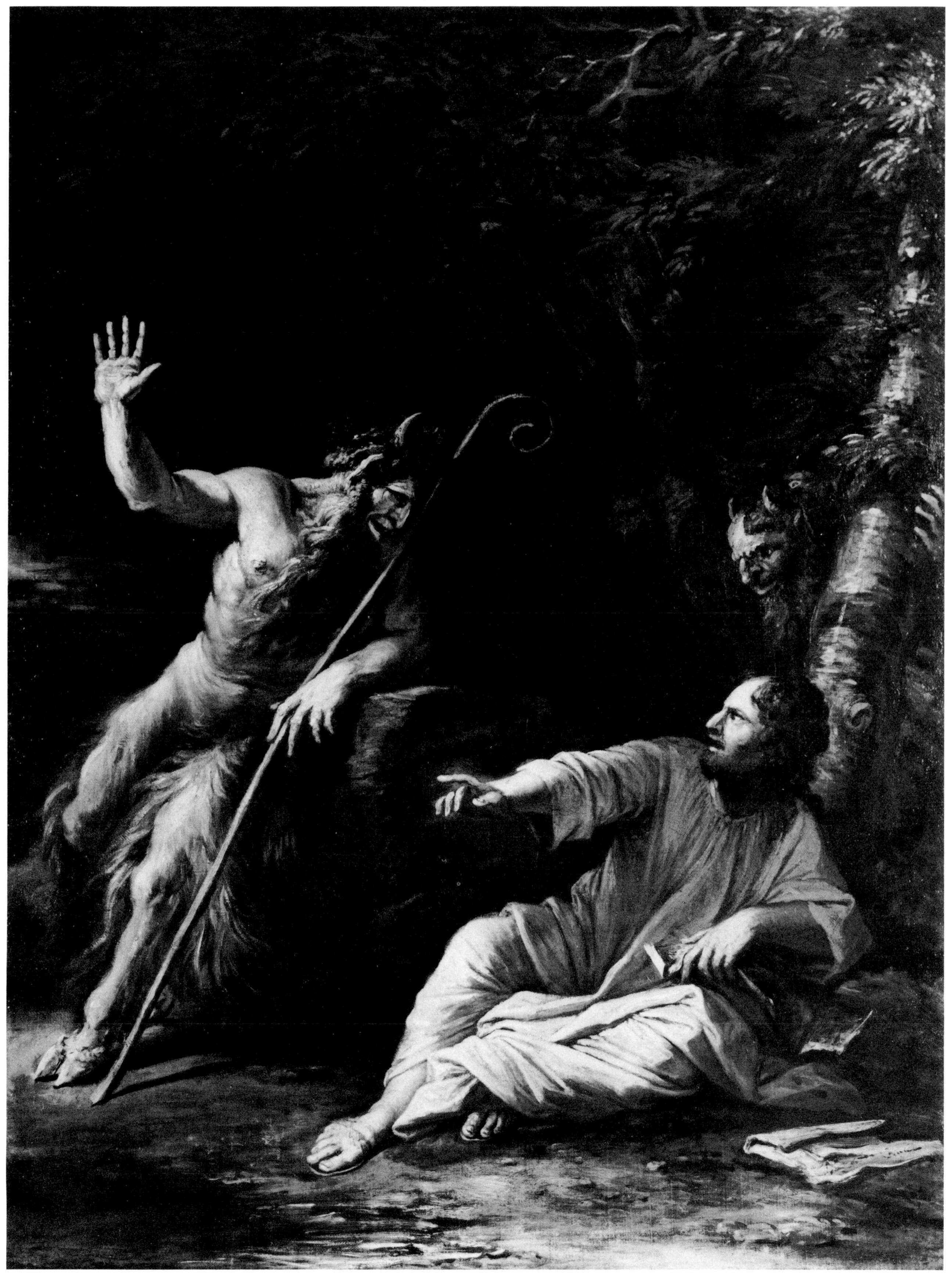

Carlo Saraceni

Venice ca. 1580–1620 Venice

After initial training in his native Venice, Carlo Saraceni, often called Carlo Veneziano, traveled to Rome about the turn of the century. He entered the atelier of Camillo Mariani, a Vicentine sculptor and painter, but Baglione reports that he soon abandoned these studies to become a follower of Caravaggio. Saraceni's earliest paintings owe much to such sixteenth-century Venetian and Ferrarese masters as Palma Giovane, the Bassani, Dosso, and Scarsellino. The lush landscapes of Adam Elsheimer, a leading figure in the reaction against Mannerist contrivance, also left a lasting impression, including a predilection for small cabinet pictures. In Saraceni's first dated painting, the *Rest on the Flight* of 1606 in the Camaldolese Church at Frascati, Venetian luminism remains preeminent, but the ample, naturalistic figures are clearly inspired by Caravaggio. As his mature manner evolved, Saraceni drew ideas as well from Gentileschi and Borgianni, two other Caravaggists who were concerned with expressive color.

In September 1606 Baglione described Saraceni and Borgianni as the leading adherents to Caravaggio's manner. Saraceni was already a member of the Accademia di San Luca by that date. At Agostino Tassi's trial in 1612 for the alleged rape of Artemisia Gentileschi, Saraceni testified that he had known the father, Orazio, for eight or ten years. (In 1618 Saraceni asserted that he had been a painter in Rome for twenty years.) During the second decade of the century, Saraceni painted altarpieces in the prominent churches of Sant'Adriano al Foro, S. Lorenzo in Lucina, and Santa Maria dell'Anima. Duke Ferdinando Gonzaga invited the artist to go to Mantua; as it happens, Domenico Fetti filled this post, although Saraceni continued to receive Gonzaga commissions. In collaboration with Tassi and Lanfranco, Saraceni executed decorative frescoes in 1616/17 in the Sala Regia of the Palazzo del Quirinale.

By November 1619 Saraceni had returned to Venice for a commission in the Palazzo Ducale. He contracted typhus and died on 16 June of the next year. The unfinished canvases were completed by an assistant, Jean LeClerc.

Saraceni's infusion of Venetian colorism into Caravaggism attracted many followers in the Roman school in general. His influence extended even to Dutch painting through the agency of Terbrugghen and other northern visitors to Rome.

43 *Martyrdom of St. Cecilia*

Oil on canvas. 132.1 × 100.3 cm. Ca. 1600.

Robert and Bertina Suida Manning, New York

St. Cecilia was a Christian martyr in third-century Rome. Having survived her sentence of death by suffocation, Cecilia was condemned to be beheaded. Three blows by the executioner failed to accomplish their purpose, and by Roman law she could not be punished further. She lived three days, making many converts. With St. Agnes, St. Cecilia was the most popular of Roman saints; since the fifteenth century she has been honored as the patron saint of music, especially sacred.

Saraceni has identified St. Cecilia by the attribute of a violin. The cult of the saint received an important stimulus in 1599, when during renovations in S. Cecilia in Trastevere, her remains were exhumed and her body was found intact and semi-decapitated.

The attribution of this *Martyrdom of St. Cecilia* to Carlo Saraceni, first proposed by Robert L. Manning, is demonstrable by comparison with the artist's early paintings, including his *Rest on the Flight* (Camaldolese Church, Frascati) dated 1606.[1] St. Cecilia's sloping profile is identical to the Madonna's in the Frascati altarpiece; in other respects the present picture is less accomplished than the altarpiece and may safely be considered earlier. The elongated figures stiffly posed in profile or frontally, as well as the pencil-thin drapery folds are typical of those paintings generally recognized as Saraceni's juvenilia, among them a *Venus and Mars* in London (fig. 20) and a *St. Sebastian* in the Castle of Prague.[2]

The *terminus post quem* for the dating of this canvas must be the artist's arrival in Rome since Caravaggesque devices are predominant. Indeed, this *Martyrdom* represents a discovery of the highest importance for our knowledge of Saraceni's artistic formation. It confirms the remark by the contemporary Baglione that Saraceni was among the very first to follow Caravaggio (as was Baglione himself). In the absense of such overtly Caravaggesque exercises as this *Martyrdom of St. Cecilia,* modern scholars have tended to discount Baglione's testimony and to regard Saraceni as more or less a casual Caravaggist, and then only during the last decade of his life.

This painting demonstrates Saraceni's fascination with

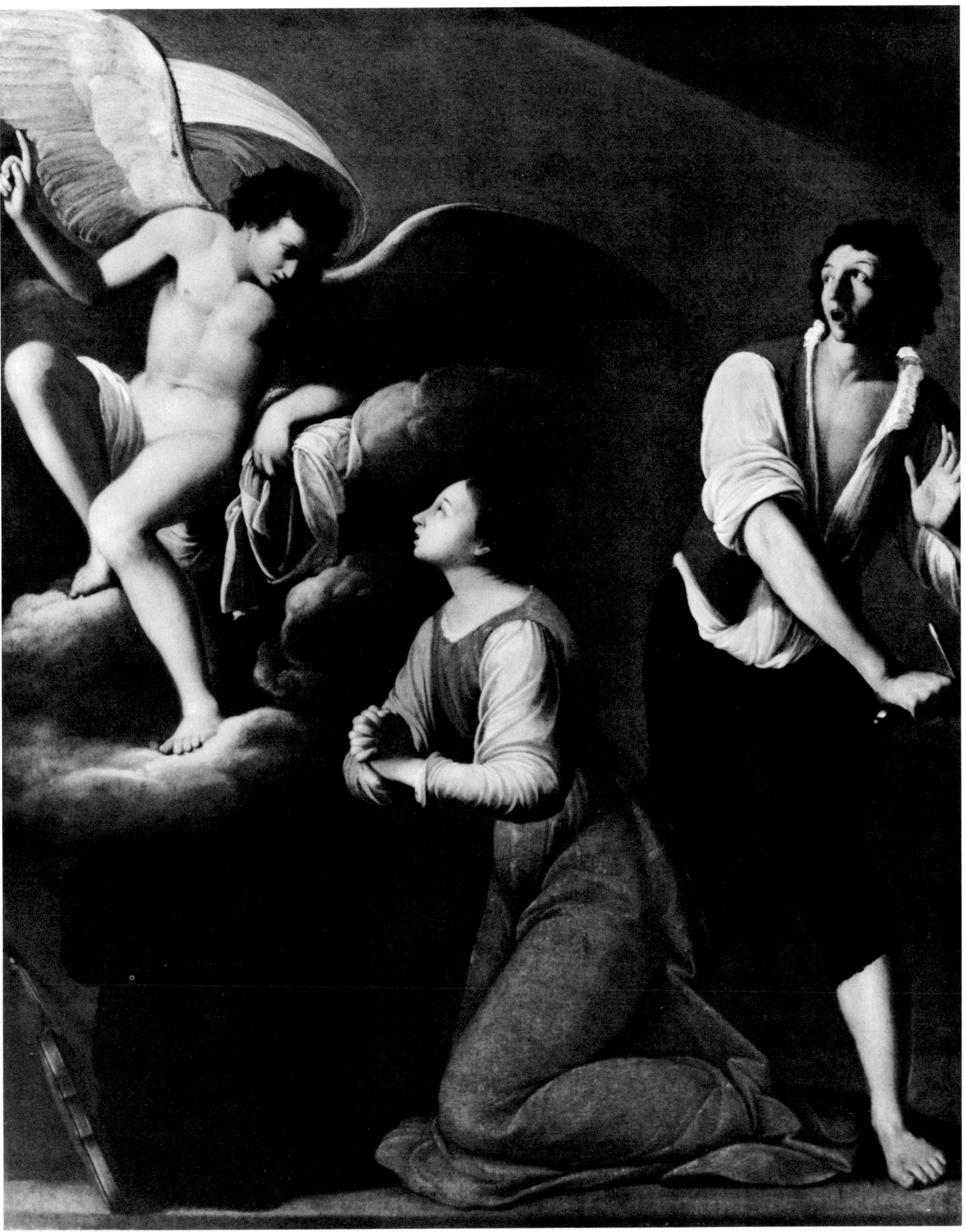

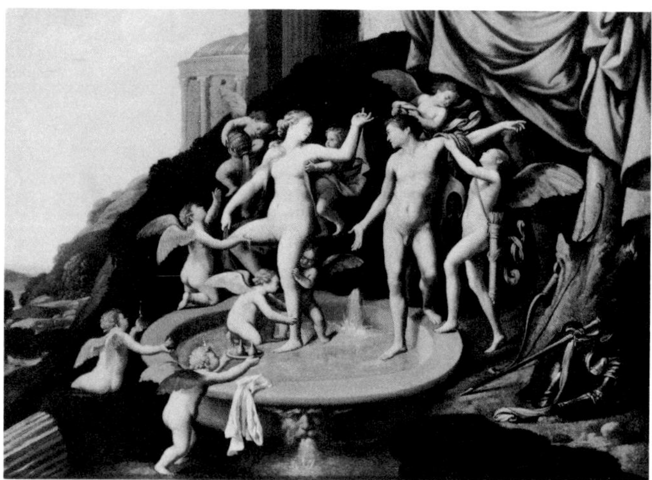

Fig. 20 Saraceni: *Bath of Venus and Mars,* oil on canvas. Heim Gallery, London

two distinct phases of Caravaggio's Roman career. Boys disguised as angels are prominent in the latter's St. Matthew cycle in the Contarelli chapel of S. Luigi dei Francesi (1599/1600), while Saraceni would have borrowed his blank background and diagonally descending ray of light, not to mention the extreme expression of the executioner, from Caravaggio's genre paintings of the 1590s.

NOTES

1 Ottani Cavina, 1968, fig. 45.

2 Ibid., nos. 32 and 51.

Ippolito Scarsella, called Scarsellino

Ferrara ca. 1550–1620 Ferrara

The son of Sigismondo Scarsella, a painter, Scarsellino must have been trained at home before embarking on the study travels to Bologna and Venice mentioned by Baruffaldi. No dates are known for the first four decades of this artist's career and very few thereafter: the chronology of Scarsellino's prolific production can be estimated only in the broadest terms.

The earliest works were devotional in subject and much indebted to Schiavone and Parmigianino: even at this stage Scarsellino employed the sensuous technique and saturated colors that distinguish paintings intended for connoisseurs.

The basis of Scarsellino's art was, however, always Dosso, and just as his great Ferrarese antecedent, Scarsellino looked to Venice for pictorial richness and even, just as Dosso, for the lyricism of Giorgione. Baruffaldi states that Scarsellino worked in the studio of Veronese for four years before returning to Ferrara. Veronesian and Bassanesque motifs were the passwords of Scarsellino's vocabulary of form. As S. J. Freedberg has pointed out, Titian was the artist's source for his naturalism, which for the sensuous immediacy of his figures led Scarsellino to solutions nearly as "modern" as the contemporary Carracci, and very influential as well (witness Saraceni and Guercino).

In 1592/93 Scarsellino contributed two paintings to the ceiling of the Palazzo dei Diamanti in Ferrara, for which decoration Ludovico and Annibale Carracci also sent canvases. Scarsellino executed his most ambitious work in fresco in the apse of S. Paolo, Ferrara, a monumental landscape with the fiery chariot of Elijah (1595/96).

After Ferrara entered the Papal States in 1598, Scarsellino was called upon to paint numerous altarpieces, of which those for S. Chiara (1609) and for the d'Este Palace chapel in Modena (*Holy Family with SS. Barbara and Carlo Borromeo*, 1615, now in the Gemäldegalerie, Dresden) have documented dates. Scarsellino's latest paintings reveal that he was sensitive to the proto-Baroque tendencies of Ludovico Carracci.

44 *The Virgin Bestowing a Scapular upon a Saint*

Oil on copper. 48.9 × 74.3 cm. Ca. 1600–1610.

Provenance: J. Weitzner, London; Mr. and Mrs. Paul H. Ganz, New York.

References: Novelli, 1959, p. 47; Manning, *Bolognese Baroque Painters*, 1962, no. 2; Novelli, 1964, p. 18, no. 104, fig. 32b.

Mr. and Mrs. Morton B. Harris, New York

The event recorded in this painting on a large sheet of copper has thus far resisted all efforts at interpretation. The complexity of the subject, the presence of two kneeling donors (at lower left, in ecclesiastic dress), and the precious quality of the medium are certain evidence that this picture was commissioned from Scarsellino by a private patron to commemorate a particular devotion. The bestowal by the Madonna of a scapular of the third order may well refer to the founding of a tertiary of the monastic order represented by the recipient (in brown habit).[1] Presumably the answer lies in an exclusively Ferrarese tradition; it is curious (and unhelpful) that no mention of this singular painting has yet been found in any old inventories.

The only common denominator, so far as we know, among this congregation of saints is that all of them pertain to monastic orders. Reading from upper left and concluding on the horizon to the right in this roughly U-shaped arrangement, the eighteen figures seem to be (1–3) St. Francis of Paola walking on water with two companions; (4) St. Anthony of Padua, in a gray habit, with heart and lily attributes; (5–6) two donors; (7) an unidentified saint receiving the scapular; (8) an unidentified Augustinian nun holding a book (St. Monica?); (9) St. Clare with the monstrance; (10) St. Catherine of Siena with a crucifix; (11) St. Dominic with a taper-bearing dog (a wordplay on *Domine cane*); (12) St. Nicholas of Tolentino; (13) St. Anthony Abbot? in a habit of the same brown color as the unidentified saint, no. 5; (14) St. Augustine? with crozier; (15) an unidentified saint in a purple-trimmed dalmatic; (16) St. Peter Martyr; (17) St. Francis of Assisi preaching to the birds (and fish); and (18) St. Raymond of Peñaforte sailing with the wind across the sea.

M. A. Novelli would date this masterly performance to the end of the sixteenth century.[2] It seems preferable to place this painting some years into the new century. The naturalness and ease with which the figures move and their highly individualized expressions reflect Scarsellino's intelligent response to the new seventeenth-century pictorial concerns that he had helped precipitate.

NOTES

1 Elizabeth Beatson kindly identified this scapular for me.

2 Novelli, 1964, p. 18.

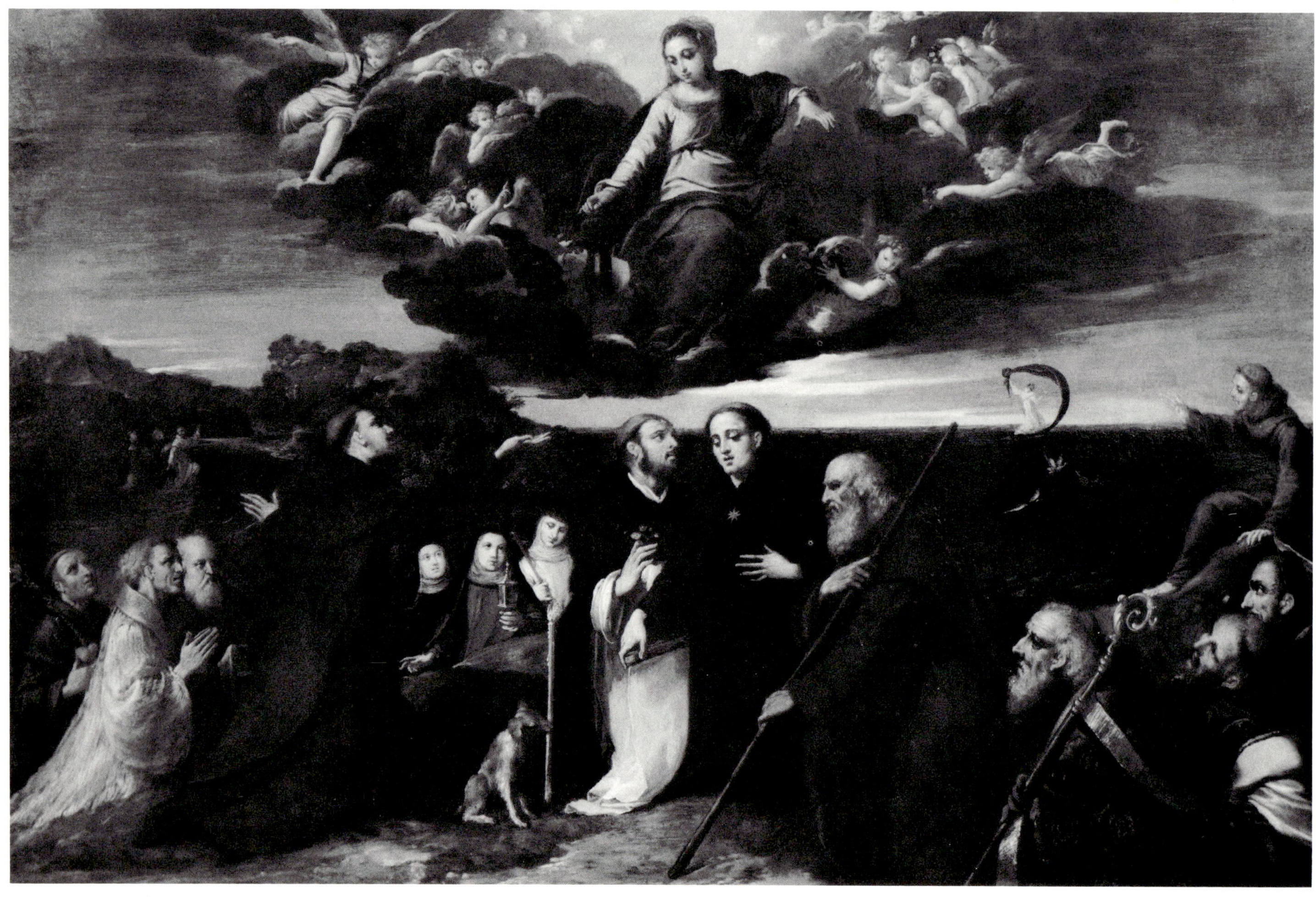

Francesco Solimena

Nocera 1657–1747 Barra/Naples

Francesco Solimena received his first instructions in art from his father, Angelo Solimena, a pupil of Francesco Guarino and Massimo Stanzione. When he was seventeen years of age, Francesco was sent to Naples, where he studied in the drawing academy of Francesco de Maria. However, he soon undertook to educate himself through independent studies of the draftsmanship of Lanfranco and Preti and the colorism of Cortona and Giordano.

In 1674 his fresco on the vault of the chapel of S. Anna in the Gesù Nuovo, Naples, was an unqualified success for the young artist. Thereafter, notable commissions are recorded for nearly every year of Solimena's long life. He placed frescoes and paintings on canvas in countless churches in Naples and abroad, as only Giordano had before him. By the turn of the century Solimena's school had supplanted *Giordanismo* as the dominant force in Neapolitan painting.

After the death of Carlo Maratti (1713), Solimena was indisputably the most famous artist in Europe. His pupils included such extraordinary talents as Sebastiano Conca, Francesco de Mura, and Corrado Giaquinto, who were amongst the most influential proponents of Rococo style in both its decorative and classical aspects.

45 *Continence of Scipio*

Oil on canvas. 43.8 × 55.9 cm. Ca. 1692.

Provenance: Sale, Parke-Bernet, New York.

Private collection, New York

The Roman general Scipio Africanus demonstrated his magnanimity in victory by returning to her parents unharmed a beautiful Celtiberic princess captured in the fall of Carthago Novo, Spain (Livy 26.50). In Solimena's representation of the episode, Scipio points to the gold and silver ransom offered by the maiden's father and declares that it shall serve instead as her dowry. Directly behind the modest princess stands her thankful fiancé.

Despite pronounced affinities with the brilliant colorism of Luca Giordano, this delightful picture should rather be assigned to the brush of Francesco Solimena during the early 1690s, the period of his closest emulation of Giordano.[1] The figures that imbue the background shadows with color derive from specifically Giordanesque types and technique. However, the exacting draftsmanship in the figures of Scipio, his page, and the princess is unmistakeably Solimena's, as is the friezelike arrangement of the actors and the attention to serious expression. These latter two qualities, influenced by

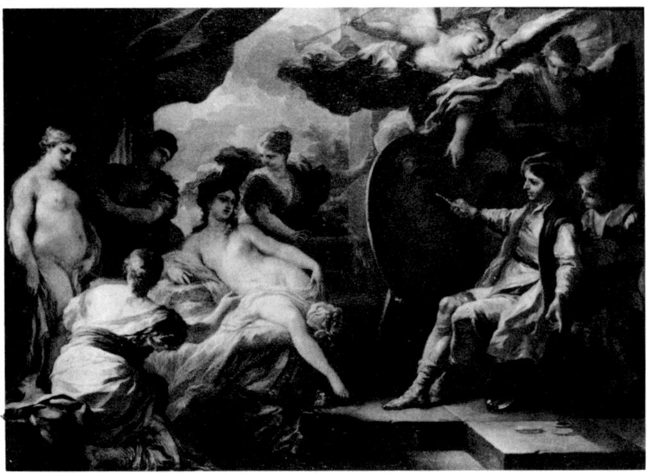

Fig. 21 Solimena: *Zeuxis and the Maidens of Croton,* oil on copper. Duke of Devonshire Collection, Chatsworth

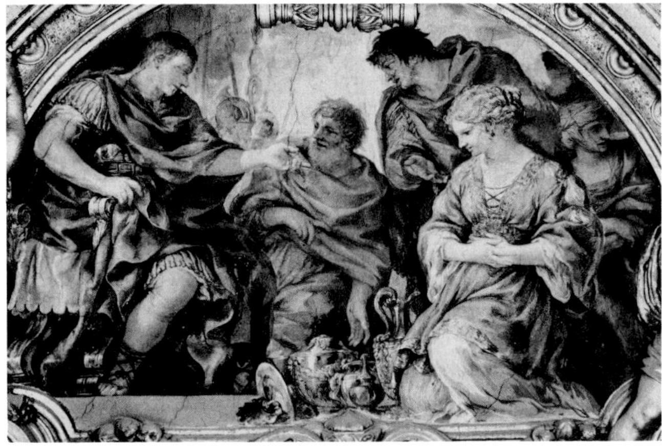

Fig. 22 Pietro da Cortona (1596–1669): *Continence of Scipio,* fresco, 1641/42. Palazzo Pitti, Florence.

Preti, appear in Solimena's oeuvre at just this moment.[2] Undoubtedly contemporary are the pendants of *Zeuxis and the Maidens of Croton* (fig. 21) and *Apelles Painting Campaspe* at Chatsworth.[3]

Solimena adapted this composition from Pietro da Cortona's fresco of this theme in the Sala di Venere, Palazzo Pitti, Florence, of 1641/42 (fig. 22).[4] Since Solimena never visited Tuscany he probably knew Cortona's fresco through Bloemaert's engraving of it. The discovery of this source vindicates De Dominici's insistance on terming "Cortonesque" Solimena's works most in the manner of Giordano.

No preparatory drawings for the New York picture have come to light as yet. On the other hand, Solimena re-used some years later certain motifs in this small painting for two drawings in Copenhagen and New York which are presumably studies for another (lost) *Continence of Scipio*.[5]

NOTES

1 Solimena's frescoes in the sacristy of S. Paolo Maggiore, Naples (1690), furnish a telling comparison; see Bologna, 1958, fig. 83.

2 See Bologna, 1968, pp. 49–50.

3 Campbell, 1977, p. 107.

4 Royal Museum of Fine Arts, Copenhagen (Collection de Solimene, II, 17; Gernsheim photo no. 73750); Metropolitan Museum of Art, New York (inv. no. 1971.222.3; see Bean, 1979, no. 358, repr.).

5 An autograph replica on copper of the *Zeuxis* picture is in the collection of Nelson Shanks, Andalusia, Pa. For other versions, see Spinosa, 1979, p. 212. It is possible that the New York painting exhibited here also once had a pendant.

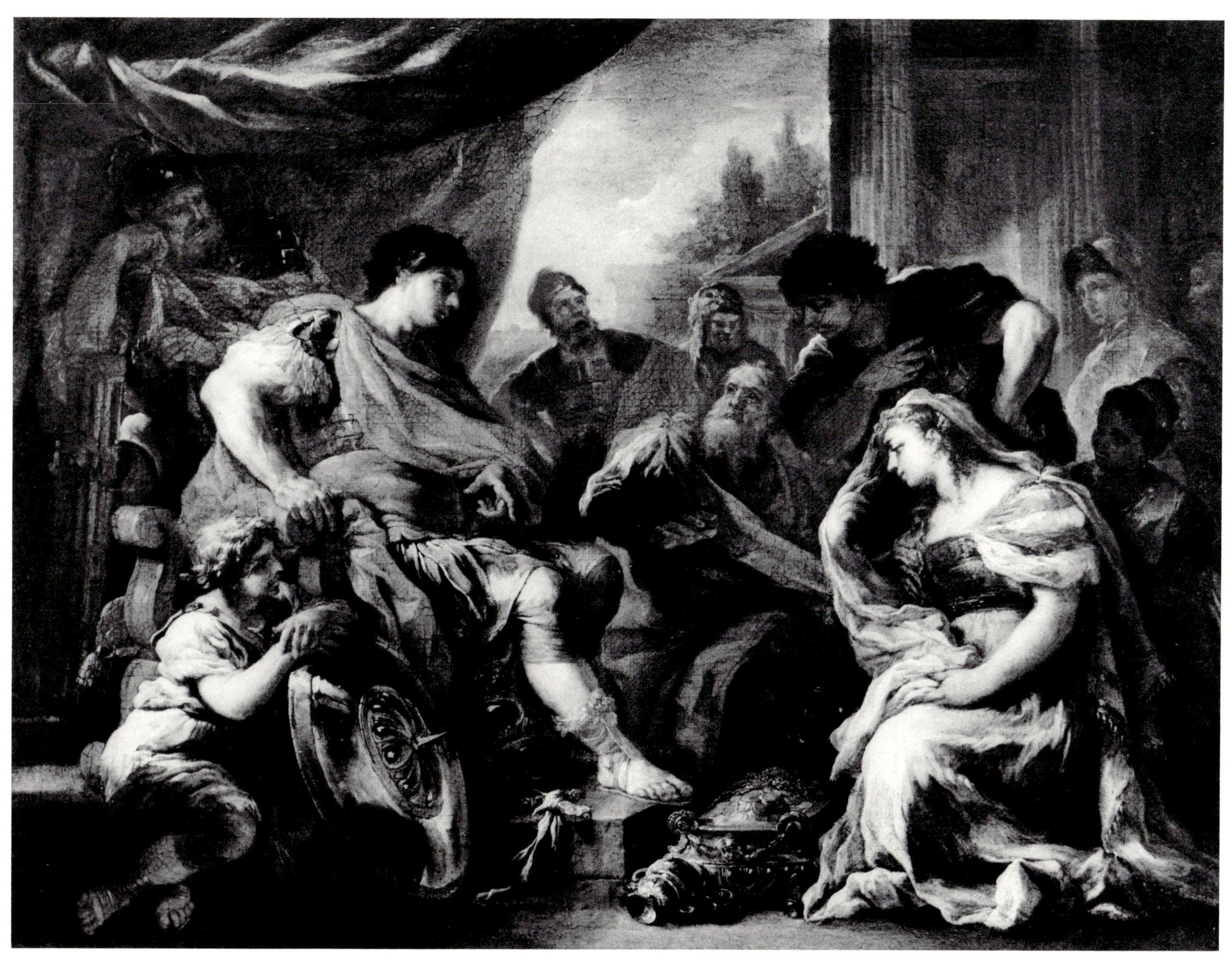

Bernardo Strozzi

Genoa 1581–1644 Venice

Bernardo Strozzi was trained as a painter by Pietro Sorri, a Sienese who visited Genoa about 1595–97 (Soprani and Ratti). In 1598 Strozzi entered the Capucine monastery of S. Barnaba in Genoa, hence his sobriquet "Il Cappuccino." His talent for painting devotional subjects, St. Francis most often, attracted much notice. His apprenticeship had drawn his attention to the art of central Italy: the nervous energy and brilliant pastels of Federico Barocci were decisive influences. During the second decade of the seventeenth century Strozzi added observations of the monumental figures of the Milanese masters G. C. Procaccini and Il Cerano: the fanciful *St. Catherine of Alexandria* in Hartford (Wadsworth Atheneum) reveals the confluence of these trends.

About 1610 Strozzi was permitted to leave the monastery to support his mother and sister. His activity was mainly devoted to private commissions and his oeuvre abounds with replicas of varying merit. At the end of the second decade a pronounced interest toward naturalism appears, at times evidently inspired by Rubens and occasionally seemingly by Caravaggism. A visit to Rome has been postulated for about 1615.

Strozzi painted his major Genoese work in fresco in the Palazzo Centurione a Sampierdarena in 1623–25, but was criticized for his slow work. During this last decade in Genoa, Strozzi emerged as a portraitist of merit, clearly sensitive to the style of Van Dyck. Upon the death of his mother in 1630, Strozzi declined to return to the monastery. He must have been granted a dispensation to be allowed to transfer to Venice (after September 1630), where he was called "Il Prete Genovese."

The lessons of the Venetian Renaissance were not lost on this inveterate colorist. His palette bloomed. Strozzi studied too the expressive power of the paintings left by Domenico Fetti. For the Biblioteca Marciana in Venice, Strozzi painted in a single month (October/November 1635) a robust *Allegory of Sculpture*, which put to shame Padovanino's accompanying effort. Among the Venetian churches graced with Strozzi altarpieces are S. Benedetto and S. Niccolò da Tolentino. Strozzi's close pupil, Armanno Stroiffi, was a witness to the ailing master's last testament of 1 August 1644, the day before he died.

46 *St. Francis Praying before a Crucifix*

Oil on canvas. 115.5 × 87 cm. Ca. 1620–25.

Provenance: Private collection, Rome.

Reference: Mortari, 1966, p. 168, fig. 7.

Private collection, New York

Born in Assisi, Francis was a wealthy and worldly youth until one day in prayer, he heard a voice: "Francis, repair my church." He immediately renounced all his possessions and devoted himself to zealous preaching throughout the countryside and solitary retreats for tearful prayer and meditation. Beloved for his gentleness and charity, Francis founded the Franciscan order in 1210.

As a Capucine prelate Bernardo Strozzi had frequent occasion to paint the devotion of St. Francis, spiritual head of his order. Mortari illustrates two autograph versions of the painting in this exhibition: certainly earlier is a canvas in a Genoese private collection[1] which evinces some of the tentativeness of a youthful artist. The version in a Sienese collection[2] is a replica with slight variations of the present picture. Mortari notes the subtle modulation of tone within a limited range and dates the *St. Francis* to Strozzi's Genoese period after 1610.[3] The fluency with which Strozzi has executed this work might in fact lead to a slightly later dating to the 1620s, not too long before his departure for Venice.

NOTES

1 Rubinacci collection, Genoa; see Mortari, 1966, fig. 1.

2 Conte Guido Chigi Saracini collection, Genoa; ibid., fig. 3.

3 Ibid., p. 168.

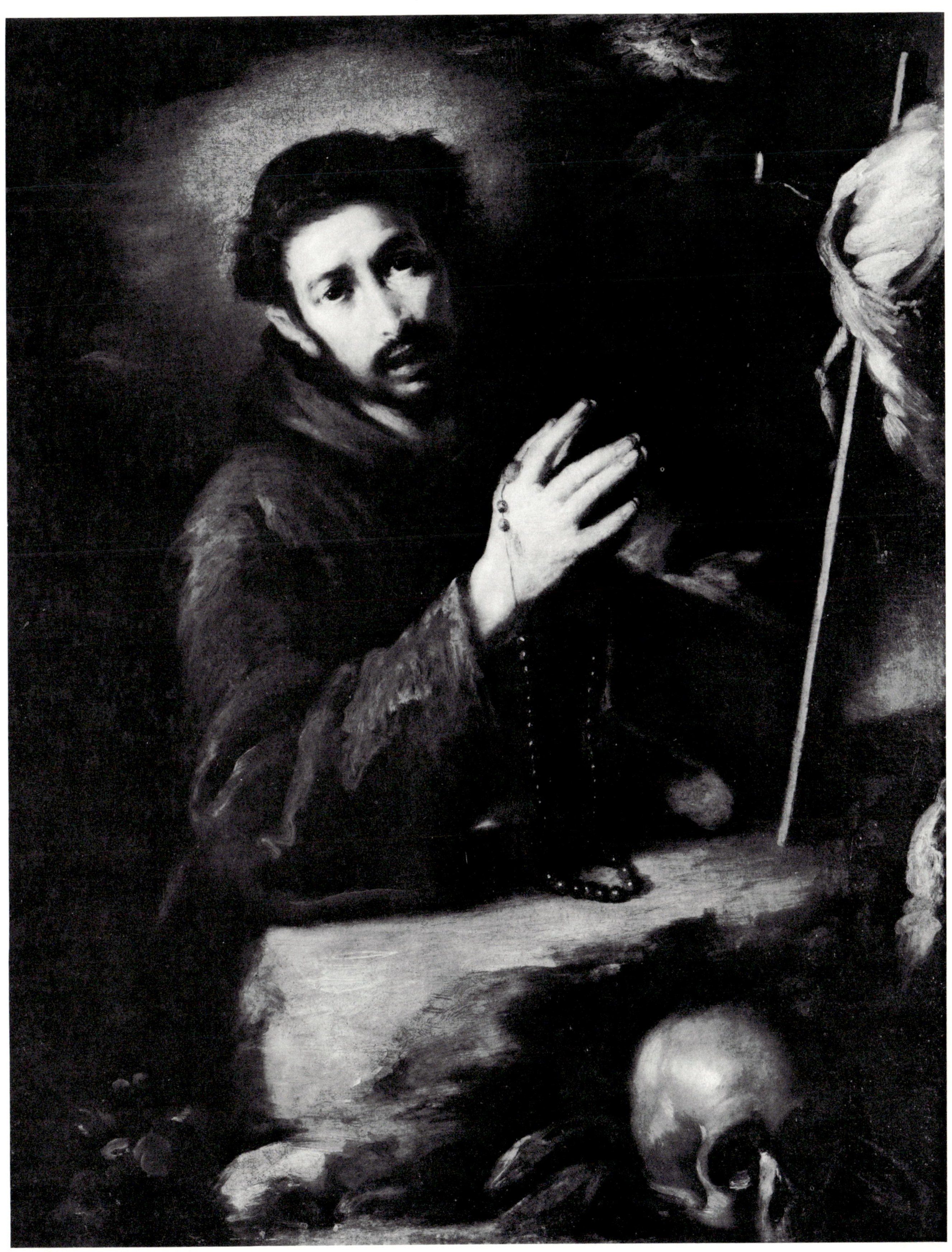

Pietro Testa

Lucca 1611–1650 Rome

Paintings by Pietro Testa are extremely rare: he seems not to have painted more than twenty during the two decades of his career. We know Testa best perhaps through his plentiful drawings and etchings in which he obsessively cast and recast his ideas for paintings and recorded his philosophical musings.

In Rome in time to study with Domenichino before the latter's departure for Naples (1631), Testa then passed a brief, unsatisfactory period in Pietro da Cortona's atelier. Testa was active in the antiquarian circle of Cassiano dal Pozzo, through whom he would have met Nicolas Poussin. Poussin inspired him, and G. B. Castiglione at the same moment, to a lush neo-Venetian style of landscape with figures and also to stoic subject matter. In this his early mode, Testa painted his *Moses Striking the Rock* (Picture Gallery, Potsdam-Sanssouci), which was documented in the Giustiniani collection in 1639.

An absence of dated works renders Testa's chronology problematic. He apparently did not travel outside of Rome save for visits to his native Lucca in 1632 and 1637. For the church of S. Romano, Lucca, he painted an altarpiece of S. Domenico in 1637/38. His most important altarpiece in Rome probably dates to the early 1640s: the *Presentation of the Virgin*, formerly in S. Croce de Lucchesi and now in the Hermitage. By this time Testa's obsession with emotive expression, proto-Romantic in its tendency, had led him to formal distortions that verge on the grotesque.

During the 1640s Testa followed Poussin's direction and carefully purged his compositions to conform to canons of classicism. He set his academic theories down in a *Trattato* (preserved in the Kunstakademie, Düsseldorf). The palette employed for the later paintings is typically restricted and dark.

Testa had no success with his aspirations to fame as a painter of monumental commissions. His plans for the apse of S. Martino ai Monti were rejected after much delay and his frescoes in S. Maria dell'Anima apparently did not survive him by long before they were replaced. Ann Sutherland Harris has suggested that news of this impending reversal may have reached him and caused his despondency. On 1 March 1650, Testa was found drowned in the Tiber, an apparent suicide.

47 *Alexander the Great Saved from the River Cydnus*

Oil on canvas. 96.5 × 137 cm. Ca. 1645–50.

Provenance: Castelbarco-Albani collection, Italy.

References: Schleier, 1970, p. 668 n. 52; Brigstocke, 1976, pp. 16 and 19, fig. 34.

Mr. and Mrs. Paul H. Ganz, New York

On the indication of the owner, the previous writers on this painting have described the subject as an unspecified episode from the life of Alexander the Great. This view has been upheld by Jennifer Montagu, who identifies Quintus Curtius (3.5) as the source for Alexander's near-fatal encounter with the river Cydnus.[1] "Hardly had he entered [the frigid river] when his limbs began to stiffen with a sudden chill, then he lost his color, and the vital warmth left almost his entire body. His attendants caught him in their arms, looking like a dying man, and carried him almost unconscious into his tent."

Testa, as he and Salvator Rosa were wont to do, has chosen a classical subject seemingly without pictorial precedent.[2] In view of Passeri's remark in relation to Testa's *Death of Cato* that the artist identified personally with his stoic subject matter,[3] the observation is irresistible that Testa read his text with more concern to describe Alexander's appearance as a drowned man, than as the survivor of this accident.

Hugh Brigstocke has proposed to date this picture amongst the artist's last works, of which there seems no possible doubt.[4] Just as in the contemporary works of Poussin with their strict adherence to decorum, such as the *Crucifixion* (Wadsworth Atheneum, Hartford) of 1644–46, Testa paints this tragic subject under a gloomy cast. Color is so rejected in the late Testa that his paintings come to resemble "drawings" in oils.

NOTES

1 In a letter of 30 July 1979, from which this translation of the text has been taken.

2 Pigler, 1974, p. 359, lists only one painting of this theme, by J. G. Platzer in the eighteenth century.

3 Passeri, 1934, p. 188.

4 Brigstocke, 1976, p. 16.

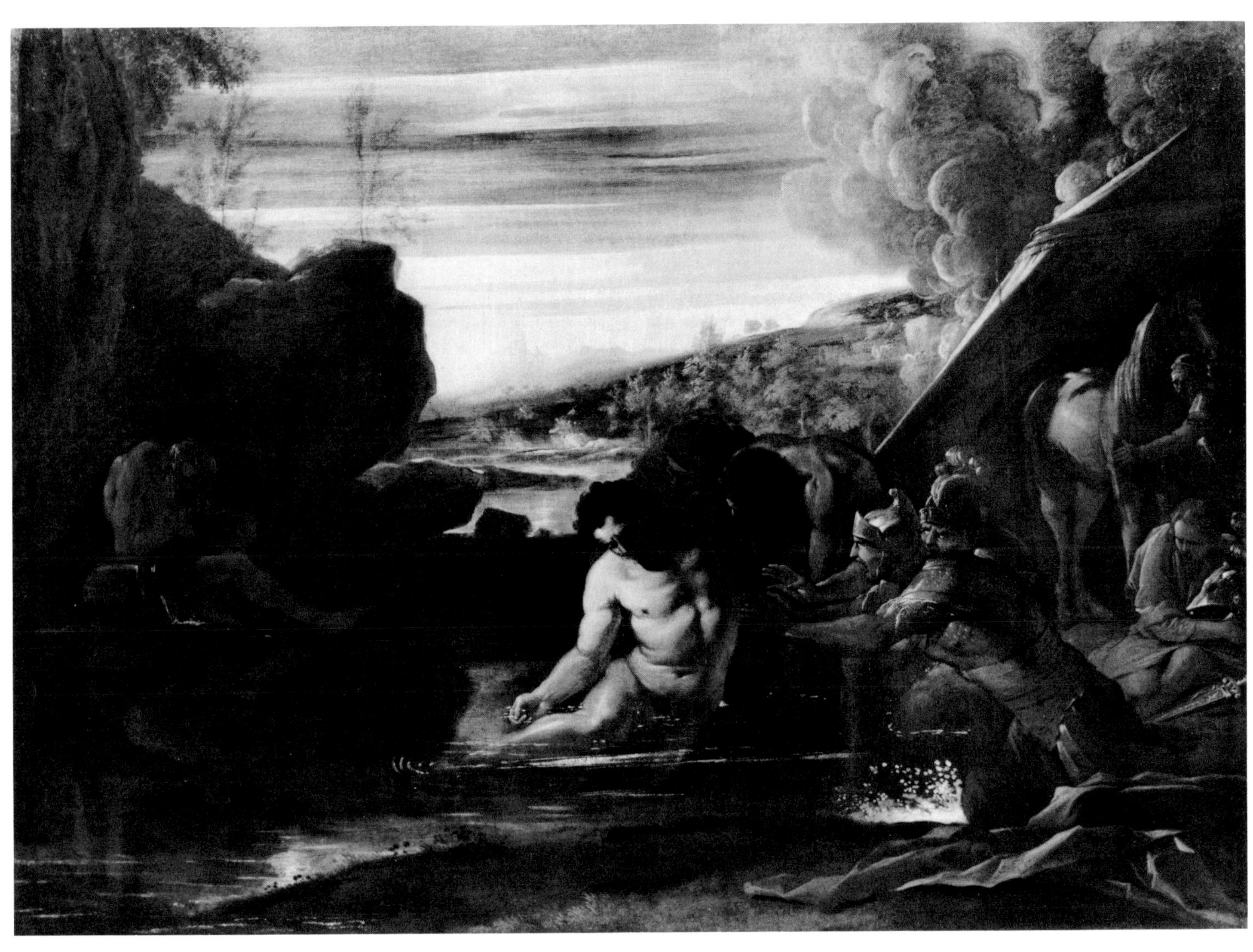

Bibliography

Andrews, K. *National Gallery of Scotland: Catalogue of Italian Drawings.* 2 vols. Cambridge, 1968.

Askew, P. "Fetti's 'Martyrdom' at the Wadsworth Atheneum." *Burlington Magazine,* 103, 1961, pp. 245–52.

———. "The Parable Paintings of Domenico Fetti." *Art Bulletin,* 43, 1961, pp. 21–45.

———. "The Question of Fetti as Fresco Painter: A Reattribution to Andreasi of Frescoes in the Cathedral and Sant'Andrea at Mantua." *Art Bulletin,* 50, 1968, pp. 1–10.

———. "Domenico Fetti's Use of Prints: Three Instances." *Print Review,* no. 5 (Tribute to Wolfgang Stechow), 1976, pp. 14–23.

———. "Ferdinando Gonzaga's Patronage of the Pictorial Arts: The Villa Favorita." *Art Bulletin,* 60, 1978, pp. 274–96.

Baglione, G. *Le vite de' pittori, scultori, architetti ed intagliatori, dal pontificato di Gregorio XIII dal 1572, fino a' tempi di Papa Urbano VIII nel 1642*. Rome, 1642. Facsimile ed. with notes by Bellori, edited by V. Mariani, Rome, 1935.

Baldinucci, F. *Notizie de' professori del disegno da Cimabue in qua.* 6 vols. Florence, 1681–1728. Suppl., 5 vols., Florence, 1847.

Baruffaldi, G. *Vite de' pittori e scultori ferraresi.* 2 vols. Ferrara, 1844.

Bean, J. *17th-Century Italian Drawings in the Metropolitan Museum of Art.* New York, 1979.

Bellori, G. P. *Le vite de' pittori scultori ed architetti moderni.* Rome, 1672.

Bertolotti, A. *Artisti lombardi a Roma nei secoli XV, XVI e XVII.* Milan, 1881.

Blunt, A. *The Drawings of Giovanni Benedetto Castiglione and Stefano della Bella in the Collection of Her Majesty the Queen at Windsor Castle.* London, 1954.

Blunt, A., and Cooke, H. L. *Roman Drawings of the XVII & XVIII Centuries in the Collection of Her Majesty the Queen at Windsor Castle.* London, 1960.

Boisclair, M.-N. "Gaspard Dughet: une chronologie révisée." *Revue de l'art,* no. 34, 1976, pp. 29–56.

———. "La Décoration des deux mezzanines du palais Borghese de Rome." *RACAR,* 3, 1976, pp. 7–27.

Bologna, Palazzo dell' Archiginnasio. *Maestri della pittura del seicento Emiliano.* Exh. cat., 1959.

———. *L'ideale classico del seicento in Italia e la pittura di paesaggio.* Exh. cat., 1962.

Bologna, F. *Francesco Solimena.* Naples, 1958.

———. "Solimena's *Solomon Worshipping the Pagan Gods* in Detroit." *Art Quarterly,* 31, 1968, pp. 35–62.

Borea, E. *Caravaggio e Caravaggeschi nelle gallerie di Firenze.* Exh. cat., Palazzo Pitti, Florence, 1970.

———. *Pittori Bolognesi del seicento nelle gallerie di Firenze.* Exh. cat., Uffizi, Florence, 1975.

Bosi, M. *S. Maria in Campo Marzio.* Le chiese di Roma illustrate, 61. Rome, 1961.

Brejon, A. "New Paintings by Bartolomeo Manfredi." *Burlington Magazine*, 121, 1979, pp. 305–10.

Briganti, G. "Milleseicentotrenta, ossia il barocco." *Paragone*, no. 13, 1951, pp. 8–17.

———. *Pietro da Cortona.* Florence, 1962.

Brigstocke, H. "Testa's Adoration of the Shepherds in Edinburgh and Some New Thoughts on His Stylistic Development." *Paragone*, no. 321, 1976, pp. 15–28.

Britton, J. *A Catalogue Raisonné of the Pictures Belonging to the Most Honorable the Marquis of Stafford*. London, 1808.

Brugnole, M. V. "Gli affreschi dell'Albani e del Domenichino nel palazzo di Bassano di Sutri." *Bollettino d'arte*, 42, 1957, pp. 266–78.

Bruno, G., et al. *La pittura a Genova e in Liguria dal seicento al primo novecento*. Genoa, 1971.

Buchanan, W. *Memoirs of Painting*. 2 vols. London, 1824.

Byam Shaw, J. *Paintings by Old Masters at Christ Church, Oxford*. London, 1967.

Campbell, M. *Pietro da Cortona at the Pitti Palace*. Princeton, N.J., 1977.

Campori, G. *Gli artisti italiani e stranieri negli stati estensi*. Modena, 1855.

———. *Raccolta di cataloghi ed inventarii inediti*. Modena, 1870.

Cannon-Brooks, P. *Lombard Paintings c. 1595–c. 1630*. Exh. cat., City Museums and Art Gallery, Birmingham, England, 1974.

Catalogue des tableaux du cabinet de M. Crozat, Baron de Thiers. Paris, 1775.

Causa, R. *La pittura del seicento a Napoli dal'naturalismo al barocco*. Naples, 1972.

Chappell, M. L., and Kirwin, C. W. "A Petrine Triumph: The Decoration of the Navi Piccole in San Pietro under Clement VIII." *Storia dell'arte*, no. 21, 1974, pp. 119–70.

Chicago, Art Institute of Chicago. *Painting in Italy in the Eighteenth Century—Rococo to Romanticism*. Exh. cat., 1970.

Clark, A. M. S.v. "Chiari" in *Painting in Italy in the Eighteenth Century—Rococo to Romanticism*. Exh. cat., Art Institute of Chicago, 1970, p. 190.

Cocke, R. *Pier Francesco Mola*. Oxford, 1972.

Cooney, J. P. *L'opera completa di Annibale Carracci*. Milan, 1976.

Cortese, G. di Domenico. "La vicenda artistica di Andrea Camassei." *Commentari*, 19, 1968, pp. 281–98.

Couché, J., ed. *La Galerie du Palais-Royal . . . .* Paris, 1786–1806.

Croft-Murray, E. *Decorative Painting in England 1537–1837*. Feltham, Middlesex, 1970.

Crookshank, A. "Two Signatures of Giovanni Battista Passeri." *Burlington Magazine*, 106, 1964, pp. 179–80.

Dal Pozzo, B. *Le vite de' pittori, degli scultori et architetti veronesi*. Verona, 1718.

Daniels, J. *L'opera completa di Sebastiano Ricci*. Milan, 1976.

———. *Sebastiano Ricci.* Hove, England, 1976.

D'Arcais, F. "L'attivita viennese di Antonio Bellucci." *Arte veneta*, 18, 1964, pp. 99–109.

De Conciliis, D., and Lattuada, R. "Unpublished Documents for Mattia Preti's Paintings in San Pietro a Maiella in Naples." *Burlington Magazine*, 121, 1979, pp. 294–301.

De Dominici, B. *Vite de' pittori, scultori ed architetti napoletani*. 3 vols. Naples, 1742/43.

Detroit, Detroit Institute of Arts. *Art in Italy: 1600–1700*. Exh. cat., 1965.

———. *The Twilight of the Medici*. Exh. cat., 1974.

D'Onofrio, C., ed. *Roma nel seicento*. Rome, 1969.

Dowley, F. H. "The Painting of Baciccio, Giovanni Battista Gaulli, by R. Enggass," review. *Art Bulletin*, 47, 1965, pp. 294–300.

Dreyer, P. "Notizen zum malerischen und zeichnerischen Oeuvre der Maratta-Schule: Giuseppe Chiari—Pietro de' Petri—Agostino Masucci." *Zeitschrift für Kunstgeschichte*, 1971, pp. 184–207.

Dubois de Saint-Gelais, L. F. *Description des tableaux du Palais Royal*. Paris, 1727.

Edinburgh, Edinburgh Festival Society. *Italian 17th-Century Drawings from British Private Collections*. Exh. cat., 1972.

Enggass, R. *The Painting of Baciccio, Giovanni Battista Gaulli*. University Park, Pa., 1964.

Ewald, G. "Simone Pignoni: A Little Known Florentine Seicento Painter." *Burlington Magazine*, 106, 1964, pp. 218–26.

———. "Studien zur Florentiner Barockmalerei." *Pantheon*, 23, 1965, pp. 302–18.

Faldi, I. *Pittori viterbesi di cinque secoli*. Rome, 1970.

Ferrari, O. "Gli studi su S. R. oggi." In *Salvator Rosa pittore e poeta nel centenario della morte (1615–1673)*, pp. 3–20. Rome, 1975.

Ferrari, O., and Scavizzi, G. *Luca Giordano*. 3 vols. Naples, 1966.

Florence, Palazzo Pitti. *La mostra della pittura italiana del sei e settecento in palazzo Pitti*. Exh. cat., 1922.

Frangipane, A. *Mattia Preti*. Milan, 1929.

Freedberg, S. J. *Painting in Italy 1500 to 1600*. Rev. ed. Baltimore, Md., 1975.

G. B. Castiglione. Fonti per la storia della pittura, II. Genoa, 1973.

G. B. Castiglione. Fonti per la storia della pittura, III. Monzambano, 1975.

Ghirardi, G. "L'attivita renana di Antonio Bellucci." *Pantheon*, 32, 1974, pp. 374–79.

"Giacomo del Po," s.v. In *Dizionario enciclopedia Bolaffi dei pittori e degli incisori italiani*. Turin, 1974.

Gilbert, C. *Baroque Painters of Italy*. Exh. cat., in *Bulletin of the Ringling Museum*, 1, March 1961.

Gould, C. *Correggio*. London, 1976.

Il Grechetto a Mantova. Fonti per la storia della pittura, I. Genoa, 1971.

Gregori, M. *70 pitture e scultore dell '600 e '700 fiorentino*. Exh. cat., Palazzo Strozzi, Florence, 1965.

Griseri, A. "Due dipinti di Lazzaro Baldi a Granada." *Paragone*, no. 153, 1962, pp. 37–39.

Hartt, F. *Love in Baroque Art*. New York, 1964.

Haskell, F. *Patrons and Painters*. London, 1963.

Heinemann, R., ed. *The Thyssen-Bornemisza Collection*. 2 vols. Castagnola, 1969.

Jameson, Anna Brownell Murphy. *The Legends of the Madonna*. London, 1903.

Kerber, B. "Giuseppe Bartolomeo Chiari." *Art Bulletin*, 50, 1968, pp. 75–86.

Kitson, M., ed. *Salvator Rosa*. Exh. cat., Hayward Gallery, Arts Council of Great Britain, London, 1973.

Koschatzky, K., Oberhuber, K., and Knab, E. *Italian Drawings in the Albertina*. Milan, 1971.

Laderchi, C. *Descrizione della quadreria Costabili*. Ferrara, 1839.

Lavin, M. A. "A Seventeenth-Century Painter's Supplies: Document of Payment to Andrea Camassei." *Art Bulletin*, 52, 1970, pp. 192–94.

———. *Seventeenth-Century Barberini Documents and Inventories of Art*. New York, 1975.

Limentani, U. *Poesie e lettere inedite di Salvator Rosa*. Florence, 1950.

London, Bryan's Gallery. *A Catalogue of the Orleans Italian Pictures Which Will Be Exhibited for Sale by Private Contract*. Exh. cat., 1798/99.

London, Hazlitt Gallery. *Baroque and Rococo Paintings and Oil Sketches*. Exh. cat., 1962.

London, Heim Gallery. *Baroque Sketches, Drawings and Sculptures*. Exh. cat., 1967.

———. *Fourteen Important Neapolitan Paintings*. Exh. cat., 1971.

———. *Italian Paintings and Sculptures of the 17th and 18th Centuries*. Exh. cat., 1976.

London, Thomas Agnew & Sons. *Baroque and Rococo in Italy*. Exh. cat., 1966.

———. *Old Master Paintings: Recent Acquisitions*. Exh. cat., 1978.

Longhi, R. "Mattia Preti (critica figurative pura)." *La voce*, 5, 1913, pp. 1171–75. [Reprinted in *Scritti giovanili, opere completa di Roberto Longhi*, I, pp. 29–45.]

———. "Ultimi studi sul Caravaggio." *I proporzioni*, 1, 1943, pp. 5–63.

———. "Presenze alla sala Regia." *Paragone*, no. 117, 1959, pp. 29–38.

———. "Codazzi e l'antologia." *Paragone*, no. 123, 1960, pp. 41–44.

———. "Note in margine al catalogo della mostra sei-settecentesca del 1922." In *Scritti giovanili, opere completa di Roberto Longhi*, I, pp. 493–512. Florence, 1961.

———. "Giovanni Baglione e il quadro del processo." *Paragone*, no. 163, 1963, pp. 23–31.

———. "G. B. Spinelli e i naturalisti napoletani del seicento." *Paragone*, no. 227, 1969, pp. 42–52.
McCorquodale, C. *Painting in Florence 1600–1700*. Exh. cat., Royal Academy of Arts, London, 1979.
———. "Some Unpublished Works by Carlo Dolci." *Burlington Magazine*, 121, 1979, pp. 142–50.
Magagnato, L., ed. *Cinquant'anni di pitturi veronese 1580–1630*. Exh. cat., Palazzo della Gran Guardia, Verona, 1974.
———. *La pittura a Verona tra sei e settecento.* Exh. cat., Palazzo della Gran Guardia, Verona, 1978.
Mahon, D. "Notes on the Young Guercino: II, Cento and Ferrara." *Burlington Magazine*, 52, 1937, pp. 177–89.
———. "An Attribution Re-studied: Sisto Badalocchio's 'Holy Family.'" *Wadsworth Atheneum Bulletin*, Spring 1958, pp. 1–4.
———. *Il Guercino dipinti*. Exh. cat., Palazzo dell' Archiginnasio, Bologna, 1968.
Mahon, D., and Sutton, D. *Artists in 17th-Century Rome*. Exh. cat., Wildenstein & Co., London, 1955.
Mahoney, M. *The Drawings of Salvator Rosa*. New York, 1977.
Malvasia, C. C. *Felsina pittrice, vite de' pittori bolognesi*. Bologna, 1678.
Mancini, A. *Considerazioni sulla pittura*. Edited by A. Marucchi and L. Salerno. 2 vols. Rome, 1956/57.
Manning, R. L. *Venetian Painting of the Eighteenth Century*. Exh. cat., Finch College Museum of Art, New York, 1961.
———. *Bolognese Baroque Painters*. Exh. cat., Finch College Museum of Art, New York, 1962.
———. *Neapolitan Masters*. Exh. cat., Finch College Museum of Art, New York, 1962.
———. *Genoese Painters*. Exh. cat., Finch College Museum of Art, New York, 1964.
———. *Venetian Baroque Painters*. Exh. cat., Finch College Museum of Art, New York, 1964.
Manning, R. L. and B. Suida. *Genoese Masters: Cambiaso to Magnasco, 1550–1750*. Exh. cat., Dayton, Ohio, Art Institute, 1962.
Marangoni, M. "Pittura secentesca nella galleria Corsini a Firenze." *Dedalo*, 1, 1920, pp. 436–51.
———. "La raccolta Cecconi di pittura secentesca." *Dedalo*, 2, 1921, pp. 362–80.
———. "Domenico Fetti—I." *Dedalo*, 3, 1923, pp. 695–710.
———. "Domenico Fetti—II." *Dedalo*, 3, 1923, pp. 777–92.
Martin, J. R. *Baroque*. New York, 1977.
Martinelli, V. "Nuovi ritratti di Guidobaldo Abbatini e di Pier Francesco Mola." *Commentari*, 9, 1958, pp. 99–109.
———. "L'amor divino 'tutto ignudo' di Giovanni Baglione e la cronologia dell' intermezzo caravaggesco." *Arte antica e moderna*, no. 5, 1959, pp. 82–96.
Mezzetti, A. "Contributi a Carlo Maratti." *Rivista dell' Istituto Nazionale di Archaeologia e Storia dell'arte*, n.s. 4, 1955, pp. 253–354.
———. *Mostra di opere d'arte restaurante*. Exh. cat., Palazzo dei Diamanti, Ferrara, 1964.
Michelini, P. "Domenico Fetti a Venezia." *Arte veneta*, 9, 1955, pp. 123–37.
Milkovich, M. *Sebastiano and Marco Ricci in America*. Exh. cat., University of Kentucky Art Museum, Lexington, 1965/66.
———. *Bernardo Strozzi*. Exh. cat., University Art Gallery, Binghamton, N.Y., 1967.
Miller, D. "Seventeenth-Century Emilian Painting at Bologna." *Burlington Magazine*, 101, 1959, pp. 206–12.
Minault, D. D. *Woman as Heroine*. Exh. cat., Worcester, Mass., Art Museum, 1972.
Mireur, H. *Dictionnaire des ventes d'art faites en France et à l'étranger pendant les XVIIIe et XIXme siècles*. Vol. III. Paris, 1911.
Moir, A. *The Italian Followers of Caravaggio*. Cambridge, Mass., 1967.
———. *Caravaggio and His Copyists*. New York, 1976.
Mola, G. B. *Breve racconto delle miglior opere d'architettura, scultura et pittura fatte in Roma . . . l'anno 1663*. Edited by K. Noehles. Berlin, 1966.
Montreal, Musée des Beaux-Arts. *Dessins italiens aux Etats-Unis et au Canada*. Exh. cat., 1970.
Mortari, L. *Bernardo Strozzi*. Rome, 1966.
———. "La 'Crocifissione' di Giovanni Lanfranco nei SS. Domenico e Sisto a Roma." *Arte illustrata,* 5, 1972, pp. 305–7.
Moschini, G. A. *Pittura in Padua.* Padua, 1826.
Newcome, M. *Genoese Baroque Drawings.* Exh. cat., University Art Gallery, Binghamton, N.Y., 1972.
———. "A Castiglione-Leone Problem." *Master Drawings,* 16, Summer 1978, pp. 163–72.
New York, Knoedler & Co. *Masters of the Loaded Brush.* Exh. cat., 1967.
New York, Pierpont Morgan Library. *William and Mary and Their House.* Exh. cat., 1979.
New York, Wildenstein & Co. *The Italian Heritage.* Exh. cat., 1967.
Nicodemi, G. *Daniele Crespi.* Busto Arizio, 1930.
Nicolson, B. "Current and Forthcoming Exhibitions: London." *Burlington Magazine,* 108, 1966, p. 211.
———. *The International Caravaggesque Movement.* Oxford, 1979.
Nieto Alcaide, V. M. "Algunos Dibujos de Carlo Maratti en el Museo de la Academia de San Fernando." *Archivo Español de Arte,* 1965, pp. 283–90.
Nissman, J. *Florentine Baroque Art from American Collections.* Exh. cat., Metropolitan Museum of Art, New York, 1969.

Noehles, K. *La chiesa dei SS. Luca e Martina.* Rome, 1970.
Novelli, M. A. "Qualche aggiunta allo Scarsellino." *Paragone,* no. 117, 1959, pp. 46–50.
———. *Lo Scarsellino.* Milan, 1964.
Nugent, M. *Alla mostra della pittura italiana del '600 e '700.* 2 vols. San Casciano Val di Pesa, 1930.
Oberhuber, K., ed. *Renaissance and Baroque Drawings from the Collections of John and Alice Steiner.* Exh. cat., Fogg Art Museum, Cambridge, Mass., 1977.
Oberlin, Allen Memorial Art Museum. "An Exhibition of Paintings, Bozzetti and Drawings by Giovanni Battista Gaulli." *Allen Memorial Art Museum Bulletin,* 24, Fall 1966.
Ojetti, U., Dami, L., and Tarchiani, N. *La pittura italiana del seicento e del settecento alla mostra di palazzo Pitti.* Milan and Rome, 1924.
Orlandi, P. A. *Abecedario pittorico dei professori più illustri in pittura, scultura, e architettura.* Florence, 1788.
Ortolani, S. *La pittura napoletana dal sei all'ottocento.* Exh. cat., Castelnuovo, Naples, 1938.
Ottani, A. "Marcantonio Bassetti." *Arte antica e moderna,* no. 26, 1964, pp. 151–66.
Ottani Cavina, A. *Carlo Saraceni.* Milan, 1968.
Ottley, W. Y. *Engravings of the Most Noble the Marquis of Stafford's Collection of Pictures in London.* London, 1818.
Paccagnini, G. "Dipinti di Domenico Feti a Mantova." *Critica d'arte,* 3, 1956, pp. 578–84.
Pane, R. *Il monastero napoletano di S. Gregorio Armeno.* Naples, 1957.
Pascoli, L. *Vite de' pittori, scultori e d'architetti moderni.* 2 vols. Rome, 1730–36.
Passeri, G. B. *Vite dei pittori, scultori ed architetti che anno lavorato in Roma morti dal 1641 al 1673.* Edited by J. Hess. Leipzig and Vienna, 1934.
Pepper, D. S. "Baglione, Vanni and Cardinal Sfondrato." *Paragone,* no. 211, 1967, pp. 69–74.
———. "Two Drawings by Baglione for the 'Gift of Constantine.' " *Master Drawings,* 8, Autumn 1970, pp. 267–69.
———. "I limiti del positivismo: L'Annibale Carracci di Donald Posner." *Arte illustrata,* 5, 1972, pp. 256–69.
———. "Annibale Carracci ritrattista." *Arte illustrata,* 6, 1973, pp. 127–37.
———. "England and the Seicento: Bolognese Painting from British Collections at Agnew's," review. *Burlington Magazine,* 115, 1973, pp. 823–27.
Percy, A. *Giovanni Benedetto Castiglione.* Exh. cat., Philadelphia Museum of Art, 1971.
Perina, C. T. "Inediti del seicento veneto: Fetti, Bassetti, Liberi." *Arte veneta,* 25, 1971, pp. 276–80.
———. "Precisazioni sul Fetti." *Antichità viva,* 10, 1971, pp. 10–19.
Picone, M. "Per la conoscenza del pittore Giacomo del Po," I and II. *Bollettino d'arte,* 42, 1957, pp. 163–72 and 309–16.
Pigler, A. *Barockthemen.* 2nd ed. 3 vols. Budapest, 1974.
Pilo, G. M. *Carpioni.* Venice, 1961.
Pio, N. *Le vite di pittori scultori et architetti.* Edited by C. Enggass and R. Enggass. Vatican City, 1977.
Posner, D. *Annibale Carracci: A Study on the Reform of Italian Painting around 1590.* 2 vols. New York, 1971.
Potterton, H. *Venetian Seventeenth-Century Painting.* Exh. cat., National Gallery, London, 1979.
Rabiner, D. "Additions to del Po." *Pantheon,* 36, 1978, pp. 35–41.
Recueil d'estampes d'après les plus beaux tableaux et d'après les plus beaux dessins qui sont en France . . . ["*Recueil Crozat*"]. Paris, 1729.
Refice Taschetta, C. *Mattia Preti: Contributo alla conoscenza del Cavalier Calabrese.* Brindisi, 1959.
Riccio, B. "Vita di Filippo Lauri di Francesco Saverio Baldinucci." *Commentari,* 10, 1959, pp. 3–15.
Richardson, G. *Iconology.* Vol. III. London, 1749.
Ridolfi, C. *Le maraviglie dell'arte o vero le vite degl' illustri pittori veneti e dello stato.* Venice, 1648.
Rinaldis, A. de. *Lettere inedite di Salvator Rosa a G. B. Ricciardi.* Rome, 1939.
Ripa, C. *Iconologia.* Padua, 1611.
Rome, Palazzo delle Esposizioni. *Il seicento europeo.* Exh. cat., 1956/57.
Rosci, M. *Mostra del Cerano.* Exh. cat., Novara, 1964.
Rudolph, S. "Contributo per Pier Francesco Mola." *Arte illustrata,* 2, 1969, pp. 10–25.
———. "P. F. Mola by R. Cocke," review. *Arte illustrata,* 5, 1972, pp. 346–54.
Ruggeri, U. "Per Daniele Crespi," I and II. *Critica d'arte,* 14, no. 90, 1967, pp. 45–56; and 15, no. 93, 1968, pp. 43–58.
Safarik, E. A. "Per la pittura veneta del seicento: Girolamo Forabosco." *Arte illustrata,* 6, 1973, pp. 353–63.
Salazzari, Brognara M. S.v. "Marcantonio Bassetti" in *Dizionario enciclopedia Bolaffi dei pittori e degli incisori italiani.* Turin, 1974.
Salerno, L. "Per Sisto Badalocchi e la cronologia del Lanfranco." *Commentari,* 9, 1958, pp. 44–64.
———. *Salvator Rosa.* Milan, 1963.
———. "Il dissenso nella pittura: intorno a Filippo Napoletano, Carosselli, Salvator Rosa e altri." *Storia dell'arte,* no. 5, 1970, pp. 34–65.
———. "Salvator Rosa at the Hayward Gallery." *Burlington Magazine,* 115, 1973, pp. 827–31.
———. *L'opera completa de Salvator Rosa.* Classici dell'arte Rizzoli. Milan, 1975.
———. *Pittori di paesaggio del seicento a Roma.* 2 vols. Rome, 1977/78.
Sandrart, J. *Accademiae nobilissimae Artis pictoriae.* Nuremberg, 1683.
Scaramuccia, L. *Le finezze de' pennelli italiani.* Pavia, 1674.
Schleier, E. "Un Lanfranco del 1620." *Paragone*, no. 147, 1962, pp. 47–53.
———. "An Unknown Late Work by Pietro Testa." *Burlington Magazine*, 112, 1970, pp. 665–68.

———. "Unbekanntes von Francesco Guarino." *Pantheon*, 33, 1975, pp. 27–33.
———. "Two Lanfranco Paintings from the Farnese Collections." *J. B. Speed Art Museum Bulletin*, July 1979, pp. 2–15.
———. "Due opere 'toscana' del Lanfranco." *Paragone*, forthcoming.
Shapley, F. R. *Paintings from the Samuel H. Kress Collection: Italian Schools XVI–XVIII Century*. London, 1973.
Shoir, D. C. "The Iconographic Development of the Presentation in the Temple." *Art Bulletin*, 28, 1946, pp. 17–32.
Soprani, R., and Ratti, C. G. *Vite de' pittori, scultori, ed architetti genovesi*. Genoa, 1769.
Soria, M. "Andrea de Leone: A Master of the Bucolic Scene." *Art Quarterly*, 23, 1960, pp. 23–35.
Spear, R. E. *Caravaggio and His Followers*. Rev. ed. New York, 1975.
Spezzaferro, L. "Una testimonianza per gli inizi del caravaggismo." *Storia dell'arte*, no. 23, 1975, pp. 53–60.
Spike, J. T. " 'The Church of St. John in Valletta 1578–1978' and the Earliest Record of Caravaggio in Malta: An Exhibition and Its Catalogue." *Burlington Magazine*, 120, 1978, pp. 702–5.
———. "Mattia Preti's Passage to Malta." *Burlington Magazine*, 120, 1978, pp. 497–507.
———. "Documents for the Renovation of the Chapel of France, 1663–1668, in the Co-Cathedral of St. John, Valletta." *Storia dell'arte,* no. 35, 1979, pp. 5–10.
Spinosa, N. "More Unpublished Works by Francesco Solimena." *Burlington Magazine*, 121, 1979, pp. 211–20.
Spinosa, N., ed. *Le arti figurative a Napoli nel settecento*. Naples, 1979.
The State Hermitage: West-European Painting. Vol. I. Moscow, 1957.
Stryienski, C. *La Galerie du Régent Philippe, Duc d'Orléans*. Paris, 1913.
Stuffmann, M. "Les Tableaux de la collection de Pierre Crozat." *Gazette des beaux-arts*, 72, 1968, pp. 11–144.
Sutherland, A. "Pier Francesco Mola: His Visits to North Italy and His Residence in Rome." *Burlington Magazine*, 106, 1964, pp. 363–68.
Sutherland Harris, A. "Notes on the Chronology and Death of Pietro Testa." *Paragone*, no. 213, 1967, pp. 35–60.
———. "A Contribution to Andrea Camassei Studies." *Art Bulletin*, 52, 1970, pp. 49–70.
———. "P. F. Mola by R. Cocke," review. *Art Bulletin*, 56, 1974, pp. 289–92.
———. *Andrea Sacchi.* Princeton, N.J., 1977.
Sutton, D. "Gaspard Dughet: Some Aspects of His Work." *Gazette des beaux-arts*, special issue, 1962, pp. 12–14.
———. *Romance and Reality: Aspects of Landscape Painting*. Exh. cat., Wildenstein & Co., New York, 1978.
Thiem, C. *Florentiner Zeichner des Frühbarock*. Munich, 1977.
Titi, F. *Studio di pittura, scoltura et architettura nelle chiese di Roma*. Rome, 1674.
———. *Ammaestramento . . . di pittura, scoltura et architettura nelle chiese di Roma*. Rome, 1686.
Turner, N. "Some Drawings by Lazzaro Baldi." *Burlington Magazine*, 121, 1979, pp. 150–55.
Valsecchi, M., ed. *Il seicento lombardo, catalogo dei dipinti e delle sculture*. Exh. cat., Palazzo Reale, Milan, 1973.
"Vecchi maestri alla galleria Agnew," review signed "H. A." *Emporium*, July 1962, pp. 41–42.
Venice, Ca' Pesaro. *La pittura del seicento a Venezia*. Exh. cat., 1959.
Vitzthum, W. "Giacomo del Po, illustrateur de Milton." *L'Oeil*, no. 190, 1970, pp. 28–31.
Volkmann, J. J. *Leben der berühmtesten Maler . . . von Anton Joseph Dezallier D'Argensville*. Vol. II. Leipzig, 1767.
Voss, H. *Die Malerei des Barock in Rom*. Berlin, 1924.
Vsevolozhskaya, S., and Linnik, I. *Caravaggio and His Followers*. Leningrad, 1975.
Waagen, G. *Treasures of Art in Great Britain*. 4 vols. London, 1854–57.
Wallace, R. W. *The Etchings of Salvator Rosa*. Princeton, N.J., 1979.
Waterhouse, E. *Baroque Painting in Rome*. London, 1937.
———. "An Immaculate Conception by G. B. Castiglione." *Minneapolis Institute of Arts Bulletin*, 56, 1967, pp. 5–10.
———. *Italian Baroque Painting.* 2nd ed. London, 1969.
———. *Roman Baroque Painting.* Oxford, 1976.
White, R. G. *Companion to the Bryan Gallery of Christian Art*. New York, 1853.
Whitfield, C. *England and the Seicento*. Exh. cat., Thomas Agnew & Sons, London, 1973.
Wibiral, N. "Contributi alle ricerche sul cortonismo in Roma." *Bollettino d'arte*, 45, 1960, pp. 123–65.
Wilde, J. "Zum Werke des Domenico Fetti." *Jahrbuch der Kunsthistorischen Sammlungen in Wien*, n.s. 10, 1936, pp. 211–19.
Wittkower, R. *The Drawings of the Carracci in the Collection of Her Majesty the Queen at Windsor Castle*. London, 1952.
———. *Art and Architecture in Italy 1660 to 1750*. 3rd rev. ed. Baltimore, Md., 1973.
Young, E. "Antonio Bellucci in England and Elsewhere." *Apollo*, 1973, pp. 492–96.
———. "Additions to Bellucci's Oeuvre." *Apollo*, 1974, pp. 300–305.
Young, J. *A Catalogue of the Collection of Pictures of the Most Noble the Marquess of Stafford at Cleveland House*. 2 vols. London, 1825.
Zampetti, P. *A Dictionary of Venetian Painters*. Vol. III. London, 1971.
Zeri, F. *La galleria Pallavicini in Roma*. Florence, 1959.
———. *Italian Paintings in the Walters Art Gallery*. Baltimore, Md., 1976.
Zeri, F., and Gardner, E. E. *Italian Paintings of the Florentine School.* Metropolitan Museum of Art, New York, 1971.

Photographs

Albertina, Vienna: fig. 1; Alinari, Florence: figs. 3 and 4; William R. Blackwell, Louisville, Ky.: fig. 14; E. Irving Blomstrann, New Britain, Conn.: fig. 2; Bowdoin College Museum of Art, Brunswick, Maine: fig. 5; Bullaty-Lomeo Photographers, New York: nos. 14 and 22; Courtauld Institute of Art, London: figs. 11, 12, 21, and 22; Bevan Davies, New York: nos. 1, 6, 8, 23, 25, 28, 34, and 35; Clem Fiori, Princeton: no. 29; Frick Art Reference Library, New York: fig. 13; Galerie Heim, Paris: fig. 8; Giraudon, Paris: fig. 19; Heim Gallery, London: fig. 20; Helga Photo Studio, Inc., New York: no. 7; Bruce C. Jones, Centerport, N.Y.: nos. 1, 3, 9, 10, 13, 21, 24, 27, 31, and 43; Kunsthistorisches Museum, Vienna: fig. 15; Kunstverlag Wolfrum, Vienna: fig. 6; Laboratorio Fotografico, Soprintendenza alle Gallerie, Naples: fig. 18; Metropolitan Museum of Art, New York: nos. 16, 33, and fig. 9; National Gallery of Ireland, Dublin: fig. 16; O. E. Nelson, New York: nos. 11 and 17; Eric Pollitzer, Hempstead, N.Y.: nos. 4, 15, 19, 20, 26, 41, 44, 45, and 47; Tom Scott, Edinburgh: fig. 7; Staatsgalerie, Stuttgart: fig. 17; Joseph Szaszfai, Yale University Art Gallery: no. 46.